SEASONS
OF FEAR

Also by Philip McFarland

A House Full of Women
Sojourners

SEASONS OF FEAR

by Philip McFarland

Schocken Books   New York

12/1983
gen. l

First published by Schocken Books 1984
10 9 8 7 6 5 4 3 2 1 84 85 86 87
Copyright © 1984 by Philip McFarland

Library of Congress Cataloging in Publication Data
McFarland, Philip James.
Seasons of fear.
1. New York (N.Y.)—History—Colonial period, ca.
1600–1775—Fiction. 2. New York (N.Y.)—Negro plot,
1741—Fiction.   I. Title.
PS3563.C363S4 1983   813′.54   83–42713

Designed by Cynthia Basil
Manufactured in the United States of America
ISBN 0–8052–3850–6

For James McFarland

Author's Note

The nature, dimensions, causes, and resolution of a social catastrophe that disrupted life in New York during one long-ago spring and summer are accurately recorded in the following pages. Three then current points of view toward issues that the catastrophe raised have been embodied by means of composites: of individuals who might have lived in New York at the time, as derived from various contemporary letters and journals. A note at the end of the book suggests what modifications of the historical record have been undertaken to evoke the events described.

I

The fifth Earl of Cavendham visited New York in his late teens, before inheriting his title and while still simply Charles Alexander Corimer, youngest son of a noble and wealthy father. Corimer came ashore from the ship *Happy Return,* Captain Rollins out of Greenwich, and set foot on Hunter's Wharf accompanied by a monkey on a chain, two greyhounds leashed, a manservant, and a slave acquired in the Shoreditch Market in days before his departure from England. Nor had the English visitor been on American soil more than ten minutes before that slave of his, a Guinea coast native named Bonny Jack, while apparently gaping in rubber-legged wonder near Hanover Square at some distance from the dock, abruptly dropped his dark head and bolted, breaking into a run that might have looked comical if so wide-armed and splayfooted a departure had not signified the loss of £40, the price one might expect to pay to replace a black that robust and well formed. Past a wagon, beyond a fruit stall and bales of tobacco, the fugitive rounded Sloat Lane and disappeared, frantic calls of his pursuers and the barking of the greyhounds notwithstanding.

To be sure, pursuit that balmy morning was halfhearted.

Much was in need of attention on the quay, and all assumed
that Jack would not get far in the little town. Yet eight months
and more went by without a word of him, despite numerous
inquiries, at least two sightings, and a notice that his owner
placed in *The New-York Weekly Journal,* which the curious may
read still, in the lower-left corner of the fourth page of the issue
for September 29, 1740:

> Run away in Dock Ward on Wednesday last, a negro slave
> about 18 years of age named Bonny Jack; a very likely fellow
> with a scar on his left cheek and a brand on his forehead that
> a cap would cover. Was wearing olive-colored cloth
> breeches, a checked shirt, and sundry old clothes. Whoso-
> ever will take up or secure this slave shall have *three pounds*
> reward and all reasonable charges paid by me, who may be
> spoke with at the Pursells in the Broad Way.
>
> *C. A. Corimer.*

* * *

Corimer's motives for coming to America remain unclear, a
minor mystery not solved by a journal that he kept fitfully
during his stay and that has survived. The journal is valuable in
any case for the picture it provides of colonial New York. My
uncle, a professor at New York University in the 1940s, located
the original (after a long search that was a detective story in
itself) in the possession of a Violet Finney of Vinton, Ohio. He
had an edition of five hundred copies printed privately, on war-
time paper, in an expurgated version, in 1942. Of course during
those years of global conflict little notice was taken of *A Standing Memorial: The American Journal of the Fifth Earl of Cavendham, 1740-41.* I own the original now, a brown duodecimo note-
book of ninety-six pages, calfbound, measuring some four by
seven inches, the final five pages blank, the others filled with a
minute shorthand that my diligent uncle and various librarians
and graduate assistants had finally determined was based on a
method devised in the late seventeenth century and published in
an obscure volume called *La Plume Volante; or, the art of short-*

hand improved. Thus keys in recent years have opened a number of doors that time had closed and locked. More years pass, and a still different ethos assures me that I need not expurgate the journal in quoting from what is a primary source for the story I have to tell.

Why had the Englishman Corimer, in his twentieth year, left London and come to remote America? The journal that extends through fourteen months does suggest that, like many of his countrymen who arrived here later, he may in part have been searching for adventure; like others he may have been fleeing debts at home. Certain early entries—and the quantity of goods he brought with him (camblet bed, medicine chest, the slave, a copper boiling pot)—imply that for a while he considered establishing himself permanently in the New World. But his movements after his arrival, his visits among New Yorkers, the few extant letters of his to England, and a later ambiguous renunciation would all lead reasonably to an assumption that he had come, at least in part, on a potentially profitable business errand. He may have been serving as agent for London merchants interested in locating an American correspondent to engage with them in the slave trade. If so, considering the life that the young man led on returning to England, the irony is evident.

* * *

About another matter entirely, Corimer writes within a week of his arrival to his older brother in Rome: "I am as yet unmarried and likely to continue so. If you knew anything of this place, you could not but know how few temptations there are here to a thing of that kind." The playful comment does show that marriage was on his mind, although even the youngest son of an earl might hardly be expected to locate a wife among moneygrubbing New York colonials. Why the jest? Why "as yet," from a gentleman of nineteen who might remain unmarried another decade without exciting comment?

Perhaps this polished specimen of classical values was falling in love. Assuming that he was, the likeliest object of his affections would have been the daughter of the merchant Benjamin Pursell, at whose home Corimer was staying as a guest through a part of the autumn after his arrival in America. By then he knew both daughter and father well, having met them in London, as the journal confirms, and traveled with them in cramped quarters over rough seas for six weeks aboard the *Happy Return* on the just-completed voyage to New York. Notes in the journal let us join the group, the sojourning Pursells, after a year's absence in England, reunited with their family in the parlor of the house on Broadway, Corimer and another English guest among the company. Late Thursday afternoon, September 25, 1740. Dinner—"a good joint of veal, pudding, and peaches from the garden"—is ended. Earlier this day slaves in a wagon have fetched chests and other possessions from the wharf across town, so that the travelers may open the horsehair trunk and extract gifts brought home to various members of the family: the wife, Pursell's sister, his son. A whistle and plated spurs for the boy, and for the women figured everlasting, velvet and damask and forest calico and cherry derry in latest patterns transported from London over an ocean. Corimer, guest in the New York parlor, may have been remembering when and exactly where some of those gifts had been purchased, during what must even then have seemed a distant August morning that had furnished the matter for the first of his journal entries: seven weeks earlier at Tomson the draper's, in Round Court, London, Corimer with Miss Pursell and her servant on a shopping expedition for Miss Pursell's Aunt Min. That early his shorthand was describing the sixteen-year-old American girl beside him in England as "a beauty, having a fine complexion and good features, black eyes and hair, and an elegant shape." And the same early entry, of August 7, preserves an exchange in an eighteenth-century dry-goods shop. A mercer is mincing about them, bowing, effusive: " . . . wonderful charming. My stars! how cool it looks! But this, madam—ye gods! would I had ten thousand yards of it!" Before the window in London's summer sunlight Corimer notes the very words of the clerk, gathering a sleeve of the "diverting silk" and placing it beside Miss

Pursell's—beside lovely Elizabeth's shoulder. "It suits your lady-ship's face wonderfully well." Amused, her escort suggests a price of ten shillings. "Ten shillings a yard?" exclaims the perfumed mercer. "Your lordship rallies me! . . ."

That exchange Corimer may have been remembering less than two months afterward on the other side of the ocean, in the colonial town, in the house of yellow brick on Broadway, where a parlor was filled with happy human sounds: a New York merchant's family gratefully assembled to receive their remembrances, including diverting silk. Later during the same fall evening of homecoming Miss Elizabeth Pursell after long absence played for them all on the harpsichord, as the journal tells us—"very pretty and agreeable, Festing and Handel"—and Corimer's white monkey, who had crossed the ocean as well, climbed on her lap, grinning like any Christian, "bussing her and handling her bubbies like an old rake.

"One might well envy the brute," the young Englishman adds, before closing that day's entry with a curious, entirely unrelated note: "Thought I saw Jack."

* * *

Jack, of course, was the runaway slave. Had Corimer glimpsed what looked like that sturdy black form, worth £40, in the checked shirt and old clothes—dark face with the brand on the forehead that a cap would hide—among slaves and bond-servants permitted to gather festively at the hall door on a late September afternoon in 1740 to watch wondrous gifts emerge from the traveling trunks of their long-absent master? From the embrasure of the window in the Pursells' parlor Corimer imagined that he saw Bonny Jack, though doubtless (since nothing more is said of the matter) he was mistaken, however accurate might be his journal on two later occasions that autumn, when it records subsequent sightings of the teenage fugitive among a street crowd and through the window of a disreputable tavern.

The other English guest at the Pursells' that early fall evening was Francis Schaw—the same who was destined to become famous—like Corimer a passenger on the *Happy Return* out of

Greenwich. A few years older than his aristocratic friend, Schaw would have been in his mid-twenties at the time of these events, although searches through church records of Gouldhurst in Kent, where he was born, have failed to uncover the date of birth or baptism. A reasonable guess would be in 1714, perhaps in February, when records of the parish are so scanty as to seem incomplete. Son of a steward on a landed estate and an inn-keeper's daughter, Schaw had risen above modest origins to become a servitor at Pembroke College, Oxford, where he was acquainted with his great contemporary, the evangelist George Whitefield. Having taken a degree at Oxford in 1736 (his name is duly recorded with Whitefield's among those on whom the university conferred the *Artium Baccalaureus* that July), he moves somewhat obscurely through the next four years of his manhood, though we can document that he spent a year or two of it at sea, apprenticed to a surgeon, and in the West Indies. What else he did is conjectural until the summer of 1740, when he was with Corimer, presumably a new friend, although perhaps an acquaintance from Oxford days, atop the Monument in the City of London: "walked to the top where Schaw measured the square gallery, which he found to be six yards square. We returned down," his friend notes scrupulously (August 9, 1740): "S counted the steps, but has forgot the number." And as the two Englishmen sailed together with the Pursells from Greenwich four days later, one of Schaw's goals in making the long voyage may already have been settled in his mind, if we may infer so from a notice that appeared promptly in both New York newspapers in early October, after his landing in America, and was repeated twice later that same month:

ENGLISH, Writing, Arithmetic, Elements of the Law, and Merchant's Accompts carefully taught at the house of Robert Hogg's in Broad Street, by Frans. Schaw, A.M. Oxon., schoolmaster, newly arrived from London.
N.B. And youth boarded reasonably by Mr. Hogg.

Schaw had found those quarters on Broad Street the day after family gifts had been distributed in the Pursells' parlor; Corimer's journal makes that clear. Together the new arrivals— Corimer and Schaw—had set out Friday morning to "take a prospect of the city" from the steeple of the Middle Dutch church. The heavy stone building, hardly ten years old then, was located on the northeast corner of Nassau and Crown (now Liberty) streets, and from its steeple the travelers who had recently surveyed London from atop the Monument would be able to see New York in panorama: the fort on its eminence at the southwestern tip of the island, red cross of St. George fluttering over it, houses and shops this side of the fort, sails in the harbor, fields on the steep Jersey shore, and farther northward on Manhattan the open land of the common and the King's Farms, where unpaved Broadway turned into the Bloomingdale road, stretching thinly between embankments and orchards and over wooded hills toward distant Harlem and Kingsbridge beyond the horizon. "Fine landskip, much shipping in the harbor," Corimer records tersely. And we later New Yorkers, two and a half centuries further into the future, would willingly trade pages of his precious journal—those conventional rephrasings of Shaftesbury's ethics, for instance—for five minutes from that height given over to recording exactly what two English eyes, now so long dust, had registered on their retinas one clear autumn morning: sunstruck weathercocks, a bedaubed Indian with his baskets on the street below, some farmer bargaining with a townsman from his scow beached by the Hudson, two slaves at horseplay by the tea pump, a woman in blue capuchin sneezing and thereby jostling her feathered parasol along tree-lined Maiden Lane. And what his ears had heard: street cries, laughter. Instead he informs us that the steeple bell behind him was cast in Amsterdam—"pretty large and handsome"—and that within the church the pulpit was "prettily wrought of black walnut," with a swiveling brass holder for the great Bible. Schaw, we learn, tested the church's echo with a hallow.

7

Outside again, on firm ground, Corimer does better by posterity, noting that morning on his "course through the town"
the brick houses, "compact and regular, several stories high,
after the Dutch fashion," the lime trees, the "large town house
at the head of Broad Street," the slave market at the foot of Wall
Street near the water's edge, the print shop in Mr. Zenger's
house near the Long Bridge, where the tourists stopped to place
the notice about Bonny Jack's absconding, and Mr. Noel's shop,
where Schaw "bought a curiosity." No mention, however, of
the offenders exhibited in the stocks that they must have passed
on Broad Street. No mention of the milk boys with their yokes
and pails, of the carmen, of the scarlet-coated soldiers, of the
covered wells and kennels, of which streets were earth, which
cobbled. Was Shakespeare's Globe round or polygonal? Not
one of all the hordes who saw the structure thought to inform
us—what scholars to this day can't agree on, a mystery that the
lowliest Londoner at the start of the seventeenth century might
have solved in an instant. And inside, were there pillars on the
outer stage? Were there sidewalks along New York's streets in
1740? Corimer as witness, like all the others who could have
enlightened us with a word, leaves the silence unbroken.

In the late morning the two Englishmen did call on Judge
Horsmanden in King Street, but that official was "from home."
By then they had tired of attracting attention: London gentlemen (Corimer in laced hat and his "plain suit of a pink color,
with gold button") with a manservant walking greyhounds before them and causing "such a deal of staring and gaping from
half the town as ever I saw." Betaking themselves to a tavern on
Broad Street, they dined on an ill-dressed beefsteak, brown
bread, and two bottles of bad Dutch claret—"elegant entertainment"—having fallen in with a company of topers whose language was all "oaths and smut." Schaw was conversing, by
means of a slate, with a "deaf doctor of Divinity. I," notes
Corimer, "found the man little but superstition, bigotry, and
nonsense, of which I often find men of the gown composed."

And with that unpromising tavern dinner concluded, the two gentlemen, before returning to the Pursells', arranged quarters for Schaw at Hogg's rooming house nearby.

* * *

Gradually from the pages of the journal Corimer's character emerges, a young nobleman imbued with a skepticism of institutional religion that many of his educated English contemporaries shared, ironical, a bit condescending to these colonials, not unobservant: a fair amount is set down about the size and feed of livestock, American market products, soil treatment, distances. He possessed, in addition, what was termed at the time a flow of animal spirits. Not always conventional in his friendships, not always purposeful in his movements, he had (so we recall of these months of 1740) no expectation of inheriting the title that subsequently came to him. His father—parliamentarian, mathematician, classicist, formidable stylist, and friend of Hartley, Voltaire, and Pope—seemed scarcely past his prime at fifty-three, flourishing with his new, third wife at their town house in St. James's Square in London or at Hinstead, the Surrey country seat that so amuses the modern visitor, with its famous labyrinth and eyetraps, those fabricated ruins and bridges going nowhere. Moreover, two older brothers, one like his father recently married and both in excellent health, were next in line respectively to succeed to the earldom. Lord Byles, the eldest, was even then serving His Majesty in campaigns against the Spanish in the Caribbean. As for the youngest of the family, Corimer had so far, since coming down from Oxford, spent his time apparently to little purpose at the card tables at White's and in various low debaucheries, sheathed against walls in London's black alleyways with the thread-stockinged Pollys and Sallys and Maggies who tramped over St. James's Park and Ludgate Hill after hours. One of the few letters that have survived from father to youngest son, although undated, probably was written shortly before Corimer's departure for America; in it his lordship refers to the "sundry things in your conduct that

9

vex and distress me," and urges, as fathers before and since have urged their progeny, that "you should strive to make prudence and discretion your pursuit."

Advice more readily given than followed. We may picture how Corimer looked, of course, from Ellys's portrait, painted only three years after this American sojourn, when the subject had returned to England as the fifth Earl of Cavendham. What gazes calmly out at us is an aristocrat in his early twenties, wearing gold-threaded waistcoat and plum-colored suit of shot silk, the face narrow, the nose like his father's, aquiline, the forehead broad and high, the eyes brilliant; years later the Countess of Hambleton recalled that they were the most penetrating eyes she had ever seen. Turrets of Hinstead rise in the left background of the portrait. Corimer's physical stature, incidentally, was average for the period, say five feet seven. His skin, according to all contemporary testimony, was fair, his gait rapid, his dress elegant but not foppish, his voice rather high but by no means disagreeable.

* * *

Such was the young gentleman who, on the Monday following the sight-seeing tour of New York, again called on Judge Horsmanden and this time found him at home. No doubt the call was made by invitation, and surely Schaw was along? For though Corimer's rather lengthy journal entry that day fails to mention him, Francis Schaw, born in Kent, would have known from his birthplace relatives of Daniel Horsmanden, Esq., barrister-at-law, and would likely have arrived in America bearing letters of introduction to so prominent a public official.

We do learn from the journal that at least Corimer and Horsmanden, a man of "good figure and esteem in his profession," spent a part of that Monday together. Michaelmas it was, September 29, and Election Day, as their visit commenced over breakfast at the magistrate's home on King (now Pine) Street. "Was warmly received; handsome rooms on the first floor, walnut furnishings." They dined, we are told, on toast, cheese, marmalade, and a dish of tea, and what they talked of we may surmise from Corimer's notations: "Indians drink rum greatly and have an ox roasted and dance all night. Papist priests." A good part of the month before Judge Horsmanden had spent making the biannual journey up the Hudson by governor's barge and dealing with the Six Nations of the Iroquois, renewing a treaty that excluded   or continued trying to exclude   the French with their Romish mumbo-jumbo from influence among the covenant chain of tribes beside the Mohawk. During days of ceremonial within the stockade above Albany, overlooking a wilderness of spruce and hemlock, the white officialdom had distributed blankets and strouds and beads and wampum and finally even some rum, in order to reaffirm among wily natives that obedience and fidelity were owing to their father and defender, the King of Great Britain. The excursion had doubtless left vivid impressions on the mind of Corimer's host. "Squaws," the journal notes, on Horsmanden's authority, we may be sure, "pick the lice of one another and eat them. Indians feast upon dogs. Three hundred above a match for a thousand regulars in the woods. Quick-sighted, bear fatigue. Fight with balls in their mouths, which prevents their being thirsty." Such converse about strange ways must have enlivened the breakfast, as did talk of schemes to develop the sturgeon fishery in the Hudson. Also some local boosterism to welcome the Englishman: how else account for this notation at a rival city's expense? "In Boston a sailor is flogged for kissing his wife in the streets on Sunday though after a three years' absence. A stallion is brought to the whipping post and lashed for covering a mare on the Sabbath day."

New Yorkers were more enlightened. For his part Corimer could chat of London with his host, for as a young man the judge had spent a number of years there before coming to America. His contemporary William Smith, who knew Horsmanden personally, tells us, in the history he wrote of colonial New York, that the magistrate was "a gentleman by birth and bred at Inn"—London's Inns of Court—"but wasting his fortune and having no hopes at the bar, he entered into partnership with a chancery collector, and after a short trial of that business he fled from his creditors to Virginia." From Virginia, the debtor had made his way to New York, arriving late in 1731, nine years before this morning and his comfortable entertainment of a noble English visitor. Those nine years had been good to Daniel Horsmanden. Now forty-six and a bachelor still, he had—through the rarity of legal skills in a land of charlatans and pettifoggers—been appointed judge of the vice-admiralty court of New York, Connecticut, and New Jersey, as well as one of three justices of the Supreme Court of the Province of New York. He was a vestryman of Trinity Church, recorder of the City Corporation, member of both the Common Council and the Governor's Council, alderman due to be reelected in his ward this very day, and coholder of the license for six thousand acres east of the Hudson in Dutchess County, up near where those recently visited Iroquois were roaming and eating dogs. He was, in fact, the very emblem of opportunities awaiting the immigrant—image by this time of prosperous rectitude, seated in morning coat before the blue porcelain of the breakfast table at a window nook overlooking King Street. And having prospered himself, he would have been urging on his young visitor the advantages of life in this New World, where a sparse population made permanent settlers from the Old World welcome.

But was there also exploratory talk about the scheme that may have prompted Corimer's journey in the first place: profits to be made from the slave trade, which would help provide hands needed to grasp the abundant riches from well-timbered, fertile land stretching in three directions away from this little city? "No friendships," Corimer quotes his host as saying, "are so strongly cemented as those carried on by mutual interest and services." Were slaves an interest they shared?

Obviously the two gentlemen did get along at this first meeting, so well that they extended it beyond breakfast to include a walk late that morning to the polls of the South Ward. Down King Street they strolled, under the locusts and elms, eastward to the river and close by the wharves and shipyards, in passing to enjoy sights of the commercial vigor of so thriving a colony. Among the oath-filled, good-natured bustle of sailors and dock-hands loading and unloading cargo, with gull cries overhead and the rattle of pulleys and the smells of spices from the ware-houses, the two of them made their congenial way along Water Street southward, around kegs and coiled hemp and masts laid out and rusty anchors—until a crowd scene of some violence abruptly arrested their progress.

In his journal Corimer sets down briefly what he saw, but details can be added from other sources. "On slip," he writes, "man cudgeling his slave, taken in the prize. Crying out with an imperious and exalted voice, 'Son of a bitch. Shitten black bas-tard.' Mr. H intervenes. Negro is sullen, speaks Spanish. Man-uel, well favored Moor."

During the preceding spring, an American privateer operat-ing out of New York had overtaken and captured a Spanish vessel on the high seas and brought her back to port as a prize of war. The battered sloop, *La Soledad*, two hundred tons burden, remained tied up for weeks at Beekman's Wharf, within sight of this incident on the quay. The vessel's cargo of quinine and cocoa and pieces of eight had been promptly confiscated and most of her crew confined as prisoners of war. Moreover, five Negroes aboard, despite their claims of being free men in their own country, had been auctioned off by the vendue master as slaves. Manuel was acquired by one Peter Wendover, chan-dler, who presumably was the nameless slaveowner of Cor-imer's entry, chastising that reluctant human acquisition these several months later for some unspecified grievance—an inso-lent glance, a dilatory response to an order. That we have the Spaniard's name suggests an admonition by Judge Horsman-den, magistrate.

Yet though unpleasant, the scene could hardly have been re-markable in eighteenth-century New York, where to preserve their faith those of benevolent disposition would have had to gaze past much, including commonplace sights of the defense-less abused. Certainly the effect of the encounter on Corimer seems to have been temporary, for we find no further mention of it. Soon afterward he is in the yard of the Crown and Thistle off Whitehall, near the Half-Moon Battery, wryly amused by the spectacle of freemen voting. Alderman Horsmanden is noisily treating his constituency to flip as they call out their loyalty among the crowd of loungers around the polling table under the buttonwood tree. The recorder of those votes is Horsmanden's choice; the hours of voting are set by Horsmanden; the results Horsmanden will bring to the city councilors among whom his predictable victory will allow him to continue sitting. Now he is treating his supporters to beer and rum as they merrily barter their franchise for what the patronizing Corimer calls a "treat and a frolic." Withal an innocent scene perhaps, passing with this late September afternoon that was like a summer gift—and about the last such benign day those lucky citizens could hope for, outdoors in the tavern yard in shirt-sleeves and good spirits: "delicious weather," says the young visitor from England, "mild and warm, so that I glowed with pleasing imagination."

* * *

Such weather would have encouraged plans that had been made earlier for an excursion next day into the country. But "I got up betimes this morning *pour prendre le frais*," Corimer begins the following entry, "and found it heavy and cloudy, portending rain." Were there breaks in the clouds as that Tuesday after Election Day advanced: sudden sunlight, patches of blue? They went on with their excursion after all: Corimer, Schaw, Miss Elizabeth Pursell, and her brother, the nine-year-old Lindsay, astride his roan pony and wearing his new spurs from London.

Up Broadway the party proceeded at a walk, on mounts from Pursell's stable. Miss Pursell rode on a pillion behind her lady's maid (whom Corimer describes as "well looked, though pock-marked"), the two of them on a slow-gaited bay mare. Milne, Corimer's manservant, "grinning and chattering like a magpie" in his cocked hat and parti-colored clothes, brought up the rear on a mule, with provisions in panniers. Early in the journey Corimer suspected that his own horse, a gray, was lame, so that he walked him carefully, past Old Windmill Lane, out past the common, past the palisades and the rope walk and the brick kiln, on into the King's Farms northward for maybe three, maybe three and a half miles. Sheep and red cattle, "smaller than those at home," were browsing in surrounding meadows. Buckwheat was ripe and golden. Along the way the party skirted "a pretty large plain about half a mile broad and two or three miles long which is marshy and overgrown with salt water hay." Blackbirds clacked in the marshes. Here and there a farmhouse was visible where the road leveled out between embankments. Gates to dismount for and open. Stone fences. A freshwater pond. A cherry orchard thickly planted on the right. Behind the wayfarers the sound of church bells came clearly from the town, and a rooster crowing.

Not long ago I made the same trip those ancestors of mine had made—mine also on a cloudy autumn forenoon, September 30, in fact, though not a Tuesday; began it from Bowling Green, site of the parade ground of the vanished fort, and walked north up Broadway alongside the financial district and past City Hall Park (which the common of old had become), then among buildings and traffic on leveled, paved ground to Hudson Street until I reached West Thirteenth and Ninth Avenue. About there, I presume, on the smaller Manhattan of that earlier time, was the farm for sale that this excursion had set out to see. But how little we finally know of the past, or of the people who lived in it. Perhaps Corimer, dutifully taking his notes about livestock and soil conditions, was considering purchasing such a rustic establishment, he who within three years, back in England as the Earl of Cavendham, would forsake rural tedium with a vow never to return to Hinstead, his Surrey seat, so marked had his preference for urban London become.

Much else about him would change in the interval. Meanwhile, he seems this cloudy morning to have considered acquiring a farm that was being advertised at the time in the New

York papers, "of 44 acres adjoining the North River, within four miles of this city, with two bolting mills, a very good grist mill, and asparagus beds. The farm is a stone house 50 feet long, 32 wide, with south lights, four rooms on a floor, cellar from one end to the other, and a new stone kitchen adjoining." Its fortunate owner would, moreover, be possessed of a breadth of forty rods of land along the waterside, with "plenty of lobsters and fish near to hand."

On that same available coastline the party from town had their midday dinner out of the panniers of Milne's mule. At one point Schaw and young Lindsay Pursell and Corimer's manservant tossed their three hats into the Hudson and ran barefoot along the water's edge, hallooing and wagering which hat would first reach the cove downstream. Their voices were lifted to cheer the hats on. Annie, the maidservant, was gathering the remains of the picnic together, and under a willow near the shore Corimer was reading aloud to Miss Pursell from *The Faerie Queene*. The journal tells us so, and without transition the journalist speaks of Elizabeth's "pretty wit. Dove's. eyes."

What words were uttered in the shade of the willow? What glances passed between those living presences? Later Corimer "was invited to sleep, but was waked by a cow eating my handkerchief, which I had put under my head. I pursued her"—and the image of the future earl is a delightful one—"for some time before I recovered it, which I suppose the snuff in it made her disgorge, but it was prettily pinked all over with holes."

And still later that afternoon, he and young Lindsay Pursell, looking southward, "viewed the town from a high rock, and saw its spires and belfries beyond green meadows."

But the weather, threatening earlier, now moved to fulfill its threat. "We had not got down from the rock before it began to rain, which wet me pretty much." Corimer more than the others, all of whom rode as fast as they could for the nearest shelter, half a mile off, a tenant's thatched cottage at the far edge of a new-sown wheat field. But Corimer's mount, which he had suspected of lameness earlier, proved to have lost a shoe,

so he must lead it through "a prodigious bad deluge. It was
very horrid, as it rained in torrents and thundered and frightened my gray." Over the furrows he dragged the rearing horse,
before he could at last hitch the creature to a fence post at the
far edge of the field and splash across the farmyard to reach
shelter beyond the cottage door.

By the time he got inside, the earlier arrivals were building a
fire in the stone fireplace. Also inside "were several young girls,
quite wild and rustic," children of the absent tenant farmer.
"They were as simple and awkward as sheep, and so wild that
they would not appear in open view but kept peeping at us
from behind doors, chests, and benches." Finally, with the help
of a handful of copper halfpence, Corimer did manage to be-
friend the children. What clothes he could decently shed were
hung before the blaze, around which all of them had gathered.
Outside, water continued pouring off the thatch eaves and
noisily overflowing the rain barrel. To pass the time the in-
truders, clearly in good spirits in the midst of their adventure,
set out to perform remembered scenes from a play that three of
them had acted together during the long, late-summer days at
sea aboard the *Happy Return*. Once more Aimwell, Archer, and
Dorinda gestured and spoke in low-ceilinged confines, among
flickering shadows:

—Pray, my lord, consider a little—
—Consider! do you doubt my honor or my love?
—Neither: I do believe you equally just as brave. But, my
lord, I'm a woman; colors, concealments may hide a thou-
sand faults in me—therefore know me better first.
—(*Aside*) Such goodness who could injure!

Clatter of a wagon outside. Under a great drenched cloak the
wife of the tenant farmer had come back from the markets, a
pursy soul babbling Dutch and English as she brought in her
half-filled basket. She and the children said grace in Dutch, then
ate their afternoon meal of fish without sauce, from a "dirty,

deep, wooden dish which they evacuated with their hands, cramming down skins, scales and all," while their guests were assuring the housewife they had already eaten. And watching the present spectacle, Corimer—that uninvited visitor—allowed himself to reflect ungenerously on the "inclination to finery amongst these poor people." A mirror with a painted frame he judged superfluous, propped against the bare stone wall. "Such an article might be sold to buy wool to make yarn. A little water in a wooden pail might serve as well for a looking glass . . ."

Perhaps the good *vrouw* was not sorry to hear the rain slackening and watch the city folk preparing to go. They left her the remains of the picnic, with a shilling besides. Milne, the manservant, would walk the shoeless gray home. Corimer rode the mule, accompanying the others in the party—Schaw, young Lindsay, Elizabeth and her maidservant Annie—back under lowering skies along muddy Bloomingdale road to the common, at dusk following the cowherds who were returning their lowing cattle down Broadway to the townsmen's various houses.

What can we know of such people? Home at the Pursells' again, in the upstairs room that the American family had provided him—room in the front hung with "genteel green paper"—Corimer we might have supposed would be reflecting on the pleasures of this day's outing, on *The Faerie Queene* under a willow, *The Beaux' Stratagem* before a cottage fire, and perhaps on certain different, amorous gazes that may for the first time have been exchanged between him and the dove-eyed Elizabeth, sixteen, black-haired, and lovely. Maybe he was. But at some point that evening pockmarked Annie entered his room for whatever reason, to bring tea or turn down the bed. An upstairs room in a commodious New York home—and how were such matters managed discreetly? The servant's return delayed, sounds through the walls, of scuffling, giggles—Nay, sir, oh Lud—bed creaks.

"Made Annie feel my roger and kissed her till I spent."

* * *

Corimer's dousing on Tuesday had consequences. "I awaked from a sound sleep about six in the morning," he records of a dismal day that immediately followed. "Found myself very unwell, being sick at my stomach, and had a great inclination to vomit, but found many attempts that way vain, such as putting my finger as far into my gullet as the wideness of my mouth or the length of my finger would permit me." At last he summoned Milne to fetch him warm water, "of which I drank plentifully, expecting it to be a means to bring off that heavy load that laid at my stomach. But instead it lulled me fast asleep. . . ."

The morning passed with him sleeping. In the afternoon the ailing Corimer did rise and hobble downstairs, only to spend much of the rest of that gloomy day huddled over the fire in the parlor, remembering to exaggeration warm weather of two days earlier—"such heat that there was hardly any going out"—now followed so soon by a drop in temperature that seemed to leave every mortal in New York "shivering with cold and burning oak, hickory, or any other combustible."

He felt miserable. Early that evening he went back to bed with a fever, which became so alarming in the course of the night that the town's only doctor was sent for. A long night it must have seemed—and just the beginning of the ordeal. "I had sixteen or eighteen ounces of blood taken from me, and took a puke in two hours after, and drank twenty-three quarts of water, which by operating downward gave me sixteen motions." One imagines those chilly, enfeebled, repeated passages over the carpetless floor to the closestool in the corner, beyond the case-of-drawers. And with daylight, he "required to be blooded again. In short, I have had a violent fit of it, with a leech and a nurse attending me."

So he wrote Thursday afternoon, propped up in bed as though the worst were over. Yet on the following morning, Friday, October 3 (as he was able to record only much later), "my whole body, legs, and hands broke out in a violent rash and peeled. Twice after I peeled also, and have had sharp pains like rheumatism. Nothing would stay on my stomach for nine days. Neither could I eat or sleep but when I took things to make me."

That report comes undated, but some time after October 11, when cannon were fired at the nearby fort to mark the anniversary of the coronation of the king and queen. In the same entry Corimer records so punctuant a signal, repeated again and again beyond his windows, as the first clear recollection after hazy, interminable days and nights: faces blurred in candlelight above him, feeble groans for the pisspot, apprehensive whispers, comings and goings, stenches of purgings and sweat, clysters and paregoric, cups heating, neck sore where the flesh was blistered, the taste of castor boluses lumpily in his throat, delirium.

Then a long, long sleep, and in time the cannon sounding; and the patient, weakly opening his eyes, found himself gazing upon filtered sunlight of a steadied morning.

Elizabeth Pursell was seated near the foot of his bed. Bending over her lap desk, she was unaware that he had wakened. She was writing a letter. Nor did Corimer disturb her, or make a sound, but lay quietly and gazed his fill, if the preciseness of his recollection is indicative. She was wearing a "robe de chambre of cherry-colored silk, with silver round the sleeves and skirts." He lay still, back from afar, and gazed at her, watching her stroke the quill feather pensively across her cheek. "She looked very handsome in every respect," so he recalled in the earliest of his entries while convalescing, "and needs neither stays nor hoop to set out her shapes, which are naturally elegant and good." When she stirred he closed his eyes. In a moment her cool palm lay briefly on his forehead, before she turned and with a rustle left the room, letter in hand, without ever knowing he had wakened and seen her.

What followed included more than a week of convalescence in an upstairs confinement, the family taking turns to watch at the bedside and, as his strength came back, to visit with the patient. Aunt Min, whom Corimer had seen not long before capering about the parlor with the gift of London cherry derry wrapped over her shoulders, now waited nearby in somber thanksgiving, "a big woman with a red face, as much like an old maid as a frying pan"; she murmured prayers in sibilant whispers. Lindsay came in, shy in the presence of what illness had transformed, with Corimer's white monkey chattering on his shoulder. Madame Pursell seated herself one morning to visit, "a good-natured woman of the sort often met with: lively without much wit. Her fault is speaking too much, which tires people." And when they were gone, "I lay abed," writes Corimer, "very gloomy. I thought York did me no good. I rather disliked it, and I thought of going back to London immediately." His eyes roamed the green room forlornly: butterflies and peacock feathers on the chimney panels, the wig box and shagreen cases and bottles of oils and pomatums stolidly on his dressing table, the empty birdcage, the washstand, those execrable pictures—on one wall of Abraham and Hagar, on another of a sheepshearing. Why had he ventured so far from home? Rising a little in bed, he could confront his own drawn face across the room, bleakly in the dressing glass.

The open door admitted sounds from below: kettles being dragged into place for more candle dipping, a servant humming a tune, the lilt of the harpsichord, and outside sounds of wood being split and stacked, somebody's laugh, a cart or wheelbarrow clattering along a path under the window. He ate a little, without relish. He read: *The Persian Letters,* Oldmixon's *Secret History of Europe.* Annie came to bank the fire at nine: "She is indeed one of the stupidest human beings that ever I met with, though very careful and diligent, and extremely good-natured and disposed to oblige."

For several days—even when sufficiently recovered to write in it—he had abandoned his journal, unwilling "to relate merely that I rose, made water, lay quiet, read a book, saw a friend or two . . ." But on Saturday, the eighteenth, he felt strong enough at last to leave his bed and, "by the help of chairs," grope his way to the window, sitting for a while and looking out on a sunny morning over the family garden down to the Hudson and across to Powles Hook on the opposite shore. "I am seated in my old clothes and nightcap and slippers bringing my journal to date. Wild ducks on the water in profusion. Fishermen raking oysters." Schaw came to visit him a second time that afternoon, Corimer back in his "lofty bedstead" and his friend reclining in a trundle bed on the floor. The two of them drank tea and conversed about the hubbub of departure, three days earlier, of transports filled with hopeful volunteers bound for a rendezvous with other colonials in Virginia, to make up an expedition that would join Admiral Vernon's fleet against the Spaniard in the West Indies. Schaw, who had been in those climes himself, might well have enhanced the report of that current event.

And that night, that Saturday night, the convalescing Corimer was obviously much recovered: "Took Annie by the cunt," he writes, without elaboration.

Sunday morning, then, after a confinement of eighteen nights and days, he could finally venture forth, his foot at last stepping on the haircloth in the hallway, and descend the stairs to the parlor. "Young Lindsay took me by the hand as his friend and led me to the couch and we talked most intimately. Then Miss Elizabeth entered and ran smiling to me, directing her bright voice to me with a most engaging liveliness. We read together a fable of Gay's and sang a smart lively song. I played my flute and did not repine."

That evening, apparently a brief relapse—"my urine is still foul, which I impute to the want of exercise"—so that he kept to the house for another couple of days, visiting with the merchant Pursell in his counting room in the ell: "He entertained me for half an hour with a sun microscope, a curious apparatus that affords a surprising intermixture of colors. I saw a small spider, the down of a moth's wing, and a fly's eye." And the two gentlemen played a hit at backgammon, over the dice and counters having "some chat of news," much of it from Europe and two months old. Sir Robert Walpole had set out for Houghton Hall again (the last time he was there war had been

22

declared against Spain); the throat distemper was raging in Connecticut; Admiral Vernon's squadron lay at Jamaica; the Catholics had their new pope at last—that anti-Christ—in the Archbishop of Bologna, as Benedict XIV; and the Reverend Mr. Whitefield, indefatigable young phenomenon, had recently raised, at a single preaching in Boston, £544 for his orphan house in Georgia. For the rest, Corimer was now well enough to have Milne dress his hair each morning, then read, write— and all the while cherish those glimpses around the house of lovely Elizabeth, once seen in "a loose deshabille which, in a manner, half hid and half displayed her charms. Fine complexion, clean and neat . . ." And at night, "had two loose stools. Slept but indifferently. Had a nocturnal pollution not altogether asleep, then dreamed I was clapped."

Outside again at last, and on a horse, well bundled against the weather even though this was a day of Indian summer, Corimer bestrode his gray "for the first time in three weeks, but now with riding I shall soon be established in health"—as he and Elizabeth and Aunt Min proceeded on a Wednesday afternoon the few paces up Broadway to the family plot in Trinity churchyard. There they lingered, among slate slabs with winged cherubs and death's heads and scythes and carved hourglasses, by the grave—only a year and a half old and the letters sharp in the stone—of Elizabeth's younger sister. The carving is worn nearly level now, so faint as to be almost illegible these two hundred and forty years later, but we can stand at the same spot still (then—though not now—in sight of the river), in the northwest corner of the yard, where those three stood about two in the afternoon of October 22, 1740, and letting our gaze wander can make out, on one of the weathered gravestones nearby, a trite inscription that they, too, might have read:

Stop here, my friend, and cast an eye.
As you are now so once was I.
As I am now so you must be. . . .

* * *

How accurately do we dare imagine those people who lived on this little island? How much of their now veiled world would please, how much revolt us? Pleasing enough the sounds of laughter beyond a window, of logs being stacked against winter; understandable the pangs of homesickness, the muted grief by the settling grave. But those hordes of flies on the butter. The stink of excrement from chamber pots. The noise everywhere in that mostly illiterate world: church bells summoning, vendors bawling their wares. Filth in the streets. The pervasive darkness.

And the formality: children like Lindsay Pursell, like monstrously shrunken adults to us—stiff nine-year-olds in flowered waistcoats striving to deny their childhood. And even lovely Elizabeth, preparing for the ball at His Majesty's garrison this Thursday evening. A daylong effort has got the young lady ready, she seated for hours while Annie used cushions and pads and puffs to compose her headpiece, then rubbed on her cheeks the paste and unguents and washes and powder and rouge, the various compounds applied to lips and eyebrows. Essences were sprinkled over her, and pastillios de bocca dissolved on her tongue, sweetening my lady's breath while reminding us incidentally of the general aversion that she and all her contemporaries felt toward the unhealthful act of bathing. So that if for one instant we could stand beside Corimer and glimpse the actual Elizabeth (my great-grandmother of seven generations back) at sixteen years of age descending the mahogany staircase in her brocade and velvet, every enhancement of beauty at last in place, would we gape in disbelief at a being so grotesquely transformed? That false hair all bedecked with curls and lappets and pins and ribbons; face plastered white like some ludicrous mask; the waist squeezed into scarcely inches; the heels of her cherished, embroidered shoes so elevated inside the hoop and multitudinous petticoats as to force on her an absurdly mincing gait—tiny steps and the shoulders far forward. But most bizarre of all, the self-gratulatory smile into which those vividly colored lips have settled on Elizabeth's face, under the spurious mole. Yet Corimer, beside us, is entranced. He sees what we may not: luxuriant tresses, arched, even eyebrows, oval cheeks and exactly regular nose, the long, finely turned neck, the highest beauty of Elizabeth's white bosom, a perfect symmetry of limbs, and a smile "that diffused light over her fair countenance." How, then, should we seek to imagine her: as she would look to us, or to him? Which is the truth? And what would Corimer make of an Elizabeth dressed in a manner we might find fetching: that same form moving supplely in, say, molded jeans and an Irish sweater?

On Thursday evening a week after the visit to Trinity churchyard the Pursell family, with Schaw and Corimer as their guests, were attending a ball at Fort George to honor the anniversary of the birthday of His Majesty the King of Great Britain, far off in Hampton Court. From eleven to noon church bells had been ringing joyfully all over town, while Elizabeth and every other belle and gallant had sat to be made ready in their separate houses. At one the company of halberdiers, with troop of horse and "gentlemen of his majesty's council, merchants, &c., following," had paraded through streets lined with militia from the fort to the City Hall, where on the piazza a ship captain just in from London had addressed an assembled crowd to reassure them of the continued health of all the royal family, including the pregnant Princess of Orange. Then, as the afternoon advanced, much loyal eating had been undertaken in taverns, and countless toasts tossed off—to the king, to Walpole and Newcastle and Admiral Vernon, to the governor and the council—and many speeches had been uttered, in which defiance was hurled at the Spaniard, the French, and every other enemy of Britannia. During the course of the afternoon one band of celebrants had got their hands on the ensign of the *Soledad,* captured Spanish prize at the piers, and in beery triumph were flaunting that bright bunting about the mob-filled streets.

Later, with dusk, came the illumination of the city, through which festive glare the Pursells and their two English guests passed, about six in the evening, the short distance over the cobbles of Broadway to the turnstile at the far end of the parade.

"Gardens and terrace walks," writes Corimer of Fort George, "from which is a pretty view of the city. Several guns are in the fort, some brass and cast in a handsome mold. The new battery is raised with ramparts of turf, 12 to 18 pounders on it." And from atop the battlements, twenty feet above the arriving guests, came the warming strains of a fiddle. A Negro in white wig and livery had been stationed to play up there; he was an old musician, a slave belonging to Governor Clarke. We know from the surviving record of the governor's effects that his name was Primus, and may presume that his fingers felt the cold of the night wind blowing off the bay. Among the music he played were "Hearts of Oak" and "Derry Down." Across the yard the Blue Artillery Company had come smartly to attention before their barracks, metal of their accoutrements silver in the moonlight. Geese waddled about the draw well. Above the fortifications, in the chapel steeple, burned a lantern that could have been seen far to the south in the bay; and alongside the chapel, from the governor's house, golden light was spilling forth, and the sounds of companionable voices.

Corimer's journal entry is full on this occasion. He seems to have enjoyed himself, alert to fresh surroundings after having been enclosed so long within the green walls of the Pursells' upstairs bedroom. Inside the governor's house he notes the wainscotted salon, on the east wall of which, under a water-stained ceiling, hung full-length portraits of King George in his robes and the late Queen Caroline. Musicians, who included officers of the garrison as well as local citizenry, were playing their viols and bass, their oboes and trumpets and flageolets at the far end of the ballroom by one of the two great fireplaces, while dancers danced minuets and gavottes to airs by Gluck, the Scarlattis, Rameau. Corimer records, in addition, the presence in mourning of the Olympian governor himself, in from his Long Island estate, the honorable George Clarke, Esq., well into his sixties, whose wife of nearly forty years had died five

months earlier and lay now in her vault in Trinity Church:
"And as it was a pleasure to her in her life to feed the hungry,
so on the day of her funeral a loaf of bread was given to every
poor person who would receive it." Attentive to the widowed
governor, somberly aloof as he sat in old-fashioned full-
bottomed wig and black velvet breeches, were members of his
council and their wives: the Livingstons and DeLanceys and
Van Cortlandts and others, mostly merchants with whom the
Pursells were sociable, as well as Councilor Horsmanden,
bachelor acquaintance of Corimer himself, and of Francis
Schaw. Conversation among those gentlemen turned on the
Caribbean campaign, on the meaning of Walpole's recent movements, on the ever-scheming French, on the need to strengthen
the defenses of the city further at a time so imperiled—while the
governor himself, vastly rich from his office but covetous still,
may all the while have been brooding over the cost from his
pocket of such an evening as this, "for they must have show and
be entertained. . . ." Liveried black servants were bringing ne-
gus and beakers of mulled canary to the numerous revelers, and
"Turkey figs, pickled mushrooms, and red herring."

The crowded hall grew warmer. Corimer, hardly recovered
from his recent illness and giddy with dancing, at one point
departed the ball briefly in company with Schaw and Miss Pursell; they may have left to view the pyrotechnics. Against the
risky night air the three of them dressed carefully, Elizabeth in
cape and calash, and descended the stairs and stepped out into
the grounds of the fort. A sentry saluted them at the gate under
the secretary's house. The three friends mounted the terrace,
and from there looked over the still-crowded streets of the illumined city and, in the other direction, toward the black, windy
Narrows beyond which the *Happy Return* had lain at anchor
hardly a month earlier, off Sandy Hook on a balmy September
night at the end of a long and boisterous passage. On that
earlier evening these three had been together as well, aboard the
crowded and too familiar ship but in sight of land at last, joyfully smelling new hay of adjacent fields: "A bagpipe and two

violins played by turns, and we danced on deck till a late hour." Next morning the ship had entered the river and anchored. Elatedly they had come ashore; and now, after a month in the town, there was dancing again, and music from within the governor's mansion—soprano voice singing "Vain Is Beauty's Gaudy Flower"—and fireworks erupting suddenly, spectacularly, over the bay, and the music louder before it ceased, as guests summoned to the ballroom windows raised them to marvel and exclaim.

Here we take note of a matter of diction. Corimer, who earlier had recorded his white monkey's impudent fondling of Elizabeth's "bubbies," who had brazenly taken Annie "by the cunt," now finds on the battlements, more poetically, that his "powers were excited; I felt myself vigorous." His language grows elevated in describing the effect of this young lady beside him, so close beside him that her presence—lips, moist eyes glistening, those caped symmetries, scent of rose water—has "awakened tender inclinations." If Schaw had not been nearby as well, that youngest son of an earl might here, at this moment, have declared himself a lover, feeling "a sort of confusion" in moonlight on the ramparts, under the pinwheels and red rockets and girandoles and tournants of brilliant fire, with his member that was sacred to Cupid tumescent, and his eyes finally opened wide to a woman's beauty.

* * *

The historical record is filled with coincidence. On the garrison battlements in colonial New York the Englishman Corimer stood fully reawakened to life, after an illness that had proved nearly fatal. And on the same night precisely, October 30, 1740, the young man's guiding fate made the first of three wrenching moves to provide him an earldom, as his older brother, who had been in sound health until eight days earlier, succumbed just before midnight, in Rome, incoherently on a pallet in a dank corridor of the convent of la Chiesa della Madonna degli Angeli, to "convulsions, fever, and the bloody flux." Ralph Philip Corimer, aetat twenty-three, "reckoned by all who knew him to have superior parts," was destined never to return to England from his grand tour of the Continent and assume the duties awaiting him there of standard-bearer to the band of gentlemen pensioners and clerk extraordinary of His Majesty's Privy Council.

News of young Corimer's demise in Rome would require two weeks to reach his father at St. James's Square, six more to cross the ocean from London to an ice-free port in the New World. Our Corimer, accordingly, returns to the ball this October evening in innocence, banquets and grows tipsy with the others on mullet and boar and wines and fatty wild goose, observes the celebration of the king's birthday ending at midnight, then accompanies the Pursells across the parade ground home, to live thereafter through the next two months and then two more, until late February, all unconscious of the death of his brother, the "Rafe" with whom he had played and been tutored through childhood, and for whom in recent years he had felt a deepening affection.

The ball was ended, the Pursells were home, and the innocent Corimer this same evening chose to accompany his friend Schaw through the streets, dark by then, to the latter's lodging house. When they arrived, Hogg, the Scots landlord, was still up, setting his downstairs in order after the day's revelry, and so urged on them a bottle of Madeira by the fire in the sitting room, and then another—"though I thought it bad wine"—as the two young friends "chopped politics" into the night, and talked "of the pursuits of men," and "of ghosts, and the immortality of the soul." At three, his condition as convalescent having finally caught up with him, Corimer fell asleep on the couch near the smoldering fire. He slept there, under his cloak, two hours and more before his friend reentered and awakened him.

Though it was not yet dawn, light gleamed through the windows. People were passing up Broad Street, usually empty this early in the morning. Multitudes of people: clogs sounded on the cobbles, and clattering wagon wheels, and the hooves of horses. Corimer followed Schaw to the door. Outside, "the street was as full of lanterns," writes the journalist, "as the Haymarket is full of flambeaux on opera night." Many passersby carried light, and all were moving in the same direction—old and young, men and women, freemen and slaves, white and black, poor people and some not poor—all hurrying mutely northward.

The two spectators at Hogg's front door crossed over the stoop. In the chilly dusk they ascended Broad Street to the City Hall and turned left, up Wall Street with the multitude toward the heights of Broadway. Glancing behind him Corimer could see lights on the water approaching the shore, ferries and small boats crossing the river from timbered Brooklyn, "running swiftly and bringing over more hordes of people." And as the sky continued to fade toward morning, he saw that not only in the east toward Brooklyn but to the west along the Hudson the land and the banks were "black with people and horses."

All that movement was converging on the Presbyterian meet-inghouse on Wall Street, a stone edifice near the north corner this side of Broadway. Ahead, at the high doors, bailiffs and constables directed the crowds that were pushing their way into the vestibule. The church was already filled downstairs. In time Corimer and Schaw were jostled among the press up the nar-row stairwell to the balcony; there the two friends were sepa-rated, though still within sight of each other. Schaw's forward motion ended at a spot by the gallery railing. Corimer held his place in the back, against the rear wall and near a window from which he might look out into the street at the crowd still swelling below.

Leaning against the plaster wall he felt faint: "Some Indians set on a bench near me who stunk so that they had almost made me turn up my dinner." To add to his discomfort, a high, strained voice from among the pews below had begun to sing, shrill notes that others joined; soon, according to Corimer—offended Anglican skeptic—all were "roaring out psalms sitting on their backsides, and vulgarly bellowing forth their hymns like tavern songs."

He had time to wonder why he had followed Schaw here. For a half hour the packed congregation continued singing, even those, as Corimer could see, still on the street in the dull morning light. Then abruptly from the street crowd arose shouts that alerted and silenced the singers inside: shouts of hosannas at the approach of a wagon coming slowly into sight, before which the multitudes were parting.

In the tottery wagon sat two elderly ministers of the gospel, with a much younger minister seated between them. He looked no older than Schaw down there—not so old—hardly past twenty, possessed of a youth that seemed to mock the gown and cassock he wore. Yet he carried himself—this smooth-faced divine on whom the attention of all the vast crowd was fixed—with the assurance of a ruler before his subjects. Indeed, the youth appeared hardly to notice the crowd, his mind elsewhere, his gaze toward the cloud-filled sky, as the multitude reconverged behind his wagon and followed it to the fence gate before the church door.

Gravely the young man alighted, entered the church, and having passed under the balcony, reemerged making his way slowly up the thronged central aisle. He reached the altar. But once in front of the congregation, he seemed reluctant to speak. For a moment he stood with bowed head before them. His stature, Corimer noted, "was rather above middle size, graceful and well enough proportioned." The older ministers, the Reverend Mr. Pembleton, whose church it was, and the other (the record shows that he was a Mr. Noble), had taken seats beneath the pulpit. The crowd had grown quiet, an "awful quiet," as it would be described in other places on similar occasions time and again. But to Corimer these worshipers seemed to have gone "seriously, soberly, and solemnly out of their wits," confronting with such mute adoration the stranger youth, now turning his gaze on them, with a pronounced squint in his eyes and a Bible held high in one hand.

("As I went to the meeting," the preacher himself, the twenty-six-year-old itinerant preacher George Whitefield, would write of this very morning, "I grew weaker and weaker and could have chose to be silent rather than speak.") But now he had

31

named his text, pausing while pages of Bibles rustled through-out the congregation; and when Whitefield's voice did sound forth, even the unsympathetic Corimer found it "musical," and the remarkable delivery—awakening memories of the London theaters—seemed "the equal of any declaimer's at Drury Lane."

"I shall displease some," the voice was intoning, "being deter-mined to speak against their assemblies for the sake of conversa-tion, gallantry, and play." Having begun hesitantly, Whitefield himself attests in *A Continuation of the Rev. Mr. Whitefield's Journal* (1741) that on this occasion—as, apparently, on most others—"the spirit of the Lord gave me freedom, till at length the word came down like a mighty rushing wind, and carried all before it":

"Do *balls* and *assemblies* tend to promote the glory of *God*? Let me warn persons of the great danger those are in who either by their subscriptions, presence, or approbation promote societies of a quite opposite nature to religion. And I would not be understood to mean only those public meetings which are de-signed manifestly for nothing else but revelings and banquet-ings, for chambering and wantonness, and at which a modest heathen would blush to be present. . . ."

The effect of that voice ringing over New Yorkers enclosed in the cold of an unheated church was extraordinary. Perhaps two thousand people had jammed themselves together in and around this narrow space, and not a cough was heard from them, not a stirring, not the smallest sound as the force of Whitefield's tongue lashed across their spirits. Corimer found himself gazing incredulously at a soot-faced urchin not far off—some layabout or sweep—who was silently raining forth tears that washed white gutters down his black cheeks. The voice from the pulpit thundered on:

"Those who value themselves most on their beauty and dress, and do not love God on earth, will be most deformed in hell." And at the word a groan escaped from the congregation below. "There is no dressing in hell, nothing but fire and brimstone there, and the wrath of God." Now the congregation was breaking into an alarming response, moaning alongside Corimer, and trembling. One decrepit old fellow had started writhing in the aisle below him, and a servant girl in the balcony was whining aloud. "O what will you do," the preacher pressed forward, "when the elements shall melt with fervent heat; when this earth, with all its fine furniture, shall be burnt up; when the archangel shall cry, *time shall be no more!* . . ."

And the Reverend Mr. Whitefield himself, who had awakened the response as he would many times again, in England and Scotland and Wales and up and down the east coast of America until his death thirty years later, that evening recorded what he saw before him now: "Look where I would, most were drowned in tears. The word was sharper than a two-edged sword, and their bitter cries and groans were enough to pierce the hardest heart. Some were struck pale as death, others wringing their hands, others lying on the floor, others sinking into the arms of their friends, and most lifting up their eyes toward heaven and crying out to God. I could think of nothing when I looked at them," the minister concluded in his evening's recollection, "so much as the Great Day. They seemed like persons awakened by the last trump."

To Whitefield they did, but to Corimer in the gallery that morning they seemed like "gibberers taunted to a frenzy by a mountebank." The sight of such "extravagancies" struck the English aristocrat as "the most outlandish infatuation that ever I witnessed." Below him, in a pew toward the front, one fat drudge in homespun had thrown out her warty arms in a fit, shrieking and falling across the uncushioned seat. "Man is half a devil and half a beast," the preacher was shouting, leaning far over the pulpit and punctuating his words by smiting the lectern. "His body is vile indeed! Subject to such vile diseases, put to such vile, yea very vile uses, and to come to so vile an end!"

Near Corimer, no more than three heads away, a comely young gentlewoman in a chip hat was gazing fixedly, ardently, toward the impassioned speaker, wringing her hands and murmuring over and over, "Oh, my Jesus, my pierced Jesus . . ."

The cries from the church that morning were heard a great way off, on Queen Street and Smith Street and Flatten Barrack Hill, and Corimer in their midst perforce heard it all—all that wailing from those "hairbrained fanatics," caught up in their "mad and ridiculous frolics," their countenances "beslobbered with tears." Pressed in among reeking colonials he watched and listened until at last the cross-eyed preacher, having ended, was making his slow progress back down the aisle, worshipful hands pawing him all the way, to reappear outside in the street by the wagon that would carry him from his devotees southward toward Georgia. Prayers in the street were being uttered loudly for him; the faithful and all the converts were striving to touch his sleeve or his ascending shoe or the backboard of his wagon, and all followed his departing form with wishful looks. Even the shabbiest among them had tossed coins into the wagon, or snuffers or thimbles or whatever else they might humbly offer for his orphan house abuilding in the pine forests near Savannah.

As for Corimer, watching disgustedly through the upstairs window, all at once he let out a cry of his own. With the crowd that was starting to leave the balcony, Schaw had been making his way closer, so that his friend at the window was able to call and gesture to him, pointing; for there, right down there in broad daylight on the street below, grinning on a fence rail at the intersection, sat the runaway slave Bonny Jack. He was wearing a cloth cap and, under a threadbare waistcoat, the same brown checked shirt he had fled in a month ago. In plain sight, right there. Struggling to make a way through the gallery toward the stairs, the slave's owner was calling again to Schaw, to the puzzled, freckled face still at some distance from him. But long before the balcony mob had thinned enough to let Corimer down to the vestibule, even before Schaw could make his way to the window to confirm what had been seen, Jack and his two black companions had left their perch and, grinning still, had ambled down Broadway and disappeared.

* * *

Many years later, as an illustrious old man, Francis Schaw would write that this morning's attendance at the sermon by Whitefield was the most important event of his life.

By that time, to be sure, the friend of Corimer's youth was in his mid-sixties and gout-ridden, so that his memory might have been fuzzy, because little in the record of the days immediately after the sermon would indicate so sharp a break with the past as his recollection suggests. We recall that Schaw had known of Whitefield at Pembroke College, Oxford. Both had been servitors, from humble families, and so paying for their education by serving wealthier scholars. But Schaw as an Oxford undergraduate had more than once (to his later mortification) joined a crowd of rowdy students congregated each week to taunt the excessively devout young Whitefield and his followers on their way to St. Mary's to receive the Sacrament. Whitefield's Holy Club members whom Schaw and others jeered at had been given periodically to shedding copious tears for their sins, then laughing uncontrollably in acknowledgment of God's goodness. They had sought to reform whores and to exorcise ghosts from haunted houses; a couple of days a week those holy ones had fasted. An odd bunch, provoking with such excesses the insults of certain of their classmates along the public ways. With others Schaw had jeered at them himself, before coming down from Oxford in form in the summer of 1736 and going off to sea. Thereafter the scoffer had lived for a while in the West Indies, had returned to London, had fallen in with Corimer, and had journeyed to the New World, where on this Friday morning at the end of October 1740, he had found himself listening once more to his old schoolfellow, whose course had driven Whitefield straight forward meanwhile across those same four intervening years, absorbed in God and now preaching as an ordained minister to a huge colonial congregation, and one no larger than the crowds that were likely to gather daily to hear him wherever he spoke, in church or field, in England or America.

Strange it must have felt, attending Whitefield's words under these different circumstances, in such distant surroundings. Yet during the remainder of the itinerant preacher's brief stay in New York there is no indication that Schaw made an effort to see him. On the contrary, reunited with Corimer, that auditor spent Friday morning after the sermon looking for Councilor Horsmanden, first in King Street, then at the City Hall, finally locating the judge at Downing's tavern on Pearl Street, where Corimer was able to report the sighting of runaway Jack, still lurking impudently in this very town. And on Saturday as well, Schaw and Corimer were congenially together during the afternoon, at the Exchange awaiting mail from the packet from England; and again on Sunday they were in one another's company on the roof of the merchant Pursell's warehouse; and nothing in Corimer's journal entries then or during succeeding days suggests a strain in their relationship, despite their entirely different responses to Whitefield's preaching, and despite the awakened interest that the same journal tells us Corimer was feeling now for Pursell's daughter. For that shift in feeling might have caused its own estrangements. On the long crossing from Greenwich aboard the *Happy Return* it was Schaw who had been mooning love-struck over Elizabeth—Dorinda to his Aimwell—while Corimer had been passing the time at sea reading Juvenal, eating roasted chestnuts, wasting compassion on the unremittingly seasick Jack, and listening to old Captain Rollins's numberless yarns about storms and maroonings.

Now on dry land, Sunday morning before church, Corimer and Schaw, together with young Lindsay, had accompanied the merchant Benjamin Pursell to the roof of the latter's warehouse, in order to approve the latest scheme of that tinkerer in the mechanic arts. The warehouse was a two-story ell, part of the Pursell home along Broadway, with its own street entrance (the brick mansion itself, gable toward the street, faced south, looking over fort and bay). Upstairs past the hogsheads of sugar and rum, on up to the garret where the bags of grain were stored, Pursell with his spyglass had led his son and guests to the dormer window at the far end that gave access to the narrow walkway on the roof, behind a low railing. They had stepped over the window ledge and out into a cloudy November morning, stiff winds greeting them from the Hudson. But Pursell was so pleased with his just completed improvement that he would show it off whatever the weather—and however much his alterations might have disfigured the lines of the house as seen from street and garden below. Earlier in the fall, in the public interest, the merchant had inserted in the *Gazette* a letter of general advocacy that allows us to know what workmen had accomplished on his home: "Let a balcony," he had urged his fellow townsmen, "be erected over the ridge of the roof of every dwelling in our city, on which tubs and pails of water may be kept against fire. The advantages of such a precaution are many. As a diversion, citizens might water their gardens from the tops of the houses, with water long standing in the sun, and thus rendered more fit for that purpose than cold water from the well. Or they might wash dust from the roofs, and thereby render water received into their cisterns more pure. When they intend their servants should sweep the streets, they may from thence sprinkle and allay the dust. Further, such a balcony would afford a commodious place for the observations of those versed in astronomy. And such observers would be as so many sentinels to discover the first breaking out of any fires in the neighborhood. . . ."

The inspiration had been made a reality atop Pursell's own mansion. Ascending a short flight of steps on the roof, the three gentlemen and the nine-year-old, bewigged like them and richly arrayed for church, stood among open, empty barrels in the raw morning. In the parade ground below, wagons were arriving from the Out Ward, bearing Dutch husbandmen and their families into town to worship; some of the horses, unharnessed, had been set to graze on the grassy plot that spread to the river's edge and the Half-Moon Battery. The chapel bell in the fort was ringing, and the bell of the old Dutch church on Garden Street. "P was full of the wisdom of his enterprise," Corimer tells us— and we imagine those rooftop listeners shivering impatiently, hugging themselves for warmth, as their host elaborated the uses of this architectural deformity. Elsewhere in his journal Corimer refers to Pursell as a "pompous simpleton" who could complacently expose himself to his fellow citizens by expressing alarm in public prints about the evils of excessive tea drinking, who collected and even cherished the handiwork of benighted Indians, who dabbled eternally in "improvements" as now, fumbling to get the mount of his spyglass in place. Simpleton he may have seemed face-to-face, though the portrait by John Watson that serves as frontispiece to Volume I of the scholarly *Pursell Mercantile Papers, 1737–1783* (New York, 1959) presents to posterity an aspect imposing enough: resplendent wig, shrewd eyes, three substantial chins, ample waist, the ringed fingers beyond the ruffled sleeve pointing toward ledgers and inkwell on a table. Simpleton perhaps, but the man could make money, as indeed could that nine-year-old beside him as soon as he grew to manhood; a portrait of Lindsay Pursell in his thirties is the frontispiece to Volume II, and the activities of Lindsay Pursell during his maturity, as recorded in the papers of the second volume, would vastly augment his family's fortune in the years ahead, until the Revolution overwhelmed it all.

Already by 1740 their fortune was substantial, as Corimer shivered beside them on the mansion roof of a Sunday morning, waiting to look through the spyglass. Pursell was earning his money in commerce, which to be so profitable in that world before laissez-faire would have had to include some gunrunning and smuggling and illegal dealings with native tribes, in defiance of the numerous mercantile ordinances of the mother country. In fact, one assumes that this same merchant was the American correspondent whom the Englishman was seeking to persuade to engage with overseas counterparts as they competed against the Royal African Company in the slave trade. Letters would be making their slow way back and forth between here and London and the West Indies, and meanwhile the agent (as Corimer doubtless was) for those Londoners must bide his time and continue to ingratiate himself with a potentially useful host. At Pursell's urging he steps forward now and places his eye to the glass: porpoises are tumbling among bleak waves near the open sea, where the glass is pointing. Behind him, Pursell gloats over being able henceforth to identify vessels a full day before they come into harbor.

Corimer raises his head from the eyepiece. Down in the garden are Madame Pursell and Elizabeth, ready for church, the older woman with her muff, the younger smiling, waving up to Schaw, who has called to her. She is wearing a green joseph and holds a gold-clasped psalm book in one hand. So charming a specimen of womanhood would assuredly provide another reason for humoring a not ungenerous host, and him her father. "Resolve," wrote Corimer in that day's entry, using the present tense, "to open my mind to E before this week is out."

* * *

Yet he seems not to have done so. On the contrary, before the week was well along he was abruptly moving to quarters of his own—not to a farm in the Out Ward of the city after all, but rather to a house in King Street, "next door to the Hon. Daniel Horsmanden, Esq.," advertised at the time as available to be leased at £48 a year. Tuesday, November 4, 1740: "Rose about six. At eight drank a pint of milk. Read from six to eleven, then shaved, dressed, and packed to be ready to go by two, at which time P[ursell] was to make a cart ready. I put up my linen in my chest with as many other things as it could hold. My clothes in a great trunk, and all things being ready"—copper pot, bedstead, the flute, the monkey, Milne with the greyhounds, Pursell's slaves aboard to help—"I dispatched them and dined with the family on a fricassee of chickens. . . ."

Why the move occurred when it did must be conjectured. Were Corimer's sensibilities finally urging him to decline further kindnesses from a host he regarded as a simpleton? Or after writing his journal entry Sunday afternoon did he speak to Elizabeth, opening his mind to her and meeting with a rebuff? Or (most likely) did the young aristocrat come to weigh matters soberly and conclude that a permanent alliance with a colonial family soiled by trade would be unseemly? Best, then, to put some distance between him and the danger that charming Elizabeth posed.

Whatever the motive, the move to his own quarters does suggest that Corimer had determined on a more or less lengthy stay in this remote town of twelve thousand souls at the edge of a wilderness. How he spent succeeding days, with winter coming on, may be inferred from journal entries, although through the next few months after the move to King Street those entries are less frequent and seldom so full as formerly. He read in the mornings, called on Schaw when that dominie was not engaged in giving lessons to his two or three pupils, at the Exchange browsed over the papers for news from Europe, dined occasionally with the Pursells, and on several evenings attended at the Hungarian Club, which met at Downing's tavern, and of which company Councilor Horsmanden had urged the visiting aristocrat to form a part. "We meet to converse, smoke, drink, pun, sing, dance, and fiddle together." Indeed, on the night following the move to new quarters Corimer was with the gentry of that club, first having stopped by the lodgings on Broad Street of his friend Schaw, who had a part to play in the activities of this evening.

The date was November 5—Guy Fawkes Day—and making their way from Hogg's rooming house to the tavern about seven o'clock, the two Englishmen found the usually dark streets lighted at several intersections by bonfires. "Rabble tossing their caps and parading about in fantastical garb, bearing effigies of the Pope and his allies the Devil and Pretender. Ragged children dragging wagons. A volley of rough-sounding Dutch from an overhead window." Corimer reports that at the intersection of Broad and Stone streets, not far from the tavern where the club was meeting, one bonfire had attracted the dames of the town as well, and its hungry flames were leaping skyward, sparks scattering into the higher darkness not to commemorate the foiling of the Gunpowder Plot but rather to acknowledge an event as recent as the Reverend Mr. Whitefield's visit. For amid "howling prayers and hymns" godly folk were feeding their fire with the world's vanities: wigs, gloves, hoop petticoats, red-heeled shoes. Past those exultant fanatics Corimer for one was inclined to hurry, eager to get inside and out of a night that was cold for the season, the air this day having "turned very sharp, it being a degree of frost."

Accordingly, the fire that the two new arrivals found in the fireplace in the front room of Downing's "was very grateful." Before them, gathered about a table, they found as well "a mixed company, among the rest Mr. Horsmanden, Mr. DeLancey, and a gentleman in a blue coat with a scarified face whose name I cannot recollect, from Antigua." Each was a bumper man, Horsmanden in particular a "jolly toper, and gives good example, and so is esteemed among these dons. One Levy played a good violin, Quinn bore another pretty good part." They had a supper that included partridge, fat bacon, sweetmeats, and jellies, after which "all put about the bowl again, the table chat running upon privateering and such discourse as has now become so common as to be tiresome."

In short, "the conversation was indifferent dull, but the viands and wine were tolerable." About nine, having passed the punch bowl from hand to hand until they were "pretty well flushed," the members got down to the business of the evening. Ten gentlemen, including Corimer, were seated around the table, wigs that had been removed earlier back on their heads as the president, Horsmanden "with his solemn nose," assumed his special seat, a more imposing one against the wall, under the club seal and the mezzotint of the Twelve Golden Rules. The club secretary, Quinn the fiddler, was standing to read the minutes, over the voice of the landlord bellowing in the hallway to a servant girl. Minutes approved, the capation followed. All donned their cocked hats. A chair was set on the table, and Corimer was helped to get up there and take his seat as inductor; Schaw on the table as a new member kneeled before him to receive the laying on of hands. With swords or pokers shouldered, fellow club members sang a fine rousing chorus of the club's anthem, which brought the landlord grinning to the half-opened door in time to witness the end of the ceremony.

The rest of that night's meeting was given over to group criticism, rather soddenly, of "a poem in the newspaper," then to a concluding speech by Mr. DeLancey, the opening of which Corimer does us the service to copy down: "It is not often that thefts can be narrated which are calculated to excite a smile; and yet I am much mistaken if my listeners do not relax their risible faculties when they are informed of a singular method of stealing garter buckles. . . ." The speech provoked a good bit of horseplay, with wigs off again, and the wags vocal, and the bumpers abounding, colonial gentlemen at their ease in the privacy of their club, one of them adding to the general hilarity by producing and inflating a pig's bladder bound to a pair of beaver's testicles, two others wrestling, a couple of others dancing a country dance, yet another snoring asleep on the floor.

However, when the club adjourned at eleven o'clock, dignity had been reclaimed, as members exited sedately into the night, wigs in place and two by two, under the stern scrutiny of neighbor women at upstairs windows nearby.

* * *

Except for Corimer. "The wine had made me frolicsome. Nothing would serve but a wench; accordingly I sallied out in search of a place of nocturnal entertainment."

Schaw hurried to follow, not in order to indulge himself but to look after his friend. The other club members seem to have headed home as grave as philosophers, but Corimer (were his frustrations with Elizabeth a factor?) would go awhoring, through streets ruddy in the light of the dwindling bonfires, through cold that his inner warmth defied. That charge of Lord Ashfield's in later years, to the effect that the fifth Earl of Cavendham reveled in the company of the drunken and profligate, seems hardly substantiated by the bulk of the surviving evidence, though for this specific evening of a life (Wednesday night it was, November 5, 1740—and into Thursday morning), his lordship would have found documentation to support the oft-quoted slur.

Corimer himself provides it, the following day, contritely, in a journal entry as detailed as his befuddled memory will let him set down, after having made his way home at last, still "more in liquor than was needful." He had been helped home in the early morning and got to bed "not so sober as becomes a young man, where I had not been long before the wine, uneasy in its confinement, made its way through the same passage by which it went in. This discharge gave me great ease, and I went to sleep. I rose at noon, after a rest not so calm nor easy as those I enjoy when not heated with wine and geneva." Thereupon, penitently, full of righteous resolves on the day after, the erring Anglican sat down to his journal and made his confession.

He remembered after the club meeting having left Downing's with Schaw at his heels. "I was elevated, and felt myself undaunted to engage in the wars of the Paphian queen." Perhaps at the fort on the night of the anniversary ball was where he had learned that "to walk out after dusk on the battery is a good way for a stranger to fit himself with a courtesan, that being the general rendezvous of the fair sex of that profession, and with a choice of pretty jades among them, both Dutch and English." To the battery he would go then, despite the coldness of the night and the lateness of the hour, and despite whatever reasons Schaw at his side might have offered to dissuade him from his purpose.

That his friend's aims were not in line with Corimer's is clear; in fact, the nobleman weaving in the wrong direction up Broad Street was doing what he could to disencumber himself of Schaw's presence. And with a drunk's cunning—a sudden bolt into a dark passageway, fleeing, hiding?—somehow he did so. Yet Corimer on his own never reached the battery, for on one of the side streets in the South Ward he encountered "a piece in a red cloak of a good buxom person and comely face." She was carrying a lighted tin lantern. The two conferred briefly: she had been on her way somewhere, but would go with him.

Now Corimer and the girl were huddled in a three-sided shed, mottled with lantern light and just out of the cold wind. The girl was giggling, while Corimer was trying to quiet her lest Schaw should hear them. A woodshed it was: board floor, cut logs piled high in back, churns and barrels around, and on the wall, above the girl's shoulder—what was her name? Peggy. Peggy, the Newfoundland Beauty—above and behind the giggling Peggy were snowshoes, a saw blade, a broom. She put the lantern out. Did she have armor? He was toying with her, while she "wondered at my size. She said that if ever I tupped a virgin I would hear her squeal. . . ."

But over her giggles movement outside beyond the shed: Schaw? They held still, Corimer's hand to her mouth. A dark figure passed some yards away, treading on gravel, and in a moment another, then a third. Slaves carrying night soil to dump in the river, waste from the chamber pots of their master's family. But did she have armor? She giggled behind his hand, caressed him, when he removed his hand assured him that it would be all right, that armor spoiled the sport.

A strong, plump, good-humored girl, though (as our reformed debauchee remembers) "her breath smelled of spirits." Was she big with child? Her belly seemed big with child. The sport, she was saying, "was much pleasanter without armor, and she was quite safe. I was so rash," writes the rueful Corimer, "as to trust her, and had a very agreeable congress, though it had been my whim to lubricate her on the battlements, with the mighty ocean roaring beyond us. . . ."

Yet when it was over—that wrestling among cobwebs against the shed wall—and though "I had dipped my machine in the canal and performed most manfully," the gallant felt a wave of self-loathing wash over him, having stooped "to make a most intimate companion, and most imprudently, of a groveling-minded, ill-bred, worthless creature." The girl was going to take him somewhere to get warm; she circled his arm over her shoulder. Corimer belched; she giggled again. And again they heard noises outside the shed.

The Beauty bent forward to peer into darkness.

Black figures were passing, one with a shielded candle, treading on gravel the same few yards away. They were carrying not tubs of waste but what Corimer now recognized as firkins of stored goods. Where would they be carrying firkins in the dead of night? Their footsteps receded. The nobleman belched again, began to moan softly, venting his self-disgust. Playfully the Beauty cupped his ballocks, then helped him adjust his clothing and belt on his sword. She retrieved her lantern and stepped with him into the yard.

Now the Englishman was in a dimly lit room, a wash area with wooden tubs about. He was seated in a draft, on a straight-back cane chair. The girl had gone to get him more drink. He was trying to remember the words of a song he wanted to sing. Rising, he staggered toward bright warmth glimpsed beyond a door that she had passed through and closed. His vision doubled the door latch. Leaning his head against the cool door he thought what he wanted to do.

His head spun lightly. The latch. But his hand had not yet reached it before the door opened, and the woman was there, and beyond her—just a glimpse, because she stepped quickly into the area and closed the door behind her—but for an instant he had hazily glimpsed a big room alight full of noisy Negroes, fifteen or twenty black men and women, some around a table laughing and drinking, others playing billiards, others dicing, one huge black by the fireplace holding a squawking fowl. Who? But the woman turned him and led him back to the chair without acknowledging the questions his lips seemed unable to phrase. She put the mug of gin in his hands, making sure his fingers were firmly grasping it. He wanted to ask—but she guided the mug to his lips, and he drank.

More time must have passed. The drafty room was lit by her reillumined lantern and a crusie on a ledge behind and above him. He watched the doubled reflection of its flame flicker in a small window in the opposite wall. His eyes closed. He dozed in the chair.

Then a tall man in a leather apron was standing over Corimer. The man was thin, bearded, with heavy eyebrows. He had a red cap on, the journalist remembers, and he was frowning, holding an earthenware pitcher. As Corimer's eyes opened, the frown dissolved into an obsequious smile. Stooping, the man retrieved the mug from the floor, put it in Corimer's hands, poured more gin into it. The woman Peggy lurked in the shadows by the door. What words would let him ask them something? They left before he could think, went back to the kitchen. Corimer had wanted to ask about the blacks, whose voices he could no longer hear. When the door to the kitchen had been opened, the light he could see had dimmed. Corimer drank, thought, drank again. He rose, staggered, fell, lay on the floor, his cheek wet in the spilled geneva.

His gaze settled on the window with night beyond it. The light of the crusie danced in reflection in the single pane. He felt his waist. Of course his purse was gone. And his sword, and watch, and pocketbook. He would rise now, soon, and find the rascal with the beard and demand them back—watch, sword . . . —after a nap here on the soft floor. He would close his eyes and nap, then rise . . .

But his eyes just before closing had made out a face pressed against the window. It was still there when he looked again. Faint beyond the dirty pane, a black face was grinning down at him: white eyeballs, white teeth, a mocking grin, the scar, the brand on the forehead. On the far side of the window was Bonny Jack.

Corimer blinked. The grin persisted.

Furious at his helplessness, the inebriate sprawling on the floor groaned and strove to get up, his weight on one arm, but the arm would not support so much. His shoulder struck the floor hard, with incipient pain, and he lay helpless, his vision blurring the grin that continued to mock his plight. Once more he struggled to rise, got to his knees finally, hurled himself crouching toward the window.

Abruptly the face disappeared, the window empty of all but

the dancing point of light. Corimer groped for a latch on the entrance adjacent, found it, threw open the door, and plunged into the vacant yard.

The house he had left was in darkness, not a noise from within, not a soul astir. Behind him the river washed the shore. He waited an instant, listening, then hurried forward away from the sound of the river, only to stumble and fall on the rutted earth. It smelled of barnyard. He rose, groped his way uncertain and shivering into the cold, his feet at last on cobbles so that he knew he had found a street leading somewhere. There was no moon, no stars, the night pitch black as he felt his way dizzily along, bumping into walls, hearing a sign creak overhead, his feet now splashing in muck at the center of the street, now thudding against the hard cobbles, his teeth chattering with the cold. Specks bothered his vision, stung his cheeks. He called aloud for the watch, called again.

Then light, and an arm was firmly around him. Schaw was beside him, holding a torch and draping a cloak over his throbbing shoulder. The watchman, that vigilant snorer no longer needed, croaked in a weary voice from a distant lane: "Past three o'clock." And Corimer, shameful and aching in his friend's charge, let himself be guided in the faintly lit direction of a burned-down bonfire. With a little shock he realized that the specks troubling his vision were falling snow.

* * *

That lightly falling snow of early November was gone by the following evening—a signal, merely, of the winter to come—but within two weeks another much heavier snow had descended, blanketing the earth to start a season of memorable severity. By then the sobered Corimer had been warned of what lay ahead; for in the interval between the snowfalls, having recovered from the effects of his carousal and after a walk with his greyhounds about town one chilly afternoon (during which he had observed the citizens at their preparations: piling logs, slaughtering stock, storing cellars with apples and beets and parsnips and potatoes), he had allowed himself to wonder "how some of these people in wintertime live here or defend themselves in such slight houses against what I am assured is violent cold."

All the more wonderful during the present winter. The surviving testimony concerning the rigors of that particular season is abundant. William Smith, colonial historian who endured those days, recorded later that the winter of 1740–41 "(ever since called the hard winter) was distinguished by the sharpest frost and the greatest quantity of snow within memory of the oldest inhabitant. The weather," writes Smith in *The History of the Province of New York,* "was intensely severe from the middle of November to the latter end of March. The snow by repeated falls was at length six feet above the surface of the earth. Cattle of all sorts perished by the want of fodder, and the deer of the forests were either starved or taken, being unable to browse or escape through the depth of the snow. The poor both in town and country were distressed for food and fuel, and by the scarcity of these articles the prices of almost everything else was raised."

Words that evoke a lengthily felt ordeal. Could we go there, the stink of eighteenth-century New York would doubtless first strike our senses, and the greater contrasts with our own world—noisier when it was noisy, silent and much darker in the depths of night. Evidence everywhere of Nature's maiming of the human form would appall our sensibilities—goiters, humpbacks, stumps, empty eye sockets—but the cold might be what would finally defeat us: window-rattling blasts of icy winter that pierced all life to the marrow, unrelieved outdoors or in, more penetrating than what many of us in our comforts would ever be able to imagine. Incidentally, in undertaking such an imaginative effort we would get only a little help from Corimer's journal, unless its very silences are suggestive. For after his evening of debauch he devotes succeeding journal pages to generalized, lofty, and hardly original reflections that rephrase current philosophical attitudes, notably those of Lord Shaftesbury conducting inquiries on Virtue and Enthusiasm. But even that much of an effort Corimer soon abandons, as winter seems to numb his writing fingers.

Instead of journalizing, he merely survives, awaiting the onset of the gleet while nursing his aching shoulder by the fire. Having reported his sighting of Jack to the proper authorities, and after making his complaint about the theft of purse, watch, and sword, he does venture to the river once—though in vain—to locate the scene of his nighttime escapade. Thenceforth the entries from mid-November until the first of March are few indeed, and for the most part uninformative: an occasional lament in this ice-bound port at the absence of news from Europe, a cautious expression of relief when time passes with his privities manifesting no sign of distemper, a notation of an excursion to the Exchange to meet a mysterious *R* (not otherwise identified), who may have been involved in his debts at home or in his slaving schemes. In early December, Corimer and Schaw and Elizabeth "went to a shew to see dexterity of hand performed"; before braving the cold "I wrapped myself well up in two pairs of stockings, two shirts, and a great coat. E had caused her foot stove to be brought by Annie." On three or four other occasions he visits the Pursells, who are better supplied than most for the season—cellar and garret full, dried fruits and vegetables strung along every beam and rafter. Pursell "has purchased considerable numbers of quails, which he keeps in cages properly sheltered from the cold, and feeds, in order to set them at liberty in the spring to preserve the breed." And indeed, "the cold has been so severe," *The New-York Weekly Journal* was not long in reporting, "that squirrels and birds have been found froze to death, and great quantities of sheep have perished. . . ."

We find more, in fact, in the newspapers than in Corimer's journal to help us imagine what those beleaguered citizens were suffering. The journalist does note randomly through December and January that "the frost is so intense that if you walk in leather shoes and gloves you are frost-bitten. It [*the frost*] gets down the chimneys. Handling brass or iron leaves a blister on the fingers. . . . See people with ears quite froze. . . . Shaving is vastly disagreeable and painful. In bed cold even with ten blankets on. . . . Ground floors dark at midday with snow over the windows. Strong punch in twenty minutes is covered with a scum of ice, and Jamaica rum quite froze in a room with a fire in it."

But those brief utterances, made as though with an effort, are all Corimer can manage until early March. Meanwhile the newspaper has recorded in December that "our streets are filled with confused heaps of snow, so that lovers of sled-riding can scarcely use them without danger. The whole mass fell in one night's time, and now the cold is so excessive that while I"—Zenger, the editor—"am writing in a warm room by a good fireside, the ink freezes in the pen." In the midst of such cheerlessness the numerous Dutch of the town were soon conjuring forth their stern and dignified Santa Claus, his sleigh drawn by reindeer, to descend chimneys and distribute gifts or switches during another Christmas season. Not long after the start of the new year, "a collection," we are told, "was made for the poor throughout the several wards in this city, when a generous spirit of charity appeared in everyone. The money collected amounted to upward of five hundred pounds—a seasonable relief for the distressed in so hard a winter." Items of individual misery were now being regularly reduced to newsprint: drownings (few knew how to swim then) when storms damaged wharves and shipping; a ship caught in ice floes and carried out to sea. "We hear that a canoe with a woman and a child at her breast and five men in it was last week [about New Year's] jammed in with the ice and drove to Cunny-Island, where they were all froze to death." A sentry froze at his post near the fort. An unidentified child, still clutching her begging basket, was discovered in woods near Fair Street; ravens circling above the treetops located the corpse, which rats had eaten at. Elsewhere, debtors confined in the unheated jail, "impressed with a grateful sense of the obligations they are under to a respectable public for the generous contributions that have been made to them, beg leave to return hearty thanks because they have been so far preserved from perishing in a dreary prison from hunger and cold." And through the ordeal the pious were urging people to humble themselves before the Lord for these "tokens of

His displeasure," evidenced "in the late excessive snows and tempests": "*And if*— quoting Leviticus—"*ye will not for all this hearken unto Me, then I shall punish you seven times more for your sins.*"

Yet prayers and humblings seemed futile. "Our winter continues very severe," the *Weekly Journal* reported as January advanced, "and, the river abounding with ice, no vessels can yet stir, and the poor are drove to the greatest extremities for want of wood. It is however to be hoped [*this allusion to Whitefield's recent appearance among them*] that the poor of our own country will meet with as much encouragement as the orphans of another, and that those who shewed their liberality in the collections for the latter will extend their charity to the former."

Bald, wrinkly, huddled old women, shaking with palsy. Infants in rags. Gray-locked paralytics. More fortunate New Yorkers responded as they could to "the deplorable circumstances this city is under." Tuesdays, Thursdays, and Saturdays were appointed for the receipt of offerings for the poor at the house of Mr. Nicholas Ray, opposite the late Black Horse tavern: "In commiseration and compassion in this extraordinary time, a great number of the good people of this city of New York have contributed their charitable benevolence for the relief of poor housekeepers, widows, and other necessitous people as may stand most in need of it." Thus clothes and provisions were found for at least some of the naked and hungry during "the severity of a distressful season."

And still no thaw came, no milder mornings to wake to. In February, "we have now a second winter more severe than it was some weeks past, and the poor in great want, the late charitable contributions being almost expended. . . ."

On three occasions citizens venturing out at night and losing their way in darkness were found dead next day in drifts. The smell of cheap rum was everywhere. There was no fodder for cattle. Timid deer were emboldened to enter the city to seek feed from pig troughs. A fat fowl now cost 1*s.* 6*d*. A turkey that could have been had for 3*s.* 6*d*. before was 5*s*. now and hard to find. Wood was up from 40 to 58 shillings a cord, "and almost half the inhabitants in want." A pound of butter was 14d., "and many other things proportionable." And the *Weekly Journal,* noting those hard facts, was led again to wonder: "Under all these disadvantages, what must our poor suffer?"

* * *

Of what the well-off Corimer was suffering, his journal reveals nothing beyond the brief observations already quoted. On the first of March, however, he does take up his pen again and records a visit, Thursday, the twenty-sixth of February, with Schaw, at Hogg's lodging house on Broad Street. He and his friend had gathered in Mrs. Hogg's goods shop, a ground-floor room with an outside entrance on Jews Alley and, inside, a single counter over which she sold rum and cloth. The fire there was substantial, the hearth the warmest spot in the four-story building. Schaw and Corimer were seated near the fire, and Mr. Robert Hogg the landlord was on hand, that bluff, rotund Scotsman bantering his shopkeeping spouse: "the discourse," notes Corimer, "turned upon hysterics and vapors in women, when Mr. H, pretending to discover to me an infallible cure for these distempers, spoke neat bawdy before his wife, who did not seem to be surprised at it. A good mowing, he said, was a cure for such complaints. . . ."

A customer entered, stomping snow off his boots and blowing his knuckles. Schaw knew him as one Wilson, a lad of seventeen or eighteen who was often about; earlier they had had a few lessons when Wilson had tried unsuccessfully to make a start at learning to read. He was a sailor assigned to the *Flamborough,* man-of-war on this station; a couple of his friends were servants of gentlemen lodging at Hogg's. But this morning he had come only to bargain for linen—a routine transaction to which Corimer paid no attention, hardly aware when Mrs. Hogg summoned her husband away from the fire on an errand.

With young Wilson gone as well, she emerged a few minutes later from behind the counter—a woman as big as Hogg himself—and approached the hearth, preoccupied with a foolish thing she had done. The lad had had Spanish coins to pay with. To weigh a coin the shopkeeper had opened her bureau, in a drawer of which were scales and "a considerable quantity of milled Spanish pieces of eight. She reflected that she had done wrong in exposing her money in that manner to an idle boy who came so frequently to her house, and had immediately shut up the bureau again." That had been the reason for sending her husband out of the house to weigh the coin next door. But by then the sailor had seen her money, and "was charmed with it," and she felt sure "wanted to be fingering of it."

All this Corimer would have forgotten. The details he writes out at length in an entry three days later, on Sunday, no doubt to distract himself from grief. For on Saturday evening at the Exchange he had received at last, by way of a packet from Dover to Charleston, and thence overland by stages to Baltimore, Philadelphia, and finally New York, the letter his father had penned the preceding November to inform him of the death of his elder brother in Rome. Presumably the recipient of that tardy news had remained alone with his thoughts on Saturday night, but early Sunday had repaired to Hogg's again, for a friend's company.

He had arrived in midmorning to find the lodging house in an uproar. Someone the night before had entered the shop by the door on Jews Alley and robbed it of snuffboxes, several silver medals, chiefly Spanish, "divers pieces of linen and other goods, wrought silver, &c., to the value in the whole of £4 and upward." Mrs. Hogg was alternately irate and in tears, her husband determined on vengeance.

And vengeance would come, more than the Hoggs could conceive of. For from that domestic mishap were to flow far-reaching consequences: an investigation, charges, imprisonments, alleged acts of retaliation by cohorts of the accused that would lead to panic and mass trials and punishment involving finally one hundred and seventy-four persons incarcerated, including Peggy, the Newfoundland Beauty. Judge Horsmanden would preside at their trials, which Schaw and Corimer would attend.

II

On the evening after the robbery at Hogg's the sixteen-year-old Elizabeth Pursell writes to a correspondent in England:

I take the opportunity of a ship bound shortly for Gravesend to acknowledge the receipt of dear Sophy's agreeable favor dated 30 October, and to assure her that it gives me sincere pleasure to hear of her and her family's welfare. My father continues well except a bad cold and cough that teases him. Indeed it has been a severe winter here for us all, with most melancholy consequences for the poor and necessitous, which we have been employed in aiding as best we can, that otherwise must have starved or froze, though I fear and grieve for the many beyond reach who are unimaginably suffering in the excessive cold. Yesterday several persons had like to perish on the ice in the river near our house. Snow is still in the woods four feet deep, and we hear of cattle froze stiff in one night in the stables.

I am obliged to you for your intelligence in regard to

persons and affairs in or about Chandos Street, and in return have many things to communicate to my friend.

We have had a sick house these four weeks past, my brother being ill of a quinsy, though he does well now and seems quite recovered. He had it violently. This afternoon I went to church with Mama and my aunt, and when we came home and was reading our books in came Mr. Schaw and soon after Mr. Corimer with his man Milne, who we see in the kitchen. Mr. C received last night the sad news of the death of an elder brother in Rome in October last. You will have read of it in the newspapers. The circumstance fills us with melancholy, and more so as it happens to a friend. It oppresses his spirits, who is usually so easy and cheerful. For his part Mr. Schaw brought news of a recent robbery in his house, where all has been excitement and confusion and dismay, suspicion falling on a seaman who frequented the place and who had been for a time a scholar to Mr. S. But the boy vowed he took nothing, which Mr. S believes, and indeed this afternoon led constables to a tavern where the thief was found. It seems the house is frequented by seamen, idle mechanics, and slaves, the thief proving to be a negro slave who is now in custody and no doubt regrets his temerity, for which my father says he is sure to pay dearly.

What pleasure would it be if I could but now and then see some of my old friends, and have a little converse with them. Last Thursday se'ennight we saw performed in the assembly rooms a pantomime entertainment in grotesque characters called *The Spaniard Tricked,* to which was added an optic showing scenes of London in perspective. Dear sweet London: judge how the scenes affected us all.

My time allows no more than to assure you that your friends here join in wishing you every happiness, and my father joins me in his best respects to you and your family;

likewise to Miss Shipley, to whom he desires to send the enclosed poem.

I am, dear Sophia, your ever affectionate friend,

ELIZABETH PURSELL

N. York
Sunday eve. March 1st, 1741.

* * *

The lost poem sent to Miss Shipley must have been innocent enough, although who that friend or relative of Sophia's family was is no longer known. Sophia herself, recipient of Elizabeth's letter, was the only daughter of the London merchant Nathaniel Milner and great-granddaughter of Henry Wharton, one of the ministers ejected from their Church of England benefices by the Act of Uniformity of 1662. In March 1743—two years after the letter just quoted—Sophia Milner married Matthew Finch, Esq., of county Northumberland, M.P. for Bridgnorth from 1751 to 1764. One of the sons of that marriage grew up to be licentiate in midwifery of the College of Physicians and *accoucheur* to the Middlesex Hospital. Descendants of the Finches flourish in England and Canada still.

Elizabeth's letter is one of six that I own, all written to the same addressee within a year of the American girl's return to New York after her extended stay in England. The letters came into my possession through the good fortune and initiative of my father, brother of the scholar of colonial New York who spent seven years tracking down Corimer's journal until he found it among papers in an old woman's cedar chest in the upstairs back room of a farmhouse in southern Ohio. During the First World War—two decades before Uncle Ted's discovery—my father had been serving with the 156th Brigade of the 78th Lightning Division of the A.E.F., arriving in France in the summer of 1918 and suffering shoulder wounds at Chevières in the Argonne that caused him to convalesce through eight weeks in a military hospital outside London. While convalescing he had received word from home of the possibility of acquiring an ancestral correspondence that he had not known existed. I quote from the holograph memorandum in Dad's hand that accompanies the precious packet: "The letters," he writes, "remained in the possession of the family of the English lady to whom they were sent until within a few years. They then passed into the hands of a London bookseller, who identified the American author of the letters and corresponded with her descendants." Upon examining the letters, Dad moved promptly to acquire such a treasure, which he proceeded to bring across the ocean in early 1919, disembarking at Brooklyn to set the tin box triumphantly beside two other family relics that had once belonged to Elizabeth: a mourning ring and a spinet hammer. I own all three now, with the journal my most cherished possessions; all three—hammer, ring, and packet of letters—are on my desk as I write.

The letters are written on rice paper with matching gray envelopes, in a calligraphy of a beautiful, almost copperplate regularity. I have considered simply reproducing the text of the documents as they appear, one after the other with no more than a line or two of commentary. But a number of passages could have no interest for the general public, and other passages seem too cryptic or allusive to be understood without clarification from supplementary sources. Moreover, one or two pages in the sequence are missing. For those reasons it seems preferable to utilize the correspondence selectively—as has been done with Corimer's journal—to provide the basis of a continuing account, elaborating Elizabeth's version of events with what may be gleaned from other documents of the period, both public and private.

I have indulged in one further liberty. Elizabeth wrote: "I take the Op^o of a Ship bound shortly for Graves^d to aknolg^e the Recp^t of d^r Sophys agreable ffav^r dated 30 Octb^r & to aſsure her . . ." Whatever quaintness attaches to such conventions is an accretion of time, no part of the impression her words would have made on their original reader. How recapture a past all bewigged and unbathed? Transcribing exactly what this eighteenth-century correspondent wrote would not only impede comprehension; it would also invest her words with a fraudulent picturesqueness. Better, it seems, because closer to her meaning and intent, to transcribe that typical sentence, the opening sentence of Elizabeth's letter of the first of March 1741, as I have done above, on page 54, and to regularize elsewhere in the same manner.

✳ ✳ ✳

The letter dated March 1 was not dispatched until nearly a week afterward. In those days a correspondent would generally undertake a communication upon hearing that a ship was due to depart soon for a destination near where a friend lived. If then, as often happened, the sailing was postponed or canceled, what had been written so far would be set aside, to be resumed at a later date. So it was with the letter in the present instance; a postponement of sailing allowed time for Elizabeth to include an addendum some days later, giving further news about the robbery at the house where Schaw lodged.

But before turning to the addendum, I extract, for the light they cast on relevant events, briefly from the three letters she had written Sophia earlier, all of them during the autumn months that have been traversed through Corimer's journal. The earliest is dated Friday, September 26, 1740, no more than a couple of days after the voyagers to America had disembarked at last from the *Happy Return:*

> I immediately set down to write my dear Sophia, who will be gratified to learn of our safe arrival at New York, after a pretty good voyage of six weeks during which I was ill no more than half the time. Papa never was ill but eat and drank all the way. Mr. Corimer pronounced the vessel scarce better than a floating refuse heap, and all of us mewed up together, you may be assured we had time on our hands, which to while away the captain's clavier took its share with Mr. C's flute and Mr. Schaw's violin, so that

we often formed a concert to pass hours as tolerably as possible, and the gentlemen and Papa and I undertook to amuse each other by performing in theatrical pieces, but you may imagine that with the first sight of land we could all but be highly pleased. Yet nothing could equal the impression I received from the affectionate welcome my dearest mama and aunt gave us as we passed through our own dear gates after so long an absence. . . .

Mr. C is vexed by the treachery of his Jack, purchased as you recall at considerable expense to him. We were not well down river from Greenwich before the negro begun complaining, and continued so on the way until even the hardest heart must be moved. Indeed, I never before beheld such suffering; nay he could not so much as stand for sickness, but would be crawling about the decks most piteously on all fours munching biscuit day and night the length of the crossing. Yet no sooner had we set foot on land, and Mr. C commiserating all the while with this fellow's feebleness and anguish, when he proves in a jump to have been a great malingerer from the beginning, for instantly in full vigor he absconds from his master and has not been seen or heard from since. Mr. C has gone this day to have a notice inserted in the papers, but Papa begins to despair of his ever recovering him, who he says has crossed into Jersey by now. . . .

My aunt has grown fat in our absence, and looks extremely well. Our weather is fine, and I have set out a good deal today in the garden. We have now in the greenhouse a beautiful white camellia, and in the front of our house a sweet-scented clematis in very great perfection. My bitch puppy Sylvia, as was when we left for England, is now a great stranger-like spaniel dozing noisily at my feet in the sunlight in the periwinkle. . . .

From a second letter, dated Saturday, October 11, two weeks after the preceding:

Whilst I am waiting for an opportunity to write to dear Sophy by some ship for London I received her agreeable letter dated August 13. Your kind favor brings to remembrance former times and so many agreeable hours I spent with you. . . .

Mr. Corimer has been gravely ill since last I wrote, but I bless God that he seems now to be mending. I watch at present by his bedside, where he rests easy though cannon are firing close at hand for the king. Near a fortnight ago Mr. Schaw, Mr. C, and I undertook an expedition into the adjacent country some three or four miles, stopping under a tree at midday to enjoy a cold repast. But a most terrific wind and rain arose of a sudden, and as Mr. C's grizzle had lost a shoe, he must needs walk the creature and so was thoroughly wetted before reaching shelter. Nor did he escape feeling the effects of such bad weather. Indeed, he has had a very unpleasant seizure, and his sufferings very great. Fomentations were applied and leeches to the temples, and the bark was given him, but he could not continue it as it disagreed with his stomach. He was obliged to submit not only to the lancet but to blister and calomel, the last which seems to have worked to good effect, though he is woefully wasted, so that you would scarce know him. This has been an abrupt and melancholy interruption. Poor Mr. C has kept his room now for the better part of two weeks, where my aunt and Mama and I have attended to administer the warmer, soothing medicines such as hemlock and assafetida. . . .

And from the third letter, dated Thursday, November 6, nearly a month after the above:

My dear Sophy will be frighted by the length of the paper, but I am resolved to write you a long scribble. I would gratify your curiosity, or rather answer your obliging inquiries about this country, and to give you an idea of our place and situation, as you are pleased to desire.

... Hudson's River is a very little way from our house, flowing from the north into the ocean; its source is not known. Our lot extends two hundred feet into the river. There is a full view that can never be obstructed of the bay with little pretty islands down to the Narrows and of the grand passage near two miles across to Jersey. We keep two cows. Our wild fowl are chiefly quails, partridge, pigeons, and robins. We never saw any larks here, though plenty of tame fowl in season. Chickens we pay 6d or 7d for. We have rabbits and hares, but very different from what they are in England. . . . The east and southern parts of the city are in general low, but the west, where we live, is situated on dry, elevated soil, hence very healthy. The streets are irregular, some paved with round pebbles and lined with brick houses, many of which are covered with tile roofs. The principal street is near fifty foot broad and follows the watershed of the island, which is itself scarce a mile across at a medium. . . .

As you was so good to give me an account how you spent your time, I must in return tell you how we go on, though I fear will sound amazing dull. The only public entertainment and amusement are in an assembly in the winter, and feasting and parties, going out into the country, having a dinner and a dance. Wednesdays and Saturdays we have company at home, seldom less than ten on Saturdays to dine with us. There are cribbage parties at each other's houses. Lately we have been diverted by a very flaming preacher, both in his sermons inflaming and in his prayers, though I only heard of 'em, did not hear him, and he is gone now. Yet so quiet do we live that such a brimstone parson signifies. Last week we went to the fort to an assembly, danced till after 11 and then came home again by moonlight. There was a bright assembly of all the first people in the town and some excessive smart beaux and officers, upon my word. We danced ten couple and vastly pleasant it was, I with Mr. Schaw and Mr. Corimer, who is quite recovered now from the disorder which attacked him. The ball began with French dances, and then proceeded to country dances. . . .

I have been writing the above while my hair was dressing; fear you can hardly read it. [*To our eyes, here as elsewhere, Elizabeth's handwriting astonishes with its proficiency, as though engraved.*] Mr. C has just come but stayed only a short while. Quite downcast and mortified; he has had his pocket picked about nine last evening of [*a?*] little cash, his handkerchief, and a watch. The last he laments the loss on most. Desires me to send his respects; his good wishes ever attend you. My papa commissions me to return his best thanks for your obliging favor and to say he would ere this have acknowledged it but on Sunday eve he unfortunately pinched his finger in a door, by which means it was most sadly bruised and he has been forbidden by the surgeon to use it for some time. . . .

We have been visited yesternight with our first snowfall. Mama says she longs to sleep like a dormouse from autumn to spring. It may be unnecessary for me to reply to dear Sophy's direct enquiry about my determinations to remain a spinster. I am not insensible to the charms of a virtuous attachment and the comforts of a well-suited connection. Pray make no more excuses about long letters, and believe yours never seem so to me, who remain your faithful and devoted friend,

ELIZABETH PURSELL.

* * *

This of November, with what seems to be a hint about her developing feelings for Corimer, was the last written until the one the first of March, which relates Schaw's news of the robbery at his landlord's. For three months and longer winter had intervened, locking New York port in ice that kept ships from arriving or leaving. But by the end of February a vessel was at last preparing to venture seaward toward Gravesend on the other side of the Atlantic. The departure was announced, then postponed, so that to the letter about the robbery at Hogg's lodging house, already quoted at the beginning of this section, Elizabeth had time to compose an addendum in a quite different tone that must have perplexed and troubled her English correspondent:

Tues. noon. March 3rd

I take up pen again to acquaint my friend of a private affair of moment, all unexpected, connected with the robbery at Mr. Schaw's of which I writ before, and causing me much uneasiness. Letters are an imperfect intelligence, yet will try to say in few words what the matter is. Within the hour has come a woman to me to ask a favor that I may not, I venture to say cannot grant. Dear Sophia would justly say my duty as a Christian is to forgive, and she that charity demands—However, I am determined that such an one shall never again with my assent be permitted to enter our home. It grieves me excessively, as I told the woman, to withhold what might save one from a life of wretchedness and worse, indeed it does, yet 'tis not possible. O might I but converse with my dear friend what to do—But I will tell all plainly.

This morning comes to the gate where our servants loiter a most disagreeable old woman who would speak with me. I see her in the parlor by the fire and knew her at once despite the years that have passed since last setting eyes upon her. She was my brother Lindsay's nurse some eight or nine years past, nor have I scarce seen her since. As it was exceeding cold I bade her warm herself, which she did. O Sophy, the woman then brings out the reason for her visit, having come on behalf of one, a child who lives at the tavern where the stolen goods of which I writ you was thought to be hidden. Indeed, she says the child may have means of discovering the goods, for which something will be owing to her, as the woman says. But that can be none of my affair, and so I told Mrs. Kannady. I told her as much. She had learned from the girl—I cannot so much as write her name—she has learned that the child was once bound to my father and had served us, though served us very ill and so had left our house under circumstances so distressing—I will not pursue that hard reflection. I no longer know what I write. Dear good Sophy, sure my dear friend will make allowances, ill-prepared as I was—My state will not suffer me to write more at present. I beg your pardon. Let me hear from you.

* * *

What had intruded into Elizabeth's life may be pieced together from other sources, including Corimer's journal and a deposition at a related trial that spring.

The woman asking the favor so repugnant to her had been, as the letter says, formerly a wet nurse in the Pursell household; she was married to a peruke maker named James Kannady. In recent days Kannady had been one of the searching constables sent at the seaman Wilson's direction to recover the goods stolen from Mrs. Hogg's shop and alleged to be hidden at a tavern on the Hudson River. The constables' first search, on the day after the robbery, had uncovered nothing. Wilson, however, did at the time of the search identify a black slave in the tavern as the culprit who had that same Sunday morning, the morning after the theft, in the room where he was then lounging, flaunted Spanish money and speckled cloth identical to what the sailor had seen at Hogg's shop earlier in the week. On Wilson's identification the luckless slave was taken into custody.

The following evening, Monday—on the night before her abrupt intrusion into Elizabeth's life—Mrs. Kannady, according to that goodwife's account of events, was visited in her house by a servant girl named Mary Burton, "come to buy a pound of candles for her master." The girl's master was one John Hughson, disreputable owner of the very tavern not far off that the constables had earlier been searching in vain.

Aware (Mrs. Kannady reports) that Mary lived at the taverner's, "I asked her did she know aught of the recent robbery?"

The girl answered no. She did not. Yet although she denied several times that she knew anything about the matter, her questioner persisted:

"I asked her if she had a mind to be freed from such a master as Hughson was?"

Of that agreeable possibility they talked. If she would discover the goods—And the girl, as it happened, would have remembered service different from what the churlish Hughson required of her, service at the Pursell mansion in a world of domestic civility sharply contrasting to low tavern life. During the course of their talk Mary mentioned the Pursells, whom by chance Mrs. Kannady also knew and had served. A plan was suggesting itself: "If she would discover the goods, I might get her freed from Hughson's."

Finally the girl did reply after a fashion. "Your husband was not cute enough," she mumbled obliquely.

Not sharp enough in his search of the tavern? "Tell me where the goods are," the older woman persevered, aware that the aggrieved Hoggs would likely reward the restoration of their cloth and coins. "Tell me, and I will take you away from Hughson's tonight."

The prospect of freedom must have been tempting, as the interest being shown her must have gratified the neglected child. She nevertheless responded provokingly, according to Mrs. Kannady, "that she would not tell me anything tonight. She would tell me tomorrow. *But that my husband searching at Hughson's had trod upon the stolen goods.*" And with that tantalizing hint Mary had made her escape with the candles, before she could be questioned further.

The hint was enough, however, to send the goodwife shuffling the following morning to the Pursell household on Broadway. Would Miss Elizabeth be so kind as to urge her esteemed father to interest himself in repurchasing Mary Burton's indentures, so that the child might be removed from base influences of the tavern and restored to more suitable surroundings?

Surprisingly, Miss Pursell had refused to undertake that charitable office, even when reminded of the consequences of her refusal. Mary, "except she help her," would keep silent. Goods stolen from the Hoggs would thus go unrecovered. Any fellow thieves of the accused Negro would escape punishment. And an impressionable, vulnerable fifteen-year-old girl would continue her squalid life among low company that could lead only to crime, whoredom, and an early and violent end.

Elizabeth, however, remained adamant. She would do nothing on Mary Burton's behalf.

At best the importunate Mrs. Kannady could not have been an attractive petitioner, meddlesome and sanctimonious and self-serving as she seems even now, across the wide gap of time. The preceding night, for example, she had begun her talk with the servant Mary, come to her place only to make a purchase, by inquiring "whether that was a black child or a white child which the Newfoundland Beauty had, which lodged at her house?" The gossip would learn the color of the infant recently born to a woman residing at Hughson's tavern. "And Mary made answer that it was as white as any of my children, or any other child. I then told her that I heard that there was a negro who kept company with the Beauty and was the father of that child. Mary answered there was a negro came thither to her, but he was not the father of that child, she believed. Then I," notes Mrs. Kannady primly, "took upon me to give Mary good advice, who was a stranger in the country. I told her to have no dealings with negroes, and to have no hand in thievery, for that would be a means of bringing her to the gallows."

Perhaps the advice was disinterested, and perhaps her continuing concern for the girl had nothing to do with a proffered reward. In any case, what the woman did next day, after leaving the Pursells', was to locate Mr. James Mills, the undersheriff, "and I told him what had last night passed with Mary. Whereupon Sheriff Mills, with the recorder, Mr. Hogg and his wife, several constables, and others including my husband and myself, went down to Hughson's house."

Among those others was Corimer. The nobleman had been lounging at the Exchange with the recorder when the woman's news was brought to that interested party. The recorder—legal counsel for the city corporation—was, in fact, Corimer's friend, neighbor, and fellow club member, the honorable Daniel Horsmanden; and while Sheriff Mills was reporting to Recorder Horsmanden about the searchers having earlier "trod upon the stolen goods," the Englishman beside them must have heard something to alert him that Hughson's tavern might be the same where his sword, purse, and watch had been purloined and where he had seen Bonny Jack's face through a window during a night of debauch the preceding fall.

His journal entry for the date is exasperatingly brief: "*Tuesday, March 3*. This day recover my watch. I and party with Judge H from Exchange to tippling house at the end of an alley. River still partly froze up, with shoals of floating ice which crash against each other. Ice blocks along the shore. Children with feet in rags chasing geese; chickens and lounging slatterns and derelict blacks about. Scold delivers from a sooty cook-wench coins and my watch. *Ex ore parvulorum*. The rogue landlord is led off for examining. Home by five. At night writ my father."

Mrs. Kannady's deposition gives additional details. "At Hughson's," she reports, "I desired Sheriff Mills to go into the house first and bring Mary Burton out to me. He staying a long time, I went in and found him and the others and Mary in the parlor. There she denied all that she had said to me the night before. But I charged her home with it, until at last the girl said she could not tell us anything there; she was afraid of her life, that they would kill her. Whereupon we took her out of the house, and when we had got a little way from thence, she put her hand in her pocket and pulled out a piece of silver money, which she said was a part of Mr. Hogg's money which the negro had given her, and in showing the coin exposed a watch which a gentleman knew as his and stolen from him some months past, and Mary says this the negro gave her as well so that she would keep silent. Whereupon I informed the recorder what I had promised Mary, that is to say, to get her freed from her master. The recorder directed that she should that night lodge with the sheriff at the City Hall for safety, and I went with Mary, and left her at Mr. Mills accordingly."

We may regret that no more vivid account of the scene at Hughson's survives. In the bare parlor, with the taverner hovering near, the girl is stoutly denying all that Mrs. Kannady attributes to her. The older woman grows shrill in her accusatory anger: "Did you not last evening say to me . . . ?" Before the woman's onslaught the child cowers, trembling, face puckered, tears starting, her eyes glancing apprehensively about. Finally braving Hughson's menacing glare she cries out: "Indeed they will kill me! I fear of my life! . . ." And being led among municipal officials into the trodden snow of the barnyard, she produces from her placket an identifiable coin, and a golden something that glitters in the wintry sunlight.

Corimer had his watch back; the humiliation of how he had come to lose it he would keep to himself. As for Elizabeth, yet another delay (before the ship *Two Brothers,* Robert McHugh, commander, weighed anchor and dropped down for Gravesend) granted her time, two days afterward, to add a final postscript to her news to London:

Thurs.

I open my letter to reassure my dear Sophy that the concerns of which I writ is disposed of to satisfaction, the girl in safety and away from vile influences. I write in haste and have not time to enlarge or copy again, as the ship sails within the hour. I beg you will disregard all above that gives uneasiness. Your friends here are well. Mr. C's watch, which was picked from his pocket earlier, is recovered, for which he is very thankful, as it was a gift from his father.

* * *

What had the child Mary Burton done while a servant at the Pursells' to forfeit Elizabeth's patronage? The answer is to be found in part in Corimer's journal, in part among the pages of Volume I of the *Pursell Mercantile Papers, 1737–1783,* compilation transcribed and edited by the late W. O. Twycross, professor of economic history at Columbia, that was published finally in 1959: a monumental labor of scholarship exemplarily executed—and for the general reader a work of surpassing dullness. Letters from Pursell to merchants in Boston, Philadelphia, Jamaica, Londonderry, Liverpool, they read for the most part like this:

> Agreeable to your request I send you by Captain Ingersoll 49 lb good bohea at 16/9 in 2 canisters cost 30/ as also balance of your account being 230 round dollars 87/4½ in small money is £92.74½. I would desire you to send 6 pieces of good black London sheloon, 3 pieces red ditto, 3 pieces of green ditto, 8 pieces of black ditto, 6 pieces of yard-wide check linen small checked, 2 blue . . .

through six or seven hundred similar pages. But dogged attention is occasionally rewarded by a hint of the living man who was the merchant: he has been on a trip and hence is late writing; his wife has been ill but is recovered. Thus, a letter of March 8, 1739, two years before the present event, discloses that Benjamin Pursell had that day acquired a couple of indentured servants just arrived from England, one as a favor to his daughters, being a child scarcely in her teens whose mother had died on the passage over.

The New-York Weekly Journal of the appropriate date carries a corroborative notice:

> In the brigantine *Conquer,* Joshua Smythe, from Bristol, a number of very likely servant lads, as farmers, shoemakers, weavers, &c., and sundry women and girls, to be sold by Nathaniel Hazard, near the Slip Market. Will be

disposed of for five years each to anyone paying their pas-
sage-money at £10 per head.

N.B. The said brig. returns directly for Bristol and will
take freight and passage agree with Hazard.

There the notice is, among others on page 4 of the friable
paper; and during a spring morning of 1739, near the Slip Market, in the street or on the porch of an adjacent tavern, the sale
of the bondservants would have taken place. The child Mary
was wearing "an old whitish cloak" at the time; to us she would
have looked younger than her thirteen years, "middling small,"
undernourished, sallow-faced, bedraggled. Mother and daughter had come aboard at Bristol. A forced or voluntary boarding?
Was the girl a bastard child? Was the father dead? The mother,
in any case, died at sea—of what does not appear. (Her name,
Martha Burton, does appear among the sixty-two that comprise
a "True List of Servants and Redemptioners on Board the *Conquer*, Bound for New York this 15th Day of January, 1739"—the
list extant in the British colonial archives.) And the forsaken
girl, lined up and darkly surveying her surroundings on these
new shores, was to be indentured now for five years to anyone
willing to pay Captain Smythe for the expense of her crossing—
for the below-decks space she had been crowded into and the
peas and oatmeal she had eaten. Pursell, there to purchase one
servant, was moved to purchase two, including this friendless
child whose age was that of his own daughter, of Elizabeth's
younger sister.

He took the child home, had her washed and clothed and fed,
and provided her with a sleeping place in the attic beside a
chimney. She was to be Susannah's maidservant. But as days
passed, the newly acquired lady's maid proved difficult. Though
physically slight, she was in fact some months older than the
mistress she was charged with serving. Before long Susannah
had cause to complain to her father: Mary was "pert," was
"saucy." Though not yet marriageable, she "likes servants' company much"—presumably the company of male servants, with

whom she idled. Needed in midmorning, she would be found asleep in the attic. When sent to fetch tea water, she would be gone two hours.

Children just entering their teens: the fortunate Susannah Pursell and the hapless Mary Burton, the older committed by law to being effectively the slave of the younger through five years before earning her freedom. Both may have been strong-willed, though little is left to help us evoke Susannah—scarcely more than a few flat words on a stone, carved when her fortune ran out, and one curious notation in Corimer's journal. The latter, set off from his regular entries, is an undated jotting on an end page that I surmise was written (in longhand, not the shorthand of the rest of the journal) soon after his recovery from his illness at the Pursells', perhaps on the day of his convalescent visit, in late October 1740, with Elizabeth and her aunt to Susannah's grave in Trinity churchyard.

The words on the tombstone they visited then, so weathered now as to be almost illegible, read:

HERE LIETH THE BODY OF SUSANNAH
DAUGHTER OF BENJAMIN F. & S. PURSELL
WHO DEPARTED THIS LIFE THE 20TH OF JUNE, 1739
AGED 13 YEARS.

For within three months of Mary Burton's arrival and purchase in the New World, her young mistress had fallen ill—though the cause of the illness had little to do with maidservants. Most likely it came from infected udders of one of those two milch cows the Pursells owned. "Attendance," writes Corimer, "on sister in a scarlet fever which turned putrid." That Elizabeth would confide to her English guest what these notations reveal indicates the degree of their intimacy. His own recent plight must have awakened painful memories for her: in the fall of 1740, in the Pursells' green bedroom, she may have watched him suffering through an illness not unlike Susannah's fatal one a year and a half earlier. (We recall that the entry in which Corimer describes his own sickness speaks of his skin having peeled, and desquamation of the skin is one of the symptoms of scarlet fever.) Of Susannah's illness: "At first [*Elizabeth*] could not help flattering herself that there was no other cause of alarm but what her mother's natural tenderness made her see." The older daughter had been briefly ill as well: sore throat, headache, loss of appetite. But she was soon better, whereas Susannah's malady grew worse. Madame Pursell and young Lindsay—then only seven—were "sent out of the house to avoid the danger of infection," retiring to a relative's seat near Flatbush on Long Island. Elizabeth, Aunt Min, and the servant girl Mary took turns at the bedside, comforting the patient, cooling her throat with cloths, altering the pressure of her bedclothes, brushing insects from her face, serving the gruel that was all she could eat. "That I"—so writes Corimer, setting down exactly what Elizabeth had told him—"was able to be of use to her in her last illness was my only comfort."

On one occasion near the end Mary Burton had been in attendance. Elizabeth was returning down the hall to relieve the girl at watching when she heard a heavy fall, a cry, then convulsive, horrifying whines. Hurrying into the room she found her delirious sister unattended, alone, and having fallen from the high bed, lying shivering in a fit on the floor; from her ulcerated throat came a foul discharge. In fright and desperation Elizabeth somehow got the limp patient back into bed. Mary had not returned—finally had to be sought for and was found by the smokehouse at the foot of the garden, giggling alongside one of the servants she had earlier been flirting with from the upstairs window. Thereafter Susannah's forehead bore the purple bruise where she had fallen—bore it the following dawn when, her illness having "'baffled all art, she sunk forever from this world.

"I do not expect," Corimer quotes Elizabeth as saying, "to regret another so sincerely. Her burial in the churchyard took place on Friday, my birthday. The morning was fine. The simple, solemn procession, without parade, moving over our lawn, my father and brother walking as mourners, was a very affecting sight. My mother, unable to bear the scene, had removed to the house of friends . . ."

That was in late June 1739. The indentures of the girl Mary were sold to a cordwainer across town. Pursell, who earlier had made plans to sail at the end of the summer for England, determined to take his grieving daughter with him. Their restorative sojourn among the distractions of London lasted a year, with evenings at Covent Garden and the Opera House, new friends in Chandos Street, excursions to Kensington and Canterbury and Scarborough. Near the end of their stay the American visitors made the acquaintance of Mr. Corimer and Mr. Schaw, and with those two English gentlemen sailed from Greenwich August 13, 1740, dropping anchor six weeks later in the East River, off New York City, where time would by then have softened the grief of a sister's passing, and—so Elizabeth assumed—would forever have removed from her world all traces of a feckless servant girl.

* * *

The servant girl was by this time under Sheriff Mills's care in the City Hall, in the stone building at the head of Broad Street that stood where the Federal Hall Memorial stands now. She was lodged for her safety in the sheriff's living quarters on the ground floor adjoining the open arcade, beneath which, in a subcellar dungeon, Caesar, the baker Vaarck's slave who three days earlier had been accused of the theft of Hogg's goods, shivered in fetters and waited.

Having spent the night with Mills's family, Mary was called the following morning, Wednesday, March 4, 1741, to appear before town officials in the assembly room on the upper floor of the same building. "This day," the record tells us, "the mayor having summoned the justices to meet at the City Hall, several aldermen with other citizens met him accordingly, and sent for Mary Burton and John Hughson and his wife." Corimer with his chained monkey was on hand, interested as much in learning news of Bonny Jack's whereabouts as in recovering his purse and sword—though doubtless disinclined to give testimony, considering the ignoble circumstances under which he had been separated from those belongings. The servant girl did testify: "Mary Burton, of the city of New York, spinster, aged about fifteen years, was sworn"—child before frowning worthies at the far side of the raised bench near the fire, with her master and mistress Hughson glowering at one end of the wainscotted room, under intimidating signs of officialdom: flags, portraits, the royal monogram.

She was alone in the world, had been alone since before stepping off the deck of the *Conquer* and setting foot on American earth. From the comforts of the Pursell household Mary's fortunes had tumbled her downward to harsher service at the cordwainer's, from there to ever less agreeable employ that had brought her in time into the unsavory surroundings of the Hughsons, alongside the Hudson River. Shrewd this child would have been to survive, and quick to look out for herself. The town clerk was urging her to speak the truth, tell all she knew of the theft.

"I hardly—"

"Speak up, child."

"I hardly dare to speak. I fear them, fear they will murder me."

But though frightened, she began timidly to answer the questions put to her. The robbery at the Hoggs' had occurred last Saturday night. At Hughson's, in the depths of that night, she had been awakened on her truss of straw by a noise from the nearby roof. Going to the window, she had "set down on my hunkies" in time to espy the slave Caesar making his way to the window of Peggy, with whom he usually slept, "which my master and mistress know of."

"What hour was that?"

"About two o'clock Sunday morning, for I soon after heard the watch cry."

Caesar's Peggy, we learn, was "one Margaret Sorubiero, alias Salingburgh, alias Kerry, commonly called the Newfoundland Beauty, a young woman about one or two and twenty; she pretended to be married, but no husband appeared. She was a person of infamous character, a notorious prostitute, and also of the worst sort, a prostitute to negroes."

"Continue."

"In the morning I went to bring water to Peggy's room, and Caesar was there, and he had some speckled linen. He gave me two pieces of silver and bade Peggy cut off an apron of the linen and give to me, which she did. And later he gave my master silver—"

Hughson, grown alarmed at the wench's loquaciousness, abruptly rose to protest, but the examiners ordered him to be seated and keep silent.

"Go on, child."

"Caesar gave me a lump of silver for two mugs of punch he drank and a pair of white stockings he bought from my master. Then during the day—"

"That was Sunday?"

"Sunday Mr. Mills and the others come to search the house, saying that Mr. Hogg had been robbed the night before of speckled linen and silver and other things, and the sailor Wilson that was with them pointed out Caesar sitting in the chimney corner, and they took him away. And when the officers had searched the house and found nothing and gone, my mistress hid the linen in the garret—"

Again Hughson was on his feet. "Please your honors, the girl lies. She is a vile, good-for-nothing girl. She was got with child by her former master—"

"Peace. Bailiff, see to that man. The witness will proceed."

"My mistress hid the linen in the garret, then took it from the place she had before hid it in and hid it under the stairs. Then the following night—"

"Monday night?"

"Monday she give it to her old mother, who carried it away."

Now Hughson, "finding that he was near going to jail, and as fearing the consequences of provoking the witness, changed his note," imploring—while his slatternly wife trembled beside him—to address the examiners. The girl was a very good girl, he told them, glancing nervously in Mary's direction, and had been a trusty servant. In the hardest weather of this past winter she used to dress herself in man's clothes, put on boots, and go with him in his sleigh into the deep snows in the common to help him fetch firewood for his family.

"Is examinant ready to bear witness about the theft? What says he?"

"On Monday last," Hughson proceeded to testify, "after Mr. Mills had been to search my house, Peggy the Beauty, who lodges there, told me the slave Caesar had left some checked linen and other things with her, which she delivered to me. I gave them to my mother-in-law, who took them in a boat on the river to hide them. Soon after, Peggy delivered me sundry silver things in a little bag, which I carried into the cellar and put behind a barrel, and put a broad stone upon them."

"Were the goods there when the constables searched the house?"

"Ay, but they did not find them."

"Are they there now?"

"Ay. They are in the cellar now . . ."

With those admissions the series of incidents that began when a sailor noticed coins in a bureau at Mrs. Hogg's shop seemed about to be concluded: foul nest of thieves uncovered at a North River alehouse, under a broad stone, as it were—black slave hiding his loot in a white whore's lodgings. Soon the slave Caesar, brought up before the examiners, was admitting in his scarcely comprehensible gibberish to sleeping with Peggy the Beauty, though he "would confess nothing concerning the robbery, and denied everything laid to his charge." He was remanded nevertheless, and returned to the cellar dungeon. Peggy, examined separately, "denied everything, and spoke in favor of Hughson and his wife"; the whore (with whom an earl's youngest son, now quietly at the hearing to observe, had earlier toyed noisily enough in a woodshed) was likewise committed. As for the Hughsons, they were admitted to bail, and recognizances were entered into with two sureties each for their appearance before the Supreme Court on the first day of the next term, in late April, seven weeks hence.

The stolen goods were expeditiously recovered and returned to the grateful Hoggs.

* * *

One is left to wonder about Wilson. What happened to the seventeen-year-old Yorkshire seaman whose glimpse of coins in Mrs. Hogg's bureau drawer the preceding Thursday had begun to forge this chain of events? Late the same week he had, by his own admission, told his tavern cronies at Hughson's about that "charming fine booty. A negro catched at the proposal, when the boy had told them the situation of the house and shop: that the front was toward Broad Street, and there was a side door out of the shop into Jews Alley, and if a body could make an errand thither to buy rum, he might get an opportunity to shove back the bolt of the alley door, for there was no lock to it, and then could come in the night afterward and accomplish his designs."

But what of Wilson's own culpability? During the morning immediately after the robbery, ambling into Mrs. Hogg's and hearing her bemoan her losses—"linen, snuffboxes, silver medals, one a remarkable eight-square piece"—he coolly informed her that he "had been earlier that same Sunday at Hughson's house and there saw one Caesar, who pulled out of his pocket a worsted cap full of pieces of coined silver, and that Mr. Philipse's Cuffee, who was there, seeing Caesar have this money, he asked him to give him some, and Caesar counted him out half a crown in pennies, and asked him if he would have any more, and then pulled out a handful of silver coin amongst which, Wilson said, he saw the eight-square piece described by Mrs. Hogg."

But was the seaman deflecting guilt from himself? Had he been trying to entrap the slave? And is the civil record mute on the white boy's share of punishment only because he was turned over to the ungentle care of the military, to be tied to the shrouds and chastised with the cowskin ("hard as a bull's pizzle") on the spar deck of the *Flamborough,* man-of-war? Or did Wilson's ready tongue allow him to escape punishment altogether, he whose fingers had, to be sure, felt none of the stolen coins? Yet one of those white fingers had pointed constables, searching in a tavern parlor, toward a lounging black man who had earlier listened too closely to the sailor's schemes; for his attention Caesar had earned a night of lusty excitement, a brief Sunday morning to bestow linen and coins and lumps of silver grandly among slaves, tapsters, whores, and servant girls, followed by the prospect of a long succession of nights and sunless days in irons in a cold subcellar awaiting the hour when he would surely dangle.

By now the case seemed clear enough in any event, the guilty parties having been identified to the city's satisfaction. Henceforth young Wilson all but disappears from the record, as days of winter pass, one week nearer spring, two weeks . . .

Then, exactly a fortnight after the hearing at City Hall, while the law was awaiting the convocation of the Supreme Court in April, a major fire broke out—a public calamity described at the beginning of the fifth of Elizabeth Pursell's six letters to Sophia Milner in my possession. This one is dated Thursday candlelight, March 19, 1741:

> My friend will allow me to trouble her so soon after my last when she learns the occasion.
>
> Yesterday, about one of the clock in the afternoon, a plumber stopping a leak in a gutter in Fort George close by our house, the roof of the governor's house in the fort took fire from a spark from his fire pot, which gradually kindled, and the wind blowing fresh from the southeast, the flames burned very fierce and were not long in consuming the roof, with a great danger arising from flying embers to dwellings beyond the fort in our direction.
>
> I was above stairs flowering a waistcoat for my father when alarms from the street and the violent ringing of the

chapel bell summoned me to a front window. Smoke was pouring from the fort above the parade scarce a hundred yards from hence, and all seen very plain. As yet I could see no flames, only much smoke rising high in the dark sky, and great numbers of gulls and other birds in agitated flight, and in the street men and boys shouting and hurrying toward the fort, and some men driving wagons. I quick fetched our fire buckets and threw them into the street just as Papa and Mr. Corimer were emerging from the countinghouse below. You will believe the whole family was soon alarmed. We scrambled quick as could be to the roof"—among those rain barrels—"from where Mama and I watched as lines formed to the river, so that water was soon brought to play, but the wind being high, the flames which we could see now was gaining ground, and the chapel that at first held good had a fierce spurt of flame as we watched, it coming from a window on the northern face that was a most cruel sight. Papa and my brother and Mr. C were not in our view, though we could see crowds in the square, and our mayor hurrying up and down with his trumpet, and the venerable governor himself shouting from a table in the quadrangle. Dear Sophy may well imagine the scene, though I hope she never has occasion to see such, which I shall never forget.

All was uproar and confusion. Mr. Schaw and others were extinguishing burning flakes on the ground with water from their hats. Behind them the sides of the chapel were rosy with firelight, and the windows of the barracks opposite the governor's house was lurid and bright with reflected glare, much as hell itself is depicted, and furniture being thrown from the windows and broke, tables and chairs and chests and the king's portrait come down until the flames drove everyone from within, and dogs running wildly about the open spaces as the flames moved toward the office above the fort gate, with soldiers there tossing papers out windows into the street, though the wind would catch and scatter many such as they fell.

Perceiving our own danger Mama and my aunt and maid and I exerted ourselves to save what we could against the fire should come closer, as it seemed determined to do. I hurried down from the roof and went from room to room repeating to myself, "Birds, silver, jewelry, silk dresses," and indeed we had got much of our possessions removed in baskets to the rear garden, where my aunt, who was sore distraught, as you may imagine, was left to watch over them whilst we returned for more, she calling to us through her tears not to forget this or that, much more remaining within. And all the while was heard shouting from the direction of the fort, and notwithstanding our fear and haste I could but pause, and perceived through the window that the flames had reached the barracks across the grounds, and flakes had leapt the ramparts and were consuming the stables without the walls, so that horses were rearing maddened as they led away [*sic*], some rigid and refusing to move. But a rain had by then begun, the sky dark, which providential aid set bounds to the flames (though some of our goods in the garden was damaged), and the engines arriving and directing water, which together with the alertness and industry of our citizens prevented the fire spreading further, though the danger was very great.

All was over within two hours, except floors of the buildings and timbers in the chapel steeple continued last night to burn within the fort, a most dismal and worrisome sight in the darkness, and the dread stench of burnt wet wood can be smelt as I write, and we have had our house completely filled and running over on this sad occasion. . . .

* * *

Corimer's journal, in this instance full and coherent enough to quote at length, brings us still closer to the calamity. He writes, under an entry for March 19, of having been "yesterday about one o'clock on business with P at his store"—concerning slaving schemes?—"when hearing the bell of a sudden at the fort and much commotion in the streets, we to the door and discover the governor's house afire, the middle of the roof in a great smoke and curling from eaves and upper windows. A woeful sight. Without ado across the parade, bearing buckets Miss P threw us down, and together we take our place in line in the governor's garden toward the battery beyond the sally port, young L[indsay] with other lads in the dry line and we across from him in the wet, where was soon soaked with water. All that could be done by the inhabitants seemed as nothing to the fury of the flames, which moved to the king's chapel, rising and billowing till the bell was silenced (though others of the town were clamoring), the wind blowing a violent gale at S. E. and the crowd crying out to see the chapel in flames. Pigeons distracted in the smoke alighted in vast numbers and mounted again and wheeled. In the line near to hand was two blacks kept dropping their buckets till a citizen incensed pushed one all soaked into the mud (as was by then) of the garden and would have done him harm, with 'Would you laugh and make game at our troubles, you black dog?' or such like, and sure the negroes seemed to grin and whistle and huzzah and as it were be dancing when the flames blazed high, though both stupid with drink, as it seemed to me, as was many others well liquored, black and white likewise. Rats ran from the flames in great numbers, with townsmen striking them in the yard with flaming brands, and one old wife with her apron over her head shrieking, and the flames consuming the roof and upper story of the governor's house, which fell with thunderous noise, moved now toward the office over the fort gate where was deposited all the records of the colony. Someone about that time cried out through apprehension that there was powder in the fort, which cry being taken up caused many to desert the premises in fear, notwithstanding assurances of the governor himself, who stood atop a table and harangued them and assured them there was no gunpowder there, yet many had not the courage to depend upon his assurance. Judge H was rallying militia and citizens to save the records, which was soon being thrown into the street, where some papers were blown briskly about, and the judge's voice all hoarse and his wig sooty and askew, with Schaw at an upstairs window calling down for more help from amongst the soldiers. Yet in less than two hours, notwithstanding the best efforts of the town, the progress of the flames had consumed the governor's house, chapel, barracks across the yard, secretary's office, and got to the stables outside the ramparts, with utmost danger to houses in the town next the North River, whose roofs were most of shingle. The engines, having played to little effect on the office and barracks in this high wind, were of little use to prevent the worst of such speedy destruction. Except the fortifications, guns, and carriages, all was destroyed, showers of flakes aloft for some time after, with the brightness of active conflagration changed to smothering smoke, and staves and boards and cordage and other articles to a large amount consumed, though the precise amount is not yet ascertained. Some little rain fell at last, and S[*chaw*]"—covered with cinders, and eyes stung red from the smoke—"shared with me a cup at a rum keg in the drizzle, of which all stood greatly in need, being very cold and wet and discouraged. Thence repaired again to Pursell's."

* * *

As stated at the start of Elizabeth's fifth letter, quoted above, and as confirmed by Governor George Clarke's address to the Provincial Assembly delivered April 15, 1741, nearly a month after the event, the devastating fire at Fort George was (in the governor's phraseology) "accidentally occasioned by mending a gutter on the roof of the house adjoining to the chapel, which having leaked all winter had much damaged and would soon have rotted the timber and floors of that part of the house, so that what was intended for its preservation unhappily turned to its destruction." A plumber's carelessness had wrought the destruction of buildings a hundred years old; the Dutch had built the house and chapel within the fort in the early 1640s, when the settlement was still Nieuw Amsterdam. Now, a century later, weary and saddened English moved about their town in sight of charred ruins—black fingers pointing skyward, smoking still. That same late dreary afternoon they gathered their colony records from the streets—"we do not hear that any very material writings are lost"—to be carried to the Common Council room, "for keeping during the present exigency until another proper place can be provided by the legislature": all those vellum-bound folios of minutes and ordinances, those blotters of the mayor's court, tax books, vestry books, books of grants, transports, deeds, mortgages, letters of attorney, conveyances, all stored haphazardly now in a meeting room of the City Hall. Fire buckets, piled in a heap in the parade, were reclaimed before nightfall by servants of the various citizens. The exhausted fire fighters took their refreshment at Pursell's or at the hands of other public-spirited merchants, then wandered to taverns or homes as their long day ended. Next morning the town fathers would be ordering more buckets, a hundred new leather fire buckets with CITY OF N: YORK painted on them, and thereafter, for a while at least, curfew each evening would be sounded conscientiously at nine, warning townsfolk to bank hearth fires for the night.

Even so, many would sleep less easily in that crowded, highly combustible settlement, some on the fourth or fifth floors of old, inflammable dwellings, under roofs of dry shingles, by chimneys that a hard winter might have fouled, above yards and stables where dry hay for the horses and cattle was kept, not far from the powder magazines and the wharves with their old sheds storing dry wood and pitch and turpentine.

New Yorkers had grounds for their fears.

Wednesday morning, the twenty-fifth of March, exactly one week after the fire at the fort, church bells were clanging again, and townsmen looking toward the southwest could see rising into the gray sky of a still-wintry day black smoke near the Long Bridge, and a fellow citizen's roof in flames. It was an old shingled roof on the ramshackle house of a Captain Warren, and toward it the engines were being dragged at full speed over the stones from the garage at City Hall: volunteers at a run towing those iron-wheeled copper tanks with their leather hoses that could throw "two hogsheads of water in a minute, in a continued stream, twelve feet above the ground," rushing to wheel the machines into place while lines were frantically forming to and from the river, the first buckets splashing seawater into the tanks as yelling firemen began working pump handles. "The roof was in flames," we are told, "supposed to have been occasioned by the accidental firing of a chimney; but the engines were soon brought thither, and they played so successfully, though the fire had got to a considerable head, that by their aid and the assistance and activity of the people it was soon extinguished without doing much damage to the dwelling."

One Wednesday, Fort George. The next Wednesday, Warren's house. And the following Wednesday, April 1—with spring in the air at last—in midafternoon Winant Van Zant's storehouse on the river toward the east end of town burst into flames. "It was an old wooden building, stored with deal boards, and hay at one end of it; the fire was said to be occasioned by a man's smoking a pipe there, which set fire to the hay." Luckily the shed was beside a slip, so that firemen and townsfolk could readily get harbor water for their two engines. "Most thought it impossible to hinder the fire's spreading further, there being many wooden buildings adjoining; but the people exerted their usual diligence, handed out boards into the slip"—all aflame and floating in the harbor—"played the engines, and threw the buckets of water with such extraordinary activity, it stopped the progress of the fire so successfully that it ended with little more damage than the consumption of the warehouse and most of the goods in it."

For old Van Zant the owner that was more than damage enough, and others that night must have gone home troubled, uneasy. Thursday passed without further incident, and Friday, and much of Saturday. But on Saturday evening occurred two more fires in succession. One was in the Fly Market, in a cow stable near a certain Vergereau's house—hay again—"but by timely assistance it was suppressed. People returning from that fire, however, were suddenly alarmed by a second cry of fire, at the house of one Ben Thomas, next door to the chandler Wendover; this was in the dusk of the evening." Smoke had been sighted pouring from that second roof, although this fire too, which had begun in the loft of Thomas's kitchen, was soon extinguished. "Upon examination," according to the record, "it was found that the second fire had been put between a straw and another bed laid together in the loft, whereon a negro slept. But who did it, or how the earlier fire had happened at Vergereau's cow stable, remained to be accounted for."

Next morning occurred something else to be accounted for, something assuredly sinister. A white servant with sharp eyes, bound for the well at the foot of the family garden of the affluent Joseph Murray, Esq., on Broadway, discovered, so we read in the record, "that coals had been put under a haystack standing near the coach house and stables of Mr. Murray. The stables were near dwelling houses"—including that of the Pursells'—"which, had the hay taken fire, would have been in great danger, but the coals went out of themselves, as supposed, having only singed some part of the stack." Singed hay was what the servant had seen; and before long, rumors arising from his discovery were spreading among the nervous inhabitants of the town. "It was said," for instance, "there were coals and ashes traced from the fence to a neighboring house next adjoining the stables, which caused a suspicion of the negro that lived there . . ."

But five fires in less than three weeks' time: "*five* several fires, viz., at the fort, Captain Warren's house, Van Zant's storehouse, Vergereau's stable, and Ben Thomas's kitchen, having happened in so short a time succeeding each other, and the attempt made of a sixth on Mr. Murray's haystack, it was natural for people of any reflection to conclude that the fires were set on purpose by a combination of villains." Toward what end? The answer seemed obvious: "so that wicked wretches might make a prey of their neighbors' furniture and goods, under pretence of assisting in removing them for security from the danger of flames;

for upon these late instances many of the sufferers had complained of great losses of goods that had been borne from their houses."

Crime abroad in a vulnerable community. A Mrs. Earle was among those apprehensive this same first Sunday after Easter. About service time she had happened to glance out her window that overlooked Broadway and saw three Negroes passing in the direction of Trinity Church. One she heard entertaining his sable companions with what she later described as "a vaporing sort of an air." He threw up his hands, so she said, laughed, and cried out: "*Fire, fire, scorch, scorch,* A LITTLE, *damn it,* BY-AND-BY"—swaggering on up the cobbled street. Odd behavior. More than that: "Mrs. Earle conceived great jealousy at these words, in particular at that juncture, considering what had so lately happened; and she putting the natural construction upon them, her apprehensions made her uneasy, and she immediately spoke of it to her next neighbor Mrs. George."

Mrs. George asked did Mrs. Earle know any of the Negroes?

No, she did not; "but about an hour after, when church was out, Mrs. Earle saw the same negroes coming down the Broadway again, and pointed out to Mrs. George the person who had spoke the words, and Mrs. George knew him, and said that it was Mr. Roosevelt's Quaco. These words of fire and scorch—and the airs and graces Quack gave them when he uttered them—the women made known to a neighboring alderman, who informed the justices thereof at their meeting next day."

That is, on Monday, April 6, 1741. The justices were not scheduled to meet until afternoon, but already by ten that Monday morning another alarm had sounded, for the chimney of Sergeant Burns's house opposite Fort Garden was aflame, and "from the great smother in the house, and some other circumstances"—for one, Burns would later insist that his chimney had been swept the Friday before—"there were grounds to suspect a villainous design in it." Volunteers got the sergeant's fire out, but only in time to answer a call toward noon to extinguish a roof fire at Mrs. Hilton's, "at the corner of the buildings next the Fly Market, adjoining on the east side of the house of Peter Wendover, chandler. It broke out on that side next the chandler's, but being timely discovered was soon prevented doing much mischief, more than burning part of the roof." Looking the ground over afterward, firemen came upon what led them to conclude that the Hilton fire must have been purposely set: a hole was found burnt deep in the wall plate next to where the shingles had ignited, "and it was suspected that the fire had been wrapped up in a bundle of tow, for some was found near the place."

Not irrefutable evidence, yet enough to stir a mob into motion. "The fact was plain, notwithstanding who did it was a question remained to be determined. But there was a cry among the people: *'The Spanish negroes; the Spanish negroes; take up the Spanish negroes.'* "

Saturday had seen the fire in the kitchen loft of Ben Thomas's house on one side of Wendover's. Monday—two mornings later—the roof of Mrs. Hilton's house on the other side was in flames. The chandler himself, with scarred houses on both sides of him, had, it was recalled, "purchased some time before a Spanish negro brought into this port, among several others, in a prize taken by Captain Lush"—indeed, it had been Wendover whom Corimer had encountered in the autumn cudgeling that same slave on the waterfront. Manuel was the Spaniard's name, one of five blacks aboard the captured *Soledad* who had been sold at vendue; "and the slaves afterward, pretending to have been free men in their own country, began to grumble at their hard usage here. This probably gave rise to the suspicion that this negro"— the well-favored Manuel of Corimer's earlier entry—"out of revenge had been the instrument of these two fires; and he behaving himself insolently upon some people's who mistrusted him asking questions concerning the fires, it was told to a magistrate who was near, and he ordered Manuel to jail, and also gave direction to the constables to commit the rest of that cargo, in order for their safe custody and examination."

So the fettered Caesar and the Newfoundland Beauty and

what other miscreants were already down there would have company in the cellar at City Hall. We imagine the tone of the questions that the ragtag mob gathering on the street that tense Monday posed "with forceful imprecations" to Manuel, dark native of a nation with which Britain and her colonies were then at war. The other four Spanish Negroes—"the rest of that cargo"—were soon being rounded up, and in the afternoon the justices of the province were meeting to examine them and ponder civic distresses. Scarcely were their deliberations under way, however, when about four o'clock they were interrupted by yet another alarm of fire. "Looking out the windows of City Hall, the blaze was seen clearly from thence, and found to be at Col. Philipse's storehouse in New Street. There was a small red streak running up the shingles, like wildfire, from near the bottom to the top of the roof, on the side directly *against the wind as it then blew*." The emphasis is in the record, presumably signifying that the unheated building could not have been fired by sparks from a neighboring chimney. In vivid language the record proceeds to describe the events that followed:

"The storehouse not being far from the engines, they were instantly brought to the place; and the fire, to one's great surprise, almost as soon extinguished. This was the middlemost of three large houses next each other in a row, old timber buildings, and the shingles burnt like tinder. While the people were extinguishing the fire and had almost mastered it, a man on top of the building assisting saw a negro leap out at the end window, from thence making over several garden fences in great haste, which occasioned him to cry out, *a negro; a negro;* and that was soon improved into an alarm that *the negroes were rising*. The negro meanwhile made very good speed home to his master's. He was generally known, and the swiftness of his flight occasioned his being remarked, though scarce any knew the reason but a few which remained at the storehouse why the word was given, *a negro, a negro*. It was immediately changed into *Cuff Philipse, Cuff Philipse*. The people ran to Mr. Philipse's house in quest of him. He was got in at the back door and,

being found, was dragged out of the house and carried to jail
borne upon the people's shoulders."

A fellow of general ill character, the mob was pronouncing
this terrified Cuff, an insolent, worthless fellow with too much
idle time as slave to a master who was a single man and seldom
at home. So Cuff was in jail now, and lucky to be alive after
rough handling over the streets to City Hall. But anyone
black—and a sixth of the town was black—attracted attention
that frantic afternoon. "Many people had such terrible apprehensions upon this occasion, and indeed there was cause suffi
cient, that several negroes (and many had been assisting at the
fire at the storehouse, and many perhaps that only seemed to be
so) who were met in the streets after the alarm of their rising
were hurried away to jail, and when they were there were continued sometime in confinement before the magistrates could spare
time to examine into their several cases, many others first coming under consideration before them, against whom there
seemed to be more direct cause of suspicion."

Specifically, the Spanish Negroes were suspect, as was Roosevelt's Quack, whose odd behavior the alderman for Mrs. Earle
and Mrs. George reported that afternoon to his fellow magistrates. Those worthies had the slave brought before them to
explain himself. "He admitted he had spoken the words he was
charged with"—*Fire, fire, scorch, scorch,* A LITTLE, *damn it,*
BY-AND-BY—"but it being soon after we learned the news of
Admiral Vernon's taking Porto Bello in Panama, he had contrived a cunning excuse, or some abler heads for him, to account for the occasion of his behavior Sunday on the Broadway,
and brought two of his own complexion to give their words for
it also that they were talking of Admiral Vernon's taking Porto
Bello—but a small feat to what this brave officer would do
by-and-by to annoy the Spaniards in the Caribbean."

Perhaps. Others, however, were apt to put a different construction on Quack's words, "considering it was but eighteen
days after the fort was laid in ashes that he had uttered them,
and the attempt upon Mr. Murray's haystack discovered that

89

very morning." Did the slave not mean that the fires we have seen so far were nothing to what we should see soon?—"for it was said he had lifted up his hands and spread them with a circular sweep over his head to include the whole city as he pronounced those words *by-and-by,* concluding with a loud laugh." Reluctantly the magistrates let Quack go for now, but henceforth they would have an eye on him—indeed, would keep a sharp eye on all his tribe, those accursed black sons and daughters of Ham.

* * *

Long Island, near York
Apr. 11. Sat.

Dear Sophia will find the enclosed [*describing the fire at Fort George*] was wrote above three weeks ago. I understood then that there was a vessel bound for Dover, but after writing it could not hear of any such opportunity.

By Capt. Walsh I had the pleasure to receive your agreeable favor of December last along with the pamphlet. Was glad to hear so good an account of you and your family. My father desires his respects to you and Mr. M, and advises him by all means to ride at least ten miles every day; it is what he does three or four days in the week and finds beneficial. He recommends to him likewise, instead of malt liquor, to drink spruce beer at meals, which is esteemed very sweetening to the blood. However, he don't pretend to prescribe as a doctor, but only desired me to mention it from him.

The burning of the fort, of which I have writ you in this, has been followed by a rash of other fires about the city so numerous as to reveal some evil design by wicked persons to prey upon the populace. Indeed, my father has concluded with others during these troubled days that it were better remove his family from thence, there being at hand a convenient dwelling in the country scarce five miles off, in my mother's family seat on Long Island. Only my dear grandmother lives here now, with a few servants, nor is she well and so keeps generally to her room, though we have no want of company, for we have been near twenty of family and friends these four days past till today. The house is a lone house so retired that not one person in fifty in York ever saw it before, yet the situation agreeable. There's no very extensive prospect, to be sure, being surrounded with hills and woods at a good distance, though this makes it more habitable and warm in winter. It is supplied with good water springs, a large lawn in front, and shrubs and flowers on the borders.

We have been here since Monday. I would have dear Sophy know of my affairs and thoughts, how trivial soever, that she might the better imagine how I get on, and desire that she will write me always with the same fullness and candor. Yet I would not burden her with our cares. Oh Sophy—what a horrid time has this been for us! I do not wish to burden my friend with our griefs, about which her benevolent nature at so great a distance can do nothing to the purpose but commiserate our lot, the more so as the times may be improved, as God wills, before ever you read these words. Yet must I write of matters so near my heart.

Since the firing of the fort has occurred a succession of fires of suspicious nature about the town, in lofts and storehouses and haystacks, indeed so many as are not to be explained except there be some dark plan afoot to stir up the negroes to rob and plunder us all. Major Van Horne had been saying as much, but none would attend his words, or worse would laugh at his fears, when at the burning of the fort he that very night drummed forth his militia company with all expedition to patrol them about the streets, having some seventy odd of them under arms all night, to the amusement of many who deemed the gentleman mad, for the major had feared from the first a rising of the negroes. Yet many, nay most thought him mad, misled by his queer manner, and Mr. Corimer, much amused, took to

calling him Major Drum—though neither Mr. C nor anyone else is laughing now.

Monday last, in the afternoon, my father hastens to us
from having been in the town and assembles the family and
servants to tell us we must quick pack and get ourselves to
the ferry, hiding what could not be carried. In few words
he explains (and even as he spoke could be heard the cries
and shouts of the people in the streets) that it was feared
the negroes were rising, and no person secure any more.
We each was given tasks. I was charged with looking up all
the pocket pistols in the house, some of which were put by
that nobody could find 'em. And ignorant of any being
charged, Annie my maid was very near shooting her mistress, inadvertently firing one off in my bedroom in the
hurry. The bullets missed within a foot of me and fixed in
the gumwood kas at my back. Here was a miraculous escape indeed, I all queasy the remainder of the day, as you
may well imagine, though we had reason to be thankful as
we readied ourselves to fly to our place of refuge. My aunt
was gathering our pets together, she remembering us in
our terror of that earlier time when the slaves revolted and
would have killed their masters, when she was scarce older
than I. Mama had hurried to the garden with Venture (our
trusted servant) to bury effects, plate and posset cups and
her cherished silver brushes and such. Meanwhile, my
father had sent forth for a boat that might take us from
thence, but none was to be had, so that we must make our
way by cart, with our trunks and cats and belongings, and
Sylvia barking in alarm, down crowded Wall Street to join
with the many others who were fleeing in consternation,
about a hundred or more of us refugees at the waterside,
with many others going north on the island into the country round about.

Our retreat at the ferry house was rendered as agreeable
as might be by the mayor's polite attention to every refu-
gee, and the governor's three barges was put at the disposal

of citizens to help them over the water. Indeed, all were well accommodated and very genteelly entertained under the circumstances. We put our horses and belongings on board ten minutes before four.

Yet it was most trying, however well our friends and neighbors assisted to make matters bearable. The frightful noises in the streets, and the rumors and fears as we waited, I can't describe and shall never forget. My mother is indisposed as a consequence, and the ordeal has given my aunt a return of her bilious disorder. The doctor attending says that exercise is too violent for her and has advised her drinking salt water, which she has done all this week, and trusts in time it may quite remove her complaint. But she is so affected that she can scarce converse, and the sight only of a black servant disorders her extremely.

In short, many scores, nay hundreds of the inhabitants of York have abandoned their dwellings in apprehension that a speedy destruction is to fall on the place, and indeed we have been so far wonderfully preserved only through the vigilance of our magistrates. Many complain of losses to those—wicked wretches indeed—who feigned to help them to remove their possessions to safety. The Lord preserve us all and grant us an happy issue out of these troubles. Such villainy cannot be conceived of. My father goes to town each morning, and Mr. Corimer with him, who tells us that N York is now a very gloomy place, the streets almost empty, so many families having removed from it, and those remaining appear some desponding, others full of rage. Mr. Schaw remains with us. We all have a deal to do. Against the worst we are provided with firearms and Mr. Corimer's greyhounds and a bell at the top of the house to give notice abroad in case of necessity.

Today is very cold and rainy. I fancy the spring has opened upon you, whilst we continue with fires, though the snow is gone except in the deep woods. A long sharp winter we have had, yet there were pleasures which even a frozen state afforded, for there were few days gone by but what we might make excursions in sleighs (carriages without wheels that travel extremely quick ten or twelve miles an hour) whilst nature smiled in a bright sky, and a white world around us. Those outings were gladsome, that seem now so long ago.

I am really ashamed of sending you this incoherent, ill-wrote scrawl, but having a deal to say I wrote fast, trusting to your friendship for an excuse for the many faults and mistakes that you will find both in the writing and style of this volume. We have been alarmed today with a report of pirates hovering about the coast, and some fear they are Spanish.

* * *

During that grim interlude there seemed so much to fear, with Elizabeth, her family, and their friends huddling among multiplying rumors in Granny Wright's home "beyond Breucklin, near the village of Flat-Bush." In addition to the perennial threat of Indians and the French, "with whom is apprehended a speedy rupture" to the north, to the south a Spanish war fleet might even now be off the coast, preparing to enter the harbor past a burned-out fort to aid savage blacks who were, as once before in living memory, rising against their all too trustful masters.

Aunt Min could remember the earlier time. That only sister of Benjamin Pursell had been born, like her brother, before the turn of the century, she in 1692, not three decades after the English had conquered the settlement of Nieuw Amsterdam and renamed it New York. Black slaves were already there, had been since within a couple of years of the founding of the bleak Dutch trading post. But the English when they came had brought, on paper at least, a brighter spirit of tolerance, if not toward blacks, at least toward the variety of whites drawn to the island outpost at the mouth of the Hudson; for as early as 1674 the English governor Andros had received royal instructions: "Permit all persons of what religion soever quietly to inhabit within the precincts of your jurisdiction without giving them any disquiet by reason of their differing opinions in matters of religion, provided they give no disturbance to the public peace, nor do molest others in the free exercise of their religion."

To our ears that sounds an admirable and refreshing strain, accompanying the ensuing immigration of numerous sects and faiths to New York: Palatine Lutherans, Moravians, Anabaptists, Six Principle Baptists, Quakers, Sabbatarians, New Lights and Dark Lanthorns, Jews. Indeed, Pursell's own father, a Dissenting shipwright, had been among those in England in the years after the Stuart restoration who chose to seek in the New World a life more congenial to their religious beliefs. Isaac Pursell (or Pursill, Purcell, Parcel—as that illiterate's name is variously spelled beside his mark on documents of the time) had landed in New York aboard the *Stout Oaks* in the summer of 1684. By 1688 he had served out his indentures. The following year, established in his craft, he had applied for and been granted the status of freeman. Another year and he was respectably married, his bride the daughter of a prospering Huguenot family. Several of the couple's children would die in infancy, but a daughter Maria, called Minnie, grew to adulthood, and a son Benjamin, born in 1694, survived to become a wealthy merchant and (returning to the fold) vestryman of the socially proper English church on Broadway. That same Benjamin was father of Elizabeth, Susannah, and Lindsay Pursell, whose maiden Aunt Min was on hand through their childhood to punctuate their thoughts with recollections of New York from the beginning of the century forward:

"You gad about so, cries my aunt, that I do not know where to have you. Hours now thrown away in dress and assemblies and visits were employed in my time in writing out receipts, or working chairs and hangings for the family. Indeed it grieves my heart, who've plied my needle these forty years, to see a couple of idle girls sipping their tea a whole afternoon in a room hung round with the industry of their ancestors." That typical complaint, recorded with good humor in a previously unquoted portion of Elizabeth's third letter to Sophia Milner, would have evoked for the children an industrious and orderly age gone by. But now, as the Pursell family found refuge from imminent calamity, Aunt Min's recollections were of a different and terrifying kind.

Sources of fear were not lacking in colonial New York. The community they had fled from, viewed in a certain light, may seem to us—if not to them—notable less for order than for the chaos of its mistrusts and hatreds. The old Dutch families doggedly resented the intruding English, who in return disdained the mean-spirited Dutch, too stingy (it was said) to cobble their streets for the wear of the stones on their wagon wheels. Dutch and English alike were contemptuous of the Quakers and all such fanatical sects. Presbyterian felt repugnance for Anglican. Mechanics found attitudes of the gentry vexing. Farmers in the Out Ward and beyond voiced scorn for the Indians, ire toward the favored merchants of the town. Long Islanders, many of them Yankees whose forebears had crossed the sound from Connecticut, verbally abused the unresponsive central authority at York; the Wrights as one example, Yankees into whose family Benjamin Pursell had married and to whose home his loved ones were fleeing, were outspoken opponents of provincial domination, as is shown in a surviving scrawl (the manuscript is at the New-York Historical Society) from Madame Pursell's father, complaining to the Provincial Assembly about some levy while crustily reminding those legislators of "our glorious monarch William the Third, who delivered us from arbitrary power and its concomitants: popery, superstition, and slavery . . ."

But almost all these factions in and around New York, mistrustful of each other, held two hatreds in common. All hated Roman Catholics. Dutch colonists, who had founded Nieuw Amsterdam in 1626, after their homeland had won its long struggle for independence from Catholic Spain, bequeathed a seething detestation of popery to their children and their children's children. The English for their part loathed and feared the Catholic French, who were harboring the Stuart Pretender (four years after 1741, Bonnie Prince Charlie would sail from France and land in Scotland in an attempt to seize the British throne). English both at home and overseas feared and loathed the French, whose busy clerics in the forests of North America were even then using Rome's pageantry to seduce the simple Indian. Inspired by that loathing a law had been passed long ago—when Aunt Min was a child, in the time of William and Mary—a law still on the books and aimed at "every Jesuit, seminary, priest, missionary, or other ecclesiastical person ordained by the See of Rome, or who shall appear to be such by practicing or teaching of others to say any popish prayers, by celebrating of masses, granting of absolutions, or using any other of the Romish ceremonies or rites of worship." Such a person even so much as entering the province of New York "shall be accounted an incendiary and disturber of the public peace and of the true Christian religion, and shall suffer perpetual imprisonment." Moreover, "if, being so sentenced and imprisoned, he shall break prison and make his escape and be afterward retaken, he shall be put to death."

Catholics in colonial New York were accordingly very few in number, and circumspect. Blacks, on the other hand, were everywhere, although they too were generally distrusted, by many feared and hated as fervently as were the absent Catholics. To the several laws on the books regulating the behavior of black slaves in the streets of the town, others were added after the insurrection of 1712 that Aunt Min, then just twenty, could remember vividly to this day. On that earlier occasion, at this same time of year, on the seventh of April, 1712, in the middle of the night as the moon was going down, Peter Vantilborough's house in the East Ward had been set alight. In the horrible moments that followed, neighbors rushing forth to help extinguish the flames were met by the twenty or thirty blacks who had lit the fire, howling and prancing with muskets, staves, swords, and hatchets. Those first unlucky whites to arrive at the flame-lit scene were promptly fallen upon and slaughtered in the miry streets.

One of Aunt Min's anonymous contemporaries set down what happened next. "Notice thereof having been soon carried to the fort, his excellency Governor Hunter ordered a cannon to be fired from the ramparts to alarm the town, at the same time detaching a party of soldiers to the fire, at whose appearance the black villains immediately fled, making their way out of town to hide themselves as fast as they could. But in their flight they killed and wounded several more white people. Being closely pursued, some concealed themselves in barns, others in swamps or woods, which being surrounded and strictly guarded till morning, many of them were then taken. Some, finding no way for their escape, shot themselves." A desperate business—the nightmare come true that whites brooded over constantly, passing their days among primitive blacks forced to their labors as carters, boatmen, water haulers, yard hands. "The end of it was that after these foolish wretches had murdered eight or ten white people, and some of the confederates had been their own executioners, nineteen more of them were apprehended, brought upon their trials, and convicted."

Aunt Min could remember so frightful a springtime that events of another April, nearly thirty years later, were calling painfully to mind. Robin, the court had ordered "to be hung up in chains alive and so to continue without any sustenance until he be dead." Five days, ten, fifteen days and nights and days before he died? Did he moan, cry out? Excrement on the chains, on the ground beneath him. Flies. Claus was to be brought "to the place of execution and there broke upon a wheel and so to continue languishing until he be dead and his head and quarters to be at the queen's disposal." Furnis's penalty was "to be burnt with fire until he be dead and consumed." Tom, the black slave of Nicholas Roosevelt, "having nothing to say for himself why judgment of death should not pass against him, was burned with a slow fire that he might continue in torment for eight or ten hours, and continued burning until he was dead and consumed to ashes."

Elizabeth's aunt would remember—and likely would not dis-

approve of stern punishment for such crimes as those wide-
eyed, suffering wretches had been guilty of. And following that
clumsy plot of 1712, more laws were on the books. From an
hour past sunset no slave above fourteen years of age could
thereafter appear "in the streets, within the fortifications, or in
any place on the south side of Fresh Water Pond, without a
lantern and a lighted candle in it, so as the light thereof may be
plainly seen." Slaves might no longer come together in groups
larger than three. A slave leaving his master's yard with a club
or staff would receive forty lashes. No white person could employ, harbor, conceal, or entertain at his house, outhouse, or
plantation slaves other than his own without their master's con-
sent; anyone knowing of such entertainment without reporting
it would be fined or imprisoned. On Sundays, day of general
rest when plots could be too easily hatched, slaves were to
indulge in no "rude and unlawful sports," no riding of a horse
"through any street or on the common," no "fetching any water
other than from the next well or pump to the slave's place of
abode." They might not purchase any article, sign their mark to
any contract, bear witness against any freeman. In addition, "all
and every slave who shall be convicted of willfully burning any
dwelling house, barn, stable, outhouse, or stacks of corn or hay
shall suffer the pains of death, in such manner as the justices
shall think fit."

Those laws were on the books, but whites of the town felt
hardly more secure. Rumors would reach them of slave revolts
elsewhere. Ships that put into harbor brought news of various
uprisings among blacks in the broiling West Indies, and as recently as 1739, just two years before the present crisis, New
Yorkers had learned of a widespread, bloody insurrection
among plantation slaves in South Carolina. In that instance,
before the rising could be put down, the dead had come to
number forty-four Negroes, twenty-nine white people.

Such news encouraged white New Yorkers to regard the
blacks in their midst warily. Skilled Negroes worked for less
and so were hated by white craftsmen, whereas the unskilled

were often creatures not long removed from a distant, heathen land, their language impenetrable, the rites that they practiced covertly in shed or loft or woods repulsive and blasphemous. Thus, during the early spring of 1741 the fear-prone city was quick to grow alarmed, and the alarm turned quickly to panic, as ten separate fires occurred in a period of less than three weeks, eight of them within six days of each other. The roof of Mrs. Hilton's house, on the other side of the chandler Wendover's, was in flames, and even before it had been extinguished that Monday noon, April 6, 1741, someone had started a cry that the angry townsmen had taken up: *"The Spanish negroes! The Spanish negroes!"* Those swarthy, recalcitrant foreigners had been promptly tracked down at their places and jailed. Yet that same afternoon magistrates deliberating upstairs in City Hall had been called to windows to see fire nearby consuming the roof of Col. Philipse's storehouse, around which building could be heard screams coming from the multitude that Negroes were inside; soon a black was indeed spotted emerging and fleeing in terror over fence and hedge. Thereafter Mr. Philipse's Cuffee was dragged from his master's home and hauled roughly to jail on the mob's shoulders. Other blacks as well, present with buckets at the colonel's fire or encountered on the streets nearby, were thrown into the crowded jail. And before the sun had set that Monday in early April white refugees were in retreat, and Governor Clarke was ordering a military watch to be kept all night about the emptying city—a precaution extended through the summer to supplement the regular town watch, deemed inadequate in the present crisis.

By now the magistrates were fully alert to the danger. For robbing Mr. and Mrs. Hogg of their cloth and coin, the slave Caesar had been languishing five weeks in jail. In times past, other slaves had been known to set fires to get back at masters who punished them. Might not this rash of fires be acts of retaliation by Caesar's vengeful black friends, led perhaps by the white suspect Hughson, who had hid their stolen goods and given them drink in his tavern? The wretched Hughson was free for the moment on recognizance, but on the eighth, Wednesday, he and his wife were ordered committed, "being charged as accessories to divers felonies and misdemeanors." The magistrates were alert now and active. By week's end, on the same Saturday that Elizabeth near Flatbush was penning her account of the Pursell family's flight to Long Island, the Common Council had assembled to hear Recorder Horsmanden turn what was a strong civic suspicion into certainty. A plot, he insisted, was abroad in the city streets, a conspiracy to burn the town. "Everyone that reflects on the circumstances attending the recent fires, the frequency of them, and the causes being yet undiscovered must necessarily conclude that they were occasioned and set on foot by some villainous confederacy of latent enemies amongst us."

A general search would be conducted. A fast day would be observed. A proclamation would be issued. The search, prepared for in elaborate secrecy, occurred the following Monday afternoon. All the streets of the town were blocked off, and no one but aldermen and constables was allowed to pass from house to house:

"It being much suspected that strangers were lurking about the city who had been the wicked instruments and occasion of the fires in order to make opportunities of pilfering and plundering in these hard times, a general search of all houses throughout the town was undertaken, whereby it was thought probable discoveries might be made, not only of stolen goods but likewise of lodgers that were suspicious and generally unknown to the settled populace." Yet though every one of the thousand buildings in town was searched that day, no stolen goods were located or suspicious strangers found. That concerted effort turned up only two pitiful Negroes, man and wife, discovered with unspecified objects (a knife? a spice box? a crystal tumbler?) "thought improper for and unbecoming the condition of slaves"; those frightened two—Cuba and her husband—were arrested and hied off to jail to join the others already there.

One is led to recall, against this public mood, a passage that occurs in the privacy of Elizabeth Pursell's third letter to her friend Sophia Milner, written the preceding fall under the date of Thursday, November 6, 1740. That morning the pretty American girl had stood waving to her father, him with his newly bruised finger, as he set off under the trees of Broadway toward the Exchange, his steps stirring the snow-frosted leaves that bestrewed the ground. She had waved, and a noise had caused her to turn. By the door of her home her cat Sappho had leapt friskily from the woodpile, dislodging kindling, and raced, seemingly in sheer high spirits, through the hedge into the garden, scattering two or three hens that had been scratching and clucking about the whitened yard. Venture, kindly old black servant, sat at the front gate beaming. The sky overhead was blue, the day crisp and bracing, the winter that was approaching almost all prepared for, the ball at the fort no more than a week in the past, Mr. Corimer recovered from his long illness and established in his new quarters for a lengthy stay. Elizabeth was happy, home in her own world and at last at peace with her loss of a sister, warm in her thoughts of an English admirer (he crapulous from the effect of his debauch the night before, though she could not have known that). On the ramparts one week earlier this lovely girl had stood close beside an earl's youngest son to watch the dazzling fireworks; and after a year's absence she was home now and happy in her town of familiar wonders—brick buildings and wharves and high ships in the harbor and gleaners in the fields beyond the palisades—home among people and sights she loved.

The community Elizabeth described in a letter to her friend in England later that day, whether real or illusory, seems serenely idyllic. A half year passes—and its magistrates are setting aside Wednesday, the thirteenth day of the coming month of May, "to be kept as a solemn fast, because his most gracious majesty, for the vindicating the honor of his crown, has declared war against Spain, and because of the severity of the cold last winter, and because many houses and dwellings have been fired about our ears, without any discovery of the cause or occasion of them, which has put us into the utmost consternation."

Those magistrates meant to get at the cause of the fires. Before the present week was out, the royal governor of the province, responding to their recommendations as urged by Recorder Horsmanden, issued a proclamation to be posted abroad and read aloud on every corner, morning and afternoon, after thorough ringing of church bells. By such means New Yorkers were to learn that rewards were being offered to whoever might know of or lately be involved in setting any fire within the city. Any slave who came forth with such knowledge would be granted his freedom. He would be pardoned if concerned in the crime. And he would receive £20, his master £25. Any white person offering such information would receive the astonishing sum of £100, and if concerned in the crime would likewise be pardoned.

Imagine the doomed in their cellar dungeon. Would the terms of that proclamation not tempt them?

* * *

The offer of rewards was published April 17, 1741. That day the Pursells had moved back from Long Island to their home on Broadway; and three evenings later, on Monday, Elizabeth concluded her long, fifth letter to Sophia Milner. She wrote in her room by a fire, Annie attending, bullets presumably still embedded in the gumwood kas but sounds from the street no longer causing concern. Spring had thawed away fear. Soon the raven-haired girl at her vanity would be receiving Pyrmont Waters that innocently cure all carbuncles and cutaneous eruptions, Italian Paste for enameling the neck a lovely white, Venetian Ointment that renders arms as soft as velvet. Her feet would be washed, and she would put on her chicken-skin gloves, worn all night to make the hands smooth and plump, then lie down in her own feather bed, in the rose room overlooking the kitchen garden in sight of the Hudson, and there sleep secure. But first she must sit a few moments at her table, with rice paper and quill pens and sand and the box of wafers, to finish this, the fifth of her six letters to Sophia that have survived:

N York. Mon. Apr. 20.

My friend will delight to know that we are escaped from dangers, and free from dreadful alarms, that we can go to bed without apprehensions and rise up without anxious thoughts, and walk out and see easy countenances instead of distress and discontented looks. I am persuaded that Sophia's benevolent heart, which will have participated in our sufferings, will delight now to share in what gives ease and satisfaction to all.

It's three days since we returned here. We find the face of things mercifully restored. To be exposed to the rage of the mob and subject to alarms and fears is a dreadful situation. But upon the appearance of law and government, those supports of society and protection of individuals, the desperate abettors of the disturbances disappear. We are assured that all are now or soon will be in jail. Peace and order has taken place, and the past scenes of confusion and disorder appear as a dream. I was for some days a little fidgety, and I dare own it to you; for dear Sophy, one can hardly credit it possible for human creatures to be so abandoned as some have been in this time of theft and firing. Yet I need only glance out our front windows at the melancholy spectacle of Fort George in ruins to confirm the truth of what appears like a fabulous story.

We have in short been engaged in a very anxious time, now happily past. I must tell you that my girl Annie sits before the fire at the same table, which often moves so suddenly that you are not to wonder at the fine black spots in this. May I ask a favor of my friend? I should be glad you would be so obliging to order for me two pair pumps and two pair shoes of good black and brown everlasting from Mr. Garnet. I shall advise again which way to send 'em, perhaps toward summer, only desire he will please to get 'em ready.

We are now preparing some pork, beef, pickles, &c.,

whatever is eatable (and proper to send them) will be acceptable by Lt. Levitt in a king's vessel which we understand to sail within the week for Jamaica to join the fleet of Admiral Vernon against the Spaniard. Have not room to say all I would. Mr. C was with us yesterday and went with us to church, but would not dine. He can't be very easy as times are—has forsook his affairs that brought him here and talks now of returning by an early passage to London. We shall miss him if he goes, though of late he has not seemed always so easeful in mind as formerly, no more have we. Notwithstanding we shall all miss his presence should he return to England, yet fear he may.

I hope to have the pleasure of hearing from you and particularly of what concerns you and yours, as I have wrote of mine, for be assured I am interested in your happiness, and having this account of my proceedings, you will assuredly acquit me of neglect, which it is not possible for me ever willfully to be to you. I indulge a secret hope of someday revisiting England, but if Providence does not permit us to meet again in this world, I trust in some happy region we shall. My compliments to all friends. I've received an obliging letter from Mrs. W, which am ashamed not to have yet answered. Papa desires to join me in best respects to your family and the young ladies, and I remain, dear Sophy, with great esteem, your most affectionate and faithful friend,

ELIZABETH PURSELL

Mr. Schaw, who dined with us today, desires to convey his remembrances and regard. The trial of the thieves in the late plot to fire the town commences tommorrow.

III

Seven generations later I'm on the fourteenth (really thirteenth) floor of a building on Nineteenth Street off Second Avenue, so that if positioned suitably at one window I can see the East River flowing south beyond the sprawling pile of glass and buff bricks that is Stuyvesant Town. Each school day I take the Lexington IRT uptown to Eighty-sixth Street, where I've been teaching for the last four years at a private school. But on weekends I'm sometimes drawn south to Lower Manhattan, a couple of miles farther below my apartment building, to walk that fragment of earth on which Elizabeth and the future Earl of Cavendham and Francis Schaw were living through days and nights two hundred and forty years ago.

The walks are instructive. Where those three picnicked one gray autumn afternoon in 1740, at what is now Thirteenth and Ninth Avenue, the Universal Screw and Bolt Company fills a six-story building on one corner, opposite the Afro-American Coffee Shop. Proceed south along Hudson Street, past warehouses and walls tirelessly scrawled on: REG, SHORTY, SISTERHOOD IS POWER. Turn west off Broadway down Liberty, alongside the World Trade Center to what is now Greenwich

Street. Hughson's tavern stood a little to the south of that intersection, at Cedar Street, along a road that was then at the shoreline. Hughson's gibbet, from which they would hang him, was set up near the water's edge to the northeast of town, across the island on the site of the later, notorious Five Points, now close by the Police Headquarters Plaza. Just above Bowling Green, near the Customs House where the old fort stood, is the site of the Pursells' yellow-brick mansion, vanished and its deed-protected view of the Hudson long since obscured.

Elizabeth in that home writing an English friend Monday, April 20, 1741, supposed her river view out the side window inviolate forever. Incidentally, the conclusion of her fifth letter to Sophia Milner (I gingerly open the original and reread it) sounds far more optimistic about the current condition of the city during an alarming spring and summer than succeeding events would justify. "We are assured," the American girl writes, that all abettors of the disturbances troubling New York since early March "are now or soon will be in jail. Peace and order has taken place," with the trial of the accused thieves and arsonists to commence tomorrow. But the trial she refers to would disclose much additional cause for alarm, as justices unmasked further villainy in the course of criminal proceedings that would put scores of others in jail—as noted, some hundred and seventy-four of them—and all in fear of their lives. Thirty-four, white and black, would surrender their lives before the proceedings ended.

Was Elizabeth meanwhile (that affectionate daughter) dreaming on those same April evenings that she might yet journey from here to England as Corimer's bride? The young nobleman "talks now of returning by an early passage to London," so she had written Sophia—then unguardedly in the same letter, a few lines later: "I indulge a secret hope of someday revisiting England . . ." And after seven generations, with tomorrow's class to prepare on the Granger decisions, I linger over the image of a dove-eyed beauty atop the benighted battlements of Fort George, under the fireworks, with young Corimer beside her in his gold-laced brown coat and scarlet breeches, on the point of declaring his love. Yet when that eighteenth-century gentleman did return home some months later, he was traveling as a bachelor still, unexpectedly elevated to his title and accompanied only by one servant, one slave, the white monkey, and the one surviving greyhound. Elizabeth for her part was indeed to be married, and before two years were out, though not to an English earl. Rather she would become, at eighteen and to the disappointment of her family, the wife of Francis Schaw.

* * *

Schaw has left his own reminiscences, justly celebrated and often reprinted. The part of them, however, that concerns what came to be called the Negro Plot presents problems. In those pages we learn that the future "Chaplain of Valley Forge," at the time no more than an obscure schoolmaster in colonial New York, was among the persons who questioned the servant girl Mary Burton outside court on the day the trial began. What occurred within the courtroom that same day is a matter of record: "At a supreme court of judicature held for the province of New York, at the City Hall of New York on Tuesday, April 21, 1741—Present, James DeLancey, Esq., justice; Daniel Horsmanden, Esq., justice. The grand jury was called. The following appeared and were sworn—viz."—and twenty-seven merchants' names are listed, including such ancestors of distinguished progeny as Anthony Rutgers, John Cruger, Jr., Adoniah Schuyler, Henry Beekman, Jr., and Benjamin Pursell. In giving the charge to the grand jury the first morning, Justice DeLancey recalled for its members "the many frights and terrors which the good people of this city have of late been put into by repeated and unusual fires, allowing room to suspect that some at least did not proceed from chance or common accident." He reminded them that "although we have the happiness to live under a government which exceeds all others in the excellency of its constitution and laws, yet if those to whom the execution of the laws is committed do not exert themselves, such laws (intended for a terror to the evildoer and a protection to the good) will become a dead letter, and our most excellent constitution turned into anarchy and confusion." He explained that arson is felony at common law, "and if any part of the house, outbuildings, barns, or stables adjoining be burned, the offender is guilty of felony, notwithstanding the fire afterward be put out, or go out of itself." He recommended in passing that the grand jury inquire "narrowly into all persons who sell rum and other strong liquor to negroes," for selling even so much as a penny dram was directly contrary to an act of assembly in force for the better regulating of slaves. And he charged the jury "to present all conspiracies, combinations, and other offenses from treasons down to trespasses; and in your inquiries the oath each of you has just now taken will," the judge concluded, "be your guide, and I pray God to direct and assist you in the discharge of your duty."

With those remarks delivered, the court adjourned until ten o'clock the following day.

Its business on reconvening was first to hear testimony from Mary Burton concerning the goods stolen from Mr. Hogg's nearly two months earlier. But the preceding afternoon Judge Horsmanden, with others including Francis Schaw, had met hurriedly to deal with a crisis of Mary's creating. They had come together at Sheriff Mills's quarters on the ground floor of the City Hall, under where the court had been sitting that morning. The sheriff lodged off the brick arcade to the left as one passed through the building from Broad to Nassau Street. (Corimer notes in his journal, by the way, that architecturally the City Hall of this colonial town "is very little inferior to the Guild Hall" in London, high praise from a visitor with a tendency toward the supercilious.) In the front room of Mills's quarters, on a bench behind a deal table, the sheriff sat with Horsmanden, Schaw, and Alderman Bancker of the West Ward. Before them stood the child Mary, between a constable and the ship's carpenter Vandursen, at whose home she had been living since leaving these same quarters three weeks ago. She was staring beyond the seated gentlemen through a window that gave on Broad Street. The rattle-watch station was nearby in the middle of the street, and next to that wooden shed were the cage (with a recalcitrant urchin spending his day inside it) and the pillory, at present unoccupied. The girl's eyes were on the pillory. She seemed, as Schaw tells us in his *Reminiscences,* "to have been under some great uneasiness or terrible apprehensions." That same morning she had sent word that "she would not be sworn nor give evidence. Whereupon," as Schaw notes, "a constable with a warrant from a magistrate had fetched her to the town house. Being some time gone he at length returned and brought the child with him," so that now she stood before these officials whom she had defied—a slight, round-shouldered girl rather masculine in appearance, with tangled brown hair and a scar through one eyebrow. She was wearing a threadbare blue jacket over her smock and petticoats. The thongs of her boots were unlaced.

Why, Alderman Bancker was asking her gently, would she not be sworn and repeat what she had already told the magistrates some weeks ago about the theft at Hogg's, about seeing the black man Caesar climbing the shed roof at Hughson's tavern at a morning hour and entering the Newfoundland Beauty's window, about entering Peggy's room herself the following day and receiving from the slave and the whore coins and an apron cut from speckled linen? Why would she not give the court that evidence?

The girl opened her mouth to speak, teeth yellow and uneven, gaps where some were gone. Her eyes darted to Sheriff Mills, then again to the street scene distorted beyond the window. She closed her mouth and was silent.

Was it perhaps that she knew something concerning the fires that had lately happened? Understandably the gentlemen had fires on their mind. Was some further, undisclosed knowledge what was frightening her?

Justice Horsmanden leaned forward and put the question directly to her. The girl looked at his grave, wig-framed face and shifted uneasily, but she offered no reply. The interrogators exchanged glances. "Her manner," Schaw says, "had awakened our jealousy that she was privy to the fires; and as it was thought a matter of the utmost concern, the justice was importunate and used many arguments with her to persuade her to speak the truth and tell all she knew. To this end he read the governor's proclamation to her, promising indemnity and a large reward."

Horsmanden's rich voice was lingering on phrases that might move the child: ". . . to any white person, confederate or not . . . the sum of *one hundred pounds,* current money of this province, and   pardoned, if concerned therein . . ." Yet the girl, says Schaw, "seemed to despise the reward, nor could the gentleman by any means, either threats or promises, prevail upon her, though she was assured withal that she should be freed from her master and pardoned, and have protection of the magistrates and her person be secure from harm. In fine, all that had been done hitherto was in vain."

They were losing patience. Abruptly Horsmanden rose from the bench and gathered his papers to leave. "Commit the wench," he ordered Alderman Bancker shortly, and started for the door. At a sign the constable seized Mary, who had moved as though to follow in the noise of the gentlemen's rising. "Commit her," the alderman repeated from behind the table, and the girl's scarred face screwed up and her gray eyes grew wide before the imagined sight, perhaps for the first time, of the jail rooms below them. She began to stammer, but the judge swept past her and through the doorway.

In the constable's grip now, Mary, struggling anew to speak, turned beseechingly to the gentlemen who remained. "I mean to tell," she cried, looking directly at Schaw. "I'll tell—whatever I know about—about—" And the officials behind the table waited, with a further show of impatience, though the alderman did signal the constable to remove his hands from the witness.

"About Mr. Hogg's goods," she went on. "And I'll acquaint their honors about the linen and coins," she managed to say, trembling violently, in tears now as she blurted out:

"But I'll not say nothing about the fires."

The expression, Schaw remembers, "thus as it were providentially slipping from her, much alarmed the company, as meaning that she could indeed give an account of the occasion of the several fires if she would; so that it highly became us in the discharge of our trust to sift out the discovery." The girl held to her resolve, however, until at length it was Francis Schaw himself, "having recourse to religious topics," who represented for her the heinousness of the crime of which she would be guilty if she was cognizant of so wicked a design as setting houses afire but would not discover it to others. "Many might lose their lives in the flames," the schoolmaster reminded her earnestly, "and this you will have to answer for at the day of judgment, Mary, as surely as if you had set the tow in place or struck the flint. A most damnable sin will lie at your door."

"Besides, child," Alderman Bancker was insinuating at her shoulder, "why need you fear divulging what you know? You rest assured of the protection of the magistrates. His honor the judge has told you as much himself."

And though for a while longer the orphan remained inflexible, at last by such means the gentlemen's arguments prevailed; so that the following day in the crowded assembly hall upstairs, before the grand jury, the fifteen-year-old indentured servant Mary Burton did stand to give evidence, "which, however, notwithstanding what had been said, came from her as if she were still under some terrible fears or restraints":

"Raise your right hand. Do you swear to tell the whole truth, so help you God?"

She nodded and, when directed by Justice Horsmanden from the bench, repeated, "I do."

"Speak so all may hear you," the justice instructed her. "Now, Mary, tell the court what you witnessed about two o'clock Sunday morning, the first of March just passed."

For a long moment the girl said nothing, her eyes shifting wildly around the room, toward the clerk, the constable at the door, the hushed group of important personages. No other witnesses, none of her fellow taverners, no Negroes were in sight.

BURTON. I saw Caesar—

COURT. The baker Vaarck's negro?

BURTON. I saw Vaarck's Caesar bring the things which he had robbed of Mr. Hogg to my master and hand them in through a window.

COURT. And could you make out who received them?

BURTON. Indeed, sir. My master and mistress and Peggy what's called the Newfoundland Beauty. The three of them was at the window, and Caesar handed them in indigo and beeswax besides.

COURT. Was Caesar often in your master Hughson's house?

BURTON. Yes, sir. He and the other negars.

COURT. What others?

BURTON. There was Cuff of Mr. Philipse used to meet there with Caesar.

COURT. Cuff Philipse, now in jail. Was there anyone else, Mary?

BURTON. Quack.

COURT. Mr. Roosevelt's Quack and Mr. Philipse's Cuffee. And for what purpose did the slaves come to Hughson's tavern?

BURTON. They talked there and junketed and refreshed theirselves.

COURT. And your master served them?

BURTON. Rum, yes, sir. That's why they come.

COURT. And what did the blacks talk of at Hughson's?

BURTON. I heard them—

COURT. Speak up, child. Don't be frightened. Tell the court what they talked of.

BURTON. I heard the negars talk of—of burning the fort.

COURT. Burning Fort George?

BURTON. Yes, sir, and that they would go down to the Fly and burn the whole town, they would. I heard Cuffee say that a great many people had too much and others too little, and that his old master as had a great deal of money soon would have less, and Cuff would have more.

COURT. And did your master overhear the slaves speaking thus together?

BURTON. Indeed, sir.

COURT. What did your master do or say?

BURTON. He said—

COURT. Proceed, child.

BURTON. He and Mistress said they would aid them as much as they could.

COURT. In firing the town?

BURTON. Yes, sir. That they did, and I heard them say when all was done Caesar would be governor, and my master would be king.

[*Tumult in the hall. Pause, while order is restored.*]

COURT. Did they talk about how they would set the fires?

BURTON. They said they would set fire to the town at night, and when the white people come to extinguish it they would kill and destroy them all.

COURT. And how would they manage that?

BURTON. With swords and guns. I've seen upward of seven or eight guns in my master's house I have, and some swords as well.

COURT. but why did you not speak of all this earlier, child?

[*Pause, the witness answering at last in a low voice, obviously agitated.*]

BURTON. Please your honor, who would believe me, a stranger and an orphan girl? Besides, my master and mistress told me—

COURT. Go on.

BURTON. They said if ever I made mention of the goods stole from Mr. Hogg they would poison me. And Caesar swore that if I discovered their design of burning the town they would burn me whenever they met me, Caesar and the other negars would.

COURT. How many negroes did you see at your master's house in all, Mary?

BURTON. Upwards of twenty, maybe thirty.

COURT. And what other white persons were involved in this hellish design, child? Tell the court.

BURTON. The design as the negars talked of, of burning the town?

COURT. When they plotted to burn the fort and the town.

BURTON. Please your honor, I never saw any white person in their company but only my master and mistress and Peggy what's called the Beauty. Only those three.

* * *

"Mary's evidence of a conspiracy," writes Schaw in his *Reminiscences* (Everyman edition, p. 27), "not only to burn the city but also to murder the townsmen, was most astonishing, and that any white people should be so abandoned as to confederate in a purpose so detestable could not but be amazing to everyone that learned of it. The court (upon hearing Mary) desiring that Margaret Kerry, prisoner, be produced to testify, the sheriff carried the said Margaret or Peggy before the grand jury and engaged to see her safe returned again."

Such passages from Schaw's book are of interest in clarifying what his attitude toward witnesses and defendants was at the time—an attitude different from what an honored old minister would remember. Yet of all the commentary that scholars have produced about *The Diary, Reminiscences, and Correspondence of the Right Reverend Francis Schaw, Minister in America* (to give it its formal title), none to my knowledge has taken note of the discrepancy. To be sure, attention has for the most part been directed toward two other sections of that invaluable work. One is the portion that recounts its author's role in the Great Awakening that was sweeping over America in the early 1740s. Schaw's optimistic narrative of spiritual struggles, soon to be entered into and in time to be couched in what Hazlitt was to call his "sweetly joyous" style, has deservedly received notice throughout the nineteenth and twentieth centuries, resulting in one great body of Schavian commentary on such matters as regeneration, unconditional election, and irresistible grace. The other body of commentary concentrates, of course, on the account of the elderly and esteemed minister's role in the Revolution, in particular on his presence, in his mid-sixties, with two of his sons at the ordeal at Valley Forge. Yet though Edgar Desmond Griffith's historical romance of 1906, *Chaplain of Valley Forge,* has no doubt fixed that epithet forever on the patriot Schaw, it hardly does justice to the range of his long, varied, and fruitful life.

My uncle, the professor at NYU—scholar of colonial New York, locator of Corimer's journal, and descendant of Francis Schaw—awakened my own interest in our illustrious ancestor, so that over the years I've read most of what has been written about him. In addition, I've inherited Uncle Teddy's papers on Schaw, including transcriptions of many unpublished documents, such as one dated April 22, 1741, signed by James De-Lancey and Daniel Horsmanden, which reads, "The Justices present appoint Fras. Schaw, Esq., to be bell ringer and secretary of the supreme court of judicature for the usual fees, and also appoint him to be messenger for the justices, and he to keep an account of his services in attending the justices and deliver his acct. to the supervisors in order to be paid for his services as the supervisors shall think reasonable. . . .' The duty of bell ringer mentioned in that appointment may have been a sinecure, for no evidence survives to show that the schoolmaster filled such a role during court sessions. But he did, as we shall see, act on at least two occasions as messenger of the court, and no doubt submitted his account to be paid for doing so, in accordance with what was almost certainly a favor by Judge Horsmanden, formerly resident of Gouldhurst in Kent, to a literate immigrant born in that same English village.

But Schaw was employed by the court. Moreover, passages from his account of these early days of the trials—passages obviously composed from notes or a lost journal kept at the time—reveal that the newly appointed messenger shared the court's impressions about major participants in those events: about Mary, Peggy, Caesar. Later he would come to feel a sympathy, eloquently expressed, for blacks caught up in the mounting terror, but not yet—not as of late April with the trials only commencing. Reminiscences of an old man in his sixties suggest the contrary, dwelling as they do upon an early morning the preceding autumn, within a crowded meeting house where a boyish preacher had been expounding to throngs of New Yorkers in and out of doors. "Some stood on the leads of the windows, and many were obliged to stand without the door. I never in my life beheld so attentive an audience," the sexagenarian Schaw would recall. "When I saw Mr. Whitefield come upon the dais he looked almost angelical, a young, slender divine with a bold, undaunted countenance before some thousands of people. He spake as one having authority, they greedily devouring every word. And my hearing him gave me a heart wound, by God's blessing, so that my old foundation was broken up, every scruple vanished, and I came home astonished, saying within myself, *Surely God is with this man of a truth.*"

From that morning, October 31, 1740, Schaw's life had changed, so the old man looking back would insist. "I began to alter the whole form of my conversation, and set in earnest upon a new life" (p. 19). Yet we have found in all our reading no external confirmation of such a change so early, not in Elizabeth's letters or in Corimer's journal of those days; and indeed, in the following spring, in April, the schoolmaster who had advertised to teach "Elements of the Law" seems still, by abundant evidence, including his own testimony based on contemporary notes, to have been not only secularly employed by the court but in agreement with its feelings and aims. Not until later—on a particular morning in June that we shall come to—would (so I think) the sight of an old acquaintance in an agony near death transform his attitude, finally and for good.

* * *

Meanwhile, in the aftermath of Mary Burton's alarming testimony, Justices DeLancey and Horsmanden at City Hall on April 23—St. George's Day and by custom an occasion of general merriment throughout New York—had solemnly "assembled all the gentlemen of the law in town to meet them in the afternoon in order to determine upon such measures as should be judged most proper in this emergency." They came, the various attorneys—Messrs. Murray and Alexander and Smith and Chambers and Nicholls and Lodge and Jamison—and reached a conclusion. Though by statute the two justices were themselves empowered to deal summarily with crimes that slaves committed, in the present instance each black defendant would receive a jury trial like any white man. So deep might be the present plot—and of such consequence to town and province—that it should be fathomed as far down as possible. Besides, had it not already been testified to that white people were confederated in the scheme? "Most probably," the record states, "these indeed were the first movers and seducers of the slaves, in a conspiracy of more dangerous contrivance than the slaves themselves were capable of." So the term for the sitting of the court would be enlarged, the assembled gentlemen of the law ("generously and unanimously offering their assistance") would each in turn help to secure king's evidence, and the jury would hear the evidence thus secured.

Members of the jury the following morning attended to the words of the Newfoundland Beauty, one of the three white people whom Mary Burton's testimony had implicated. So that they might, Sheriff Mills had brought the woman before the court at ten sharp—no beauty by then, having languished seven weeks and longer below the courtroom in the cellar jail. Its stench had seemed to accompany Peggy up the two flights of stairs and into the crowded hall. She squinted against sunlight. Pallid she looked, and frowzy, markedly thinner than was the strapping, red-caped doxy whom Corimer had zestfully embraced last fall in a woodshed. Now he would scarcely have recognized her, coarse linen chemise hanging loosely on her back. Her hair was cropped short; soil was on her smock, and a sore inflamed one muddy cheek. She rubbed her arm, staring at the floor all the while Justice Horsmanden was exhorting her, according to the record, "to make an ingenuous confession and discovery of what she knew. He gave her hopes of his recommending to the governor for a pardon if the court could be of opinion that she deserved it, assuring her (as the case was) that he had his honor the governor's permission to give hopes of mercy to such criminals as should confess their guilt."

Mercy would mean transporting the woman from the colony, but alive still in her early twenties and able to start a new life somewhere. Did she understand? Only admit to the slave's gift of the speckled linen. Name (as she may already have realized) one or two other blacks besides Caesar as plotters against the peace of the town. What did it matter to her? Confirm what the tavern-maid Mary had said, about overhearing careless words of a black man who would be governor after the town was fired, and a white man who would be king. Then mercy would be shown her; no longer would she slump in a cellar waiting darkly in fear. What says the witness?

The words that Peggy Kerry uttered were mumbled, hardly articulate, words that the judges had to strain to hear and comprehend out of the mouth of a morose, ignorant woman. What did she say? Was the slut denying what Mary had charged her with?

"If I accused anybody," she was insisting before the court, "it must be only innocent people. I never heard nothing of a plot. John never plotted, no more did Caesar. I must accuse innocent people if I said that they did, and so must wrong my own soul."

* * *

Return the prisoner to the dungeon to think that answer over. The court was by no means finished with her.

Dungeon and *trial* and *defendant* and *counsel* are words used at the time, but in us they stir images different from those they would have awakened then. For instance, although a defendant was allowed to make a statement in the course of the trial, he could not, as an interested party, testify on his own behalf. Nor could any of the present defendants, male or female, white or black, obtain counsel; none of the gentlemen of the law in the city would undertake to handle their defense. (But then, "it requires," as was thought, "no manner of skill to make a plain and honest defense, the artless and ingenuous behavior of one whose conscience acquits him having something in it more convincing than the highest eloquence of persons speaking in a cause not their own.") As for trials themselves, they were customarily over the day they began, with punishment meted out on the morrow. Hence, jails were not intended for long incarcerations. A crime would be committed, the culprit caught and promptly tried, and promptly he would pay the penalty—by our standards invariably a stiff one. In that age when no adequate police force existed, citizens were confident that the law's severity was the principal deterrent to crime. Thus the criminal who was caught was very soon either dead or free—maimed perhaps, but free—and the matter closed.

Accordingly, there was little need for numerous dungeon cells, no need for cells as we know them at all in a colonial town. New York debtors might be imprisoned for extended periods under the rafters in the attic of City Hall, but the two or three common criminals awaiting their trials at any one time were lodged almost casually in a couple of secure rooms in the basement, where little had been provided for stays longer than a night or two.

In the spring of 1741, however, the cellar of the City Hall in New York was already unusually crowded, and some had been down there awhile. The black man Caesar, for instance, had been there nearly two months, ever since Wilson off the man-of-war had pointed him out to constables at Hughson's tavern on the winter day after the robbery at Hogg's. Peggy had been down there since Mary Burton first testified against her, soon after the robbery, as one who had received stolen goods. Mr. Philipse's Cuffee was still down there—had been since a street mob enraged by the succession of fires in town had yanked him from his absent master's house on John Street and brought him there on its burly shoulders. A fellow named Price was in the dungeon too: Arthur Price, white servant accused of stealing goods belonging to the provincial governor that had been temporarily removed to the home of Price's master when the fort had burned. Price, whose chances looked dismal, was awaiting his trial with the others. Manuel and four more Spanish Negroes were down there, and Cuba and her husband, and various slaves who had imprudently volunteered to help at the fire at Philipse's storehouse. Roosevelt's Quack, named by Mary as a black plotter at Hughson's tavern, was down there, as were the white innkeeper Hughson and his wife, both accused by their maidservant Mary and accordingly crowded with all those others into the dungeons under City Hall.

Before the court Peggy Kerry, freed for a while from that congestion, had stood and stubbornly denied knowledge of any plot. The same day, Friday, April 24, she and Hughson, his wife, and the slave Caesar were all four summoned to the bar to be arraigned. They severally pleaded not guilty. "Ordered, that the trials of the negro, the Hughsons, and Kerry do come on tomorrow morning." So reads the record, although on the morrow, for reasons not stated, the prisoners' trials were put off "till Tuesday the 28th instant," and when Tuesday arrived they were postponed again, until the first day of May.

May 1—traditionally Moving Day in New York—was when Francis Schaw, in company with his friend Corimer, undertook a couple of errands around the town, one for the court and the other for Elizabeth Pursell. The appropriate passage in Schaw's *Reminiscences* and an extended entry in Corimer's journal together provide an unusually detailed account of the activities of the two of them that Friday, so that we may confidently picture them side by side near the Fly Market sometime before noon, the servant Milne preceding them on their way across town. The gentlemen were missing the proceedings at court, but perhaps they had been indoors long enough. Both at any rate record details of their outing with a gratifying fullness: poles from upper windows bearing clothes to dry, the crowded market, "the dirty and disagreeable street around it," the glum mood of farmers and housewives and servants among the stalls and gut-strewn cobbles on a day unseasonably listless, with no breeze stirring. Corimer grumbles that the market "greatly obstructs the agreeable prospect of the East River," and he comments on the confusion of carts, down from Harlem and Westchester, impeding passage along the thoroughfares.

Beyond the carts and up Rutgers Hill the two gentlemen were making their way behind Corimer's servant, in order to search out the quarters of the ship's carpenter Vandursen. That freeman they found in his cellar-kitchen mending stockings. Earlier Miss Pursell had besought her friends to inquire after the welfare of the girl from the tavern, the one whose plight had interested Nurse Kannady two months before. The carpenter, so Schaw had learned, owned the girl's indentures now. This morning, however, Mary was not at home, as Vandursen explained to his callers—was next door but two houses where she had been sent to fetch water. And at neighbor Masters's the gentlemen did in time find the court's young witness, by the well with her keg, talking to Masters's wife.

Word that these friends brought Elizabeth after that encounter could hardly have been reassuring. Listening to Mary, Schaw became convinced that she was in fact in danger—should not be left at large unprotected. The girl seemed fearful, ever close to tears, voluble about the frights that had already been inflicted on her for testifying. "For only telling the truth. But they will not believe me."

"Who will not, Mary?"

"Their honors will not, the gentlemen in court, though the judge himself, him with the large nose, said he would take care of me. Me without friends and a stranger, and it will end ill for me, mark my words. Saturday last I was on my way to the hatter's and passed by the baker Vaarck's in the Broad Street, and Bastian was at the front door fixing the steps, him the negars call Tom Peal, who put down his work and come and whispered me fiercely in his French way if I'd discovered about the fires. And I shook my head and started to go, so afeard was I, and him calling after me, 'Damn you,' says he, 'best you don't for fear you be burnt in the next one.' "

"Bastian is Vaarck's?"

"A big negar with a fierce look and half an ear gone, as speaks French. And Sunday with all at church—"

"This Sunday past?"

"Indeed, and the master and mistress at church and the house all empty. I was in Mr. Vandursen's cellar-kitchen when a negar I'd not seen come down and asked if there was a barber there. No, says I, and then he goes to send the boy out, the only body in the whole house besides myself, mind, to fetch him a barber to shave him. But I was afraid he had some ill design, so would not let the boy go. And at last when church was near out the negar went away, and people beginning to come into the streets, the negar took to his heels and run away, and I thought to have got somebody to have laid hold of him, but he made too much haste out of reach."

Had she told others of these happenings? Only Mrs. Masters here, this morning, for who would believe her, all alone as she was in the world? Schaw was late on his errand to do the court's bidding, but even so, he felt uneasy leaving the vulnerable Mary exposed as he had found her. Thus he and Corimer accompanied the girl back to the carpenter Vandursen's so that she might gather her few belongings together and from there return with them to the safety of City Hall. She and Milne preceded the gentlemen the few blocks down Smith and along Wall Street, where Corimer's servant led the child inside to take up her lodgings once more in Sheriff Mills's household.

Having seen her attended to, Schaw with his friend continued up Wall Street to Broadway. There the gentlemen turned at the post-and-rail fence before Trinity Church and walked south along the mall (Corimer's entry mentions sounds of the many birds in the locust trees that warm morning, and "a fife playing from an open window," and glimpses at the ends of cross streets of vessels plying up and down on the rivers both sides of the island, "the distant shores seen to great advantage"). Somewhat tardily he and Schaw were meeting Alderman Bancker by prearrangement at the sign of the Crossed Keys. On arriving, the two were content to find that the alderman had a constable with him. Now a foursome, they proceeded back up Broadway until reaching a narrow alley, beyond Little Queen Street, that made its cramped way over to the Hudson.

Along the western shoreline near the end of that alley stood Hughson's tavern, one of several flimsy structures elevated on a bluff a few feet above the pebbly, belittered beach. Having passed among puddles, scavenging pigs, and "confused heaps of sheds and wooden storehouses," the party on court business reached the end of the alley, where they paused a moment so that Corimer might adjust a loose shoe buckle. A flat-bottomed ferry from the foot of Oswego Street could be seen weaving under oars among limp-sailed vessels that were coasting upriver on the tide. The clouds broke, and a bit of sunlight illumined a portion of the wooded banks on the Jersey shore. With the town's odors behind them, the four might have lingered a moment longer to breathe in the scene, but sounds of a disturbance caused them to turn abruptly toward the tavern nearby.

Voices were raised at its porch, under a sagging roof, where a man was beating his fist violently against the front door—a short stout man in green coat and bagwig. "How dare you talk so saucily to an old woman!" he was shouting through the door. And a girl's clear voice inside was answering him as loudly:

"Shit pot! I'll kiss your filthy breech an you have me out of here!"

"We'll have you out soon enough. Impudent hussy! This house belongs to Mr. Campbell now—."

And the girl's voice again, shouting so distinctly as to be heard by a couple of gaping fishermen on the beach below:

"I care not a fart for that, you son of a whore! Remove your Goddamned arses from out my father's yard or I'll take his musket to the lot of you—"

The lot consisted of the short man at the doorway and two others, man and woman, all three turning gratefully as the court officials hurried through the front gate toward them, the constable freeing his cudgel as he came on. Having hastily identified themselves, the new arrivals were soon informed of the cause of the disturbance. Mr. and Mrs. Campbell, the elderly couple, had set out this morning with their lodger Mr. Ury ("a small man of civil bearing," according to Corimer, "though his clothing poor and mean") to take possession of the Hughsons' house, which having escheated to the king, the inoffensive Mr. Campbell had purchased some days earlier. Hughson's daughter was refusing, however, to vacate the premises. She had been feeding her scraggly hens by that heap of oyster shells when the Campbells had come up a few moments ago, and no sooner had they made their purpose clear to her—Mrs. Campbell speaking kindly to the girl throughout—than she fell to swearing at the good woman "like a life guardsman." Mrs. Campbell's husband (so Mr. Ury the lodger felt) not being sufficiently forward to protest the wench's behavior, Mr. Ury had stepped forth to rebuke her for her language. At that, she had turned from them with a round oath and dashed inside, bolting the door before they were able to follow.

The rest the magistrates themselves had heard. But would the jade open the door to the alderman and the court messenger? An answer was not long in coming: "You may go to hell and be damned!" she was screaming through the door. However, it took the constable no more than a minute or two, while his superiors were distracting her, to enter the house by a side window and make his way swiftly through the kitchen to seize the child in her bonnet, still bawling profanities through the bolted entranceway. And though she continued screeching her protests, he dragged her outside and through the gate and not gently down the alley and along crowded Broadway, the alderman, Corimer, and Schaw with his warrant following behind. Thus did the Campbells emerge into the record long enough to take possession of their new home; and thus was Sarah Hughson, single woman, "committed as one of the confederates in the conspiracy, being apprehended by Alderman Bancker and a messenger of the court while the court was sitting."

* * *

Sarah had been implicated during the course of Mary Burton's second body of testimony, given as a deposition earlier that same week.

(About those oaths that the newly charged confederate had been overheard bellowing through Hughson's front door: in that age of more pervasive faith, her "Goddamned" would have outraged the sensibilities of the Campbells and good Mr. Ury far more than would the girl's scatology. A century or so after these various people had died, members of a later, Victorian age, whose faith had weakened, would turn elsewhere for means to voice their rage. God's blood and wounds had lost some of their power to shock by then—though that later, proper time could be made to gasp at the mention of bodily functions that their great-grandparents had taken more in stride. And again the problem: how to represent the past accurately? For the modern reader Sarah's oaths awaken a response different from and in some instances tamer than what they did for her contemporaries. Substituting corresponding oaths that might sufficiently shock the modern ear—if such words exist—would likely yield sexual and scatological slang that the auditor of the eighteenth century would have found less offensive than profanity, or incomprehensible.)

Before Justice Horsmanden and a court secretary, Mary Burton the preceding day had deposed as follows, in answer to questions: Of the twenty or thirty blacks she had observed at one time or another at Hughson's tavern—"especially on a Sunday—many were drinking drams whose faces she could remember if she saw them again. She believes that of those, many were concerned in the conspiracy about the fires, and some country negroes, particularly one Jamaica. Hughson and his wife, and Peggy, and Sarah Hughson the daughter used, at the meeting of the negroes, to be the forwardest of any in talking about fires, to which all the negroes present were consenting; and by name Cuff, Caesar, and Auboyneau's Prince. That she has seen Vaarck's Jonneau at Hughson's a drinking with other negroes, but don't remember he was present at any time of the discourse about the fires or killing white people. That she has seen Jack (Sleydall's, the tallow chandler) often at Hughson's house, and believes he was very well acquainted with Hughson's eldest daughter Sarah. Does not remember she ever saw him there at the times of the meetings of the negroes, when they talked about fires, but from the kindness shewn to him by Hughson, his wife, and daughter aforesaid, she had great reason to think he was in their secrets."

The deposition concludes: *Signed with her mark X;* and the record proceeds tersely to note that "Jonneau, Jack, and Prince were immediately apprehended and committed." Sarah Hughson, the aforesaid daughter, was apprehended as well on the strength of this deposition, and with a promptness that may have encouraged Mary to trust that the court was ready to believe her after all.

Hughson's eldest child was, in fact, committed to jail during the very morning that the Negro slave Caesar came to trial, Friday, May 1, 1741. Caesar, we remember, was being tried "for entering the dwelling house of Robert Hogg of this city on the first day of March then last past, with intent then and there to commit some felony; and for feloniously stealing and carrying away then and there the goods and chattels of the said Robert Hogg, of the value of four pounds five shillings sterling, against the form of the statutes in such case made and provided, and against the peace of our sovereign lord the king, his crown and dignity."

The king against Caesar, Negro. On trial.

To the indictment defendant pleads not guilty. Counsel for the king proceeds to examine the witnesses: Robert Hogg, Mrs. Hogg, Christopher Wilson, James Mills, James Kannady, Mary Burton. The prisoner upon his defense denies the charge against him. The evidence being summed up, which to the court seems very strong and full, and the jury charged, they withdraw; and being returned, find him guilty of the indictment.

Ordered, that the trials of the Hughsons and Margaret Kerry be put off until Wednesday the sixth inst., and that Caesar be sentenced at that date.

Court adjourned until Wednesday morning, sixth May, at ten o'clock.

Thus the record: crisp and spare. One might wish that *la plume volante* with which Corimer was keeping his shorthand journal had been employed in recording words spoken in the courtroom that Friday morning. The testimony of the Hoggs and Sheriff Mills and the young tar Wilson. The defense by Caesar, that illiterate black, enfeebled from nine weeks of imprisonment in the subcellar, hampered by ignorance and a lack of English that would have left incommunicable much of his mulish denial of the charge against him. But Corimer was not in court that day—was accompanying Francis Schaw on an official errand to Hughson's tavern. Nor indeed would a verbatim recording of proceedings in criminal trials be routinely undertaken in America for another century and more. But what defense could the black slave have offered in any case, he who two years earlier had been caught stealing gin from a Mr. Kipps's cellar in this same city and for that whipped soundly at the public whipping post? Though he later told a story in extenuation to Mrs. Hogg when she visited him in jail, for sure Caesar was guilty of theft, in itself a capital offense—and the only offense that the court had chosen to try him for. "It has been thought proper," in fact, "to try him for the robbery and not wait to bring him to trial for the conspiracy, notwithstanding the proof against the fellow is strong and clear concerning his guilt as to that also. Yet it is imagined that as stealing and plundering is a principal part of the hellish scheme in agitation amongst the inferior sort of these infernal confederates, an earnest of example and forthcoming punishment may break the knot and induce some of the others to unfold this mystery of iniquity, in hopes thereby to recommend themselves to mercy."

Send the slave swiftly to his doom. Those others crowded into the dungeons below would not have long to wait before learning of Caesar's fate at the hands of the court above them. And to be sure, that same Friday evening the white servant Arthur Price, alleged sneak thief in jail for stealing goods of the governor's after the fire at the fort, whispered to a guard that he had information to impart in confidence to one of the magistrates. For Price had been talking to Hughson's daughter and the whore Peggy. Justice Horsmanden accordingly agreed to see the prisoner in the sheriff's quarters at nine. When he came, Horsmanden brought along Francis Schaw, schoolmaster and court official, to record what Price might say.

The prisoner being interviewed was suffering from a cold, voice hoarse and nose running throughout his story, so that standing before the deal table behind which the gentlemen had taken their seats, he would from time to time lift his manacled wrists and draw them across the lower part of his face, studying his reflection in the black window as he did so. A constable watched him narrowly. Somewhat humpbacked, the culprit was almost bald, though apparently only in his mid-twenties; two fingers of one hand were missing.

Peggy Kerry (so Price recounted), now in jail, came to the hole in the door of the room where he was confined and told him she had no stomach to eat her victuals. That bitch, she said, had fetched her in and made her as black as the rest.

"Whom did the woman mean?"

"Why, John Hughson's maid, as I supposed. Mary Burton, who has told of Hogg's goods and the indigo. And Peggy said she was afraid those fellows would discover something of her now."

"Those fellows?"

"Meaning the negars, as I understood."

"When did your discourse with the woman take place?"

"Sunday last it was, on Sunday afternoon." That would have been a couple of days after Peggy had appeared before the court and denied any knowledge of a plot to fire the town. "She calls me to the hole and says she's afeard they will tell something of her. But, says she, if they do, by God I'll hang them every one. What, says I. Is it about Mr. Hogg's goods? No, says she, by God, it's about the fires."

The justice bade the prisoner wait while Schaw's pen, its scratching the only sound in the room, caught up with his words.

"Proceed."

"So I asked her. Peggy, I says, were you going to set the

town on fire? And she answers me through the door that she was not; but by God, she says, since she knew of it they had made her swear."

"Swear to what?"

"Sure and she would not tell me that. But it was John made her swear, for I asked her was John Hughson and his wife in it? And she answered me yes, by God, they were both sworn as well as the rest."

Price stopped to cough, watching shrewdly as the gentleman in the buff coat wrote on. When the quill slowed, the prisoner resumed:

"I asked Peggy was she not afeard that Caesar would discover her? And she said no, for Cuff and Quack and Caesar were all true-hearted fellows, by God. She was afeard of some of the others discovering though. And, says she, if they hang that poor fellow below—meaning Caesar, as I understood, below in the subcellar—the rest of the negars would be revenged on them yet. If they only send him away, why, it's another case, says she, but if they hang him, the others will have their revenge for that. I asked her, what, do you think they mean to poison Mary Burton? But before she could answer, the guard comes for her victual bowl, and she whispers me quick through the door, 'For the life and soul of you, you son of a bitch, don't speak a word of what I've told you. By God, and you do, I'll cut your throat!' "

On the other side of the table the justice had set his face in a stern mask that hid his thoughts. Schaw laid down the quill. It was beginning to rain beyond the dark window, drops clicking on leaves among sounds of a breeze passing.

"So then she moved to the other side of the room," said the prisoner.

"Have you more to tell us?" the justice asked.

Price bobbed his head. "I spoke with Sarah, who was committed this morning."

"Hughson's daughter?"

"I whistled her to the hole, like Peggy, please your honor."

"And made what discoveries?"

"Please you, we talked of the late fires in town. And she told me she had been with a fortune teller who said that in less than five weeks she would come to trouble if she did not take good care of herself. She asked about her father's fortune and was told he would be tried and condemned, but not hanged. He was to go over the water."

"But said the girl aught to the purpose concerning the plot?"

"Please you, I told her that the serving maid had discovered about the plot, upon which Sarah said she did not know of any plot. Said she knew of no plot, and thereupon I told her that Mary had discovered and was bringing them every one in, all the negars and whites. Upon which she colored, and put her bonnet back, and changed color several times, as I could see through the hole. And then she asks me, when had I heard that? I told her I'd heard it by the by, and it was kept quiet but was true. Upon which she made a long stop."

As did Price now, sniffling vigorously, seeming to relish the attention being paid him in warm, homely surroundings.

"Proceed."

"I told her, sure you had better tell everything you know, Sal, for that may be of some service to your father. But no, says she, for they're doing all they can to take his life away; and she would sooner suffer death, says she, and be hanged with her daddy (if he is to be hanged) than give them the satisfaction of telling them anything. And then she begins to cry, and says that she was to have gone up into the country (like a fool that she was that she did not go) but stayed to see what would become of her mammy and daddy; but that now she would go up in the country and would be hanged if ever they should get her in York again."

The justice allowed himself a brief smile. "Did she say aught else, Arthur?"

"We talked of the fires. I told her your honors have been at me about the fire at the fort, and she said, please your honor, that your honors was putting the saddle on the wrong horse when you accused Arthur Price of knowing aught of the fires.

And she told me, please you, that if they—and I took her to mean the people of this city—have not better care of themselves, they'll have a great deal more damage and danger in York than they're aware of (or such like words), and that if they do hang her daddy, they had better do something else, though what she meant thereby she did not say. . . ."

Nor did it matter—idle threats from the mouth of a whining wench at the prison door. They would hang Sarah's daddy all right, and indeed were trying him with all dispatch, as scheduled, on Wednesday, the sixth of May—him and his wife and Peggy Kerry, "for feloniously, &c., receiving on the third day of March then last past, divers stolen goods, knowing the same to have been stolen against the form of the statute, &c., and the king's peace, &c." All three pleaded not guilty, but it did them no good. Nor did Sarah's pitiful threats. Nor did the muttered rumors of black vengeance deter the court from doing its duty. Before the end of that day's session, "the charge against them being fully proved, the evidence summed up, and the arguments closed, the jury withdrew; and being returned, found them all guilty."

Even then the day's business in court was not finished. Vaarck's Caesar was sentenced that afternoon as well, at the end of a speech by Justice DeLancey wherein the slave was reminded that for his trial he had put himself upon God and the country, "which country having found you guilty, it now only remains for the court to pronounce that judgment which the law requires, and the nature of your crime deserves. But," intoned the justice over the head of the unblinking black, "before I proceed to sentence, I must tell you that you have been dealt with in the same manner as any white man guilty of your crimes would have been. I have great reason to believe that the crime you now stand convicted of is not the worst of those that you have been concerned in, for you are a worthless fellow and a hardened sinner, ripe and ready for the most daring, enormous enterprises. Yet as the time you have left to live is to be but short, I earnestly exhort you to employ it by confessing your sins, repenting sincerely of them, and praying God of His infinite goodness to have mercy on your soul. For depend upon it, Caesar: if you do not truly repent before you die, there is a hell to punish the wicked like you eternally. And as it is in your power to make restitution for the many injuries you have done the public, I advise you to prevent further mischiefs by discovering such persons as have been concerned with you in endeavoring to burn this city and destroy its inhabitants. If you do not, be assured that God Almighty will punish you for it, for eternity, and with a pain far beyond any that we here can inflict. Therefore, Caesar, consider well what I have said to you."

The justice waited meaningfully. As for the slave to whom those words were addressed, he stared straight ahead. Was he attending, who earlier had allegedly stolen along black, wintry streets of the town to enter a shop and stealthily open a bureau drawer that had Spanish coins inside? Motionless, expressionless, he stared at the bench before him. "Then nothing further remains to say," the justice resumed at length, "but that you, Caesar, are to be taken to the place whence you came, and thence to the place of execution, and there you are to be hanged by the neck until you be dead. And I pray the Lord to have mercy on your soul."

* * *

Ordered, that the execution of Caesar be on Monday next, the eleventh day of this instant, between the hours of nine and one. And further ordered, that the gibbet on which the body of the Negro is to be hanged be fixed on the island near the powder house, and that after the execution of the said sentence, the body of the Negro be hung in chains.

On the eleventh of May, as ordered, Caesar's execution was carried out. He died, it is recorded, "very stubbornly, a person of most obstinate and untractable temperament, without confessing anything about the conspiracy, and denied he knew anything of it to the last." On that date Schaw was away from the city with Corimer on another court errand, so that neither witnessed the passage of the mule-drawn cart that carried the bound and tight-lipped black man up Wall Street and along thronged Broadway to the gallows on the common beyond the edge of town. Nor did they learn until their return of the condemned Peggy Kerry's change of heart that had led her, shortly before her black provider's death, voluntarily to confess knowledge of the conspiracy after all.

In company with the unattached Corimer, Schaw had left for Albany at noon Wednesday, May 6, the day that the court had convicted Peggy and the Hughsons and had sentenced Caesar to hang. "This is the first time this season that I have been upon the river," writes Corimer pleasantly in that day's journal entry. "Whilst we waited the tide at pierside, flocks of wild pigeons flew in great numbers very high overhead, many more than ever I saw before. S had provided us a sea-store and bed, and things fitting for the voyage. We sailed with a gentle wind at noon, and by 1 o'clock were passing to starboard the little town of Greenwich, consisting of eight or ten neat houses. . . ."

Schaw remembered later—or more likely was reminded by notes kept at the time and now lost—that he had watched on deck that afternoon a long while, "affected with a weight of distress" from causes not specified. Their sloop was passing scows returning upriver from the city, "whither they had brought provisions for sale"—but the notation is from Corimer, not from the despondent Schaw. How explain the schoolmaster's mood on setting out? He had, as he recalls, spent many days "of late in wet weather in the streets of a city where was dirtiness underfoot and the scent arising from that filth which more or less infects the air of all thick-settled towns." Yet something more than a disagreeable physical atmosphere would seem needed to account for his dejection. Was he troubled by this second errand he had been charged with performing, the fetching back a York Negro under suspicion who had recently been sold to an Albany timber merchant? "I had all along been deeply affected with the oppression of the negroes," the minister in his old age would write at the beginning of a passage, often cited, that appears a few pages further along in his *Reminiscences*. Was he, then, already burdened by early May with a sense of the plight of those ignorant, terrified blacks whose names in weeks ahead would pass in increasing numbers fatefully between the lips of the servant girl Mary? Or was it the poignancy of the condition in which the whites of the city found themselves that spring, hardly relieved of struggle after a brutal winter, food scarce, bakers in town even now striking—a "general combination of the bakers not to bake"—because of the scarcity of flour, other goods at the markets still few and costly despite those carts in the streets and scows on the river, with the fort in ruins, plot in the air, and the fear-ridden city open to enemies from without and within?

Whatever the cause of his disheartenment, Schaw's three-day voyage aboard the sloop the hundred and fifty miles upriver proved to be a tonic for it. Nowhere else, by the way, is the difference between his temperament and Corlmer's so evident as on this trip they took together. Good friends before, they were becoming better ones; so that in the course of the journey Corimer finds opportunity to describe the schoolmaster as "a rational and agreeable companion with whom I might interchange sentiments on all occasions." But whereas the aristocrat studied to control his emotions, Schaw's dipped and reared through the passing moments of such a journey. Corimer limits his remarks on the trip mainly to observable facts, sometimes dryly set down—the cabin "well stocked with flies," pease in blossom along the shore and beans five or six inches high, farmhouses on both sides of the river surrounded by plowed land and orchards. By contrast, Schaw, depressed at the start, is cheered by sights that he is soon describing with a feeling positively joyous:

"Befriended by the tide," the sloop (he tells us) was before long passing fields that "afforded a verdure which, with the reflection of the sun whose rays struck obliquely on the plain, made one of the most beautiful prospects I ever beheld." Upriver the following morning, the tide spent and the wind gone, he and his friend rowed ashore and at an alehouse "had a bass fish taken out of the river by the door before our eyes. With an Indian we entered into friendly conversation and gave him biscuit. He having killed a deer gave us some of it." A fair wind springing up from the southwest soon after noon on that second day, they weighed anchor and made good progress, sometimes keeping so near the shore "that the extremity of our boom rustled among the leaves of branches hanging from the bank. The river at places was no broader than a musket shot." Before sunset they found themselves among mountains with barren summits, the western shore uncultivated; and after nightfall, Schaw tells us, they heard the splash of sturgeon jumping and were "visited by fireflies in large numbers settling on the rigging." Not until late that second night, in fact, did they cast anchor, in twelve fathoms. The following day they tacked against the wind, and Schaw pondered "the roughness of the stones" among which they were passing on either side, "with the steepness of the echoing hills and the cavities between them, and the kindness of Him whose works in these mountainous deserts appear awful, and toward whom my heart was turned during this day of travel." Through the whole of that third night out the wind favored their voyage, so that at dawn they were "but nine miles from Albany," which they reached on its hillside by eight in the morning.

"Their women in general are hard favored," Corimer reports succinctly of the town, and notes that its streets "are dirtied by cattle" and that its predominantly Dutch inhabitants suffer from "scorbutic gums." The gentlemen had little trouble locating the timber merchant they had been sent to find, a Mr. Groesbeck, at an inn "next the town hall close by the river," so that before midafternoon they had completed their business and taken refreshment, in time to board what Corimer calls "a stinking fur boat" for the journey downriver. Their prisoner was fettered on deck beside a constable. From the stern the gentlemen watched the town and the fort on its steep hill disappear behind a bend, then settled themselves once more for the passage south, among "woods, low rocks, and stony fields."

The prisoner they had acquired from the merchant was a black slave named Sawney, sold some weeks earlier by his New York master, Mr. Niblet, because of "mischievous and insolent behavior," involving the setting of fires. The Negro, dressed in a short jacket and wide knee breeches tied with a rope, looked to be fifteen or sixteen, slight of build, a slack smile on his lips and a blank expression from his chestnut eyes as he hunched beside the constable and gazed through much of the voyage at the ring bolt on deck that secured his chain. The return was uneventful until just north of Manhattan, where the hold of the sloop was discovered to be taking in water. A boat was put ashore promptly, and Corimer and Schaw, with the constable and their prisoner, rented horses at Kingsbridge to ride on down the thirteen miles "of very good road near the length of York island, which"—Schaw remembered—was "very narrow but beautiful, with many handsome seats belonging to the gentlemen in York, where we arrived about sunset."

That was Monday evening, May 11, the evening of the day when Caesar had been hanged on the common. And the travelers completing court business, who would have passed close by the slave's gibbet (but made no mention of it), could not have been back in town long before learning that the prisoner Peggy Kerry had the day before volunteered a confession confirming much that until then had depended for credence on the testimony of Mary Burton alone:

"I declare," the Newfoundland Beauty was recorded as telling the undersheriff, "that at the house of the shoemaker John Romme I several times saw meetings of negroes; and in particular in the months of November and December last past, I saw assembled there, in or about, ten or twelve in number, viz.— Cuff, belonging to Mr. Philipse; Brash, Mr. Jay's; Curacoa Dick, a negro man; Dundee, Pintard's; Patrick, English's; a negro belonging to Mr. Breasted in Pearl Street; and Cato, Alderman Moore's. The rest of the names that were in the combination I cannot remember, or their master's names. They proposed to burn the fort first, and afterward the city, and then steal, rob, and carry away all the money and goods they could procure, which was to be carried to Romme's, where they were to be joined by the country negroes. They were to murder everyone that had money, and all the rest of the negroes in city and country were to meet in one night.

"The reason why I did not make this discovery before, John swore them all never to discover, and swore me too; and I thought I would wrong my soul if I discovered it. All the above I am ready to declare upon oath."

* * *

It was presumed at the time (so the record asserts) that the approaching execution of Caesar, and the conviction of the Hughsons and Peggy herself as accessories in receiving stolen goods, had so alarmed the Beauty that "she thought it needful to do something to recommend herself to mercy; and this confession coming voluntarily from her, it gave hopes that she was in earnest and would make some material discoveries." Whether in earnest or not, she was assuredly in terror, and in terror for her life the woman appeared ready to confirm before the court much of Mary Burton's evolving story. Though with this one difference: She swore the plot had been hatched not at Hughson's, but at the nearby house and shop of a John Romme, who had subsequently left the province and was not to be found.

Even so, her confession would serve to reassure any who might be starting to wonder about the very existence of a conspiracy, confirmation of its existence having depended until then solely on the word of a single disgruntled servant girl. Peggy's change of heart in the cellar of City Hall had occurred over the weekend before Caesar's execution Monday, May 11. Two days later, the thirteenth of May, "being appointed by the governor's earlier proclamation to be held throughout the province as a day of public fasting and humiliation, the same was reverently and decently observed, particularly in this city, by persons of all persuasions," including presumably the Pursells, Corimer, and Schaw. "Shops were shut up, and townsmen of every rank resorted to their respective places of divine worship, where they seemed deeply affected with a sense of the calamities with which we have of late been visited, calamities succeeding upon the heels of each other so fast as most surely to awaken us to our duty and to a due sense of our demerits."

Old Governor Clarke, who throughout a long public life had preferred comforts of his Long Island estate to quarters in town, was nevertheless often in the city during these days of spring, while the jail filled and the trials were unfolding their alarming discoveries and the citizens grumbled together and worried and prayed. With his mansion in the fort in ruins, the governor would stay as guest at Attorney Murray's on Broadway, and from there Friday, May 15—two days after the public fast—His Honor reported in writing to London, to the Duke of Newcastle as Secretary of State for the Southern Department, that the succession of conflagrations in New York had "wonderfully distressed the minds of the people throughout the province, who are in continual apprehensions of having their houses set on fire in consequence of an horrid conspiracy of the negroes (which we now begin to have some hopes of discovering—and even that the fort itself was willfully set on fire by them, notwithstanding that the circumstance of time and place led me at first to think it was accidentally done by a plumber). I now keep a night guard of the militia, who constantly patrol."

Thus matters stood by mid-May. In that anxious atmosphere the following afternoon the Pursells, within sight of the fort, were entertaining friends at home, as was their Saturday custom, on the occasion to which Schaw refers in his *Reminiscences* in the passage beginning, "I now come to a spring day which to me is memorable. Some time that morning I had spent in reading a pious author . . ." (pp. 29–30). Which author is not specified, nor is the name of the reverend gentleman from New Jersey whom Schaw met at the Pursells' at dinner. Scholars have conjectured one of the Tennents, though no evidence has been produced to confirm that either brother visited New York in

1741. Whoever it was, he was that afternoon in the company of the rector of Trinity Church, the Reverend Mr. Vesey, as a guest at the merchant's table.

Ten others were there as well: Mrs. Vesey, Schaw, Corimer, Judge Horsmanden, the Reverend Mr. Charlton (catechist and assistant to the rector), Pursell, his wife, his sister, and his two children. The dinner they partook of during the afternoon included tomcod, boiled ham, a spicy haunch of venison, goose in sauce, salt cheese made of hog's head, "which might have been fresher," with hot biscuit, pudding, and shortcake, all accompanied by spruce beer and Rhine wine, followed by cordial waters. To divert the diners, their merchant host at the end of the table had been holding forth on an innocent enthusiasm: "P[*ursell*] now refers everything to exercise," Corimer's journal entry notes at the day's conclusion. "Riding the most manly, most healthy, and least laborious of exercises, shaking up the whole machine, promoting universal perspiration and secretion of all the fluids, and thereby variously twitching the nervous fibers to brace and contract them. Grows eloquent in that vein over dinner." But inevitably conversation had made its way to the conspiracy, after some further talk of the West Indian campaign, of Admiral Vernon's bold strike at Cartagena, of privateers nearer home. "As for our men-of-war," Horsmanden pronounced, "they are as fit to go after privateers as a cow after a hare." And at one side of the table the lovely Elizabeth and her brother are recorded as having "sat mute" through the judge's pronouncements, "only now and then smiling or registering astonishment at what was said."

To Pursell's sister and the Reverend Mr. Charlton, the judge was speaking of the prisoner Kerry's most recent, welcome testimony before the court. Corimer would have been attending for his own reasons. ". . . that some negroes," Horsmanden was in the midst of relating, "went by her late at night as she stood under Hunt's shed toward the water side, coming toward her with each of them a firkin upon their shoulders. She watched them turn into the shoemaker's gate. Guy Fawkes night it was,

between eleven and twelve, for the wench remembers the bonfires and the first snow."

He paused to sample a strawberry from a lacquered bowl,
removing the stem meticulously before proceeding. "Now mark
the sequel. She goes later that evening to Romme's, a man
employed to make shoes for her six or eight months past when
she was living with some free negro fronting the New Battery,
three or four doors from his house. She goes to Romme and
finds the firkins nowhere in sight, but in the shoemaker's
kitchen are ten or twelve negroes, all in one room, and she hears
Romme observing to them how well the rich people at this
place live. He is telling them that if they would be advised by
him they should have the rich people's money."

Was it at the shoemaker Romme's, then, that Corimer had sat
last autumn drunk in the ladder back chair, mug of gin rolled
from his hand to the floor? Was it at Romme's or at the
taverner Hughson's, some blocks north, that Bonny Jack had
peered at him mockingly through the window?

" 'How will you manage that?' cries Cuff, who was present.
And the wench testifies she heard Romme answer, 'Well
enough, lad. Burn the houses of them that have the most
money, and kill them all.' He, Romme, should be captain over
them, and would send into the country for the rest of the negroes to help, because he could write, and he knew several
negroes in the country that could read. 'Never fear, my lads,'
says this Romme, 'the sun will shine very bright by-and-by.' "

Such a pledge would have multiplied dark memories already
formed and haunting many New Yorkers, including Pursell's
impressionable sister. "What they once have done they would
do again," she observed in dread to the justice, recollecting the
rising of blacks among them thirty years before.

"Indeed, ma'am, what they once tried they would try again.
Yet the wench Kerry will help us. To be sure, she may for now
be amusing us with a narrative—Romme for Hughson—but
Dick was there, she says, and Jay's Brash, and Moore's Cato,
new names all. And those and the others she spoke of have since

been apprehended, and last evening we brought them one by one and passed them in review before her. And she distinguished them every one, called them by their names—Pintard's Dundee and English's Patrick and the others—and declared they were all at the meeting."

The ingratitude of it was what dismayed Pursell, member of the grand jury and close to the proceedings throughout. The monstrous ingratitude of the black tribe was what "exceedingly aggravates their guilt," so he opined over the cordial waters, stroking the spaniel at his feet. "Why, their slavery amongst us is generally softened with the greatest indulgence. Is it not so? They live amongst us with little care and are commonly better fed and clothed and put to less labor than the poor of most Christian nations. Are they not in the end far happier here than in the midst of the continual rapine and cruelty of their native lands?"

Thus Pursell at the head of his table that Venture and two or three other family servants were clearing. "Sir, the fault is ours," Horsmanden was assuring his host. "By our own actions we've led our slaves to value themselves too highly. Too much kindness, and they grow obstinate. But Peggy shall tell us more of their doings. About this Romme she lies, of course. Price in jail with her has already told us it was to Hughson she swore. She lies, and thus must not flatter herself with hopes of being soon recommended for mercy."

Aunt Min supposed that "the bloody scheme has been brooding at both places, at the shoemaker's and the taverner's both."

"Nay, depend upon it," the judge answered that lady, "the wench and her advisers have thought merely to shift the scene to this Romme's, knowing him to have fled safely out of reach. I warrant you she has it in her power to unfold a great deal of this hellish business in any case, and will do so—having been told of the pardon prepared, which shall not pass the seal till she be thought amply to merit it."

Already convicted of receiving stolen goods, the Beauty was now to be arraigned and tried with other white prisoners on the

even more serious charge of conspiracy, "upon the supposition," as the judge put it, "that this step may bring her to a
resolution of making a full discovery." Meanwhile, the servant
girl Mary Burton yesterday had also been shown the Negroes—
Cato and Patrick and Brash and the others—impeached and
committed on Peggy's information. Mary had looked and
frowned and declared that she did not remember that ever she
saw any of those particular blacks at Hughson's, which, so Aunt
Min thought, "seems to add strength to what that strumpet to
the negroes has said, that the villainous scheme was carrying on
at the shoemaker's as well as the taverner's." After all, Hughson
and Romme were intimately acquainted; Mary Burton did confirm that. They frequented each other's houses and talked Dutch
together, "retiring often to a private room to have a great deal
of discourse together."

Peggy, for her part, had told the court still more; and in the
Pursells' front parlor after dinner and toasts, while some played
quadrille and others conversed near the window, Horsmanden
at the fireplace shared further details of her testimony with the
Anglican rector and his wife, speaking loudly because the Reverend Mr. Vesey was "in a good old age" and hard of hearing.
The firkins contained butter, from a Frenchman's storehouse
near the Long Bridge and belonging to a countryman who had
stored them there in the fall. Romme had offered 15 shillings a
firkin for the stolen butter, but Caesar had insisted on twenty.
They were stowed under the wood in an old house in Romme's
yard, and were to be sent to Carolina in the spring. The blacks,
whom Romme referred to as his "parcel of good children,"
regularly brought him firewood in the winter; a blue cloth coat
and cape that the shoemaker wore had been stolen by Caesar
from a countryman's boat, for which Romme had given the
slave ten shillings. At the meeting Guy Fawkes night Peggy had
heard Romme say he would stand by the Negroes and if need
be lead them into Mohawk country, where he had lived before.
Or he would carry them to a strange land and set them free.
And how did they like his proposals to grow rich by firing the

town? Philipse's Cuff, Peggy recalled for the judge, "answered him that there was great talking and no cider. Whereupon they drank together and soon broke up; only Romme after the blacks left made the Beauty swear herself to secrecy and kiss a book, though which one it was she did not know. . . ."

"We played at quadrille at a penny a fish," Corimer notes of that spring evening at Pursell's. The merchant "P deplores civil disruptions, whatever interferes with a peaceful exchange of the fruits of labor. P's sister mighty apt to fret upon the having ill cards and losing. Says herself she cannot bear to lose. Is very big," he adds bluntly of Aunt Min, "which makes her look dull and heavy." Young Lindsay sat opposite his father, while Elizabeth at the harpsichord played canzoni, a galliard. Schaw was conversing first with Madame Pursell, later with the minister from out of town whose words impressed him so deeply that years afterward they would find their way into his *Reminiscences*. Pursell's wife had "a great deal of civility in her conversation"— a conversation that Corimer earlier, from a sickbed, had noted flowed freely enough, though hardly a word survives of all she uttered ("Her fault is speaking too much, which tires people"). Of those various guests, however, it was the reverend minister from New Jersey, seated at the far end of the room by the escritoire, whose discourse made the clearest impression this day on Francis Schaw. The anonymous "gentleman spoke feelingly of his care to live in the spirit of peace and furnish no just cause of offense to any of his fellow creatures, all which are equally related to our Heavenly Father. He believed"—and ventured to say as much with considerable temerity, if perhaps less tact, in this place at this time—"that liberty was the natural right of all men equally. He thought that to all rational creatures bondage is uneasy, frequently occasioning sourness and discontent, which must affect not the bondman only but all such as claim mastery over others."

* * *

In addition to an impunible minister passing through from New Jersey, some closer at hand would have words to say on the slaves' behalf. John Roosevelt, house painter, testified at the ensuing trial of Cuffee and Quack that the latter slave, who belonged to him and who was being tried for setting Fort George on fire, "was employed most part of the morning that the fort burned, from the time my son and I got up, in cutting away ice from the yard. Quack was hardly ever out of our sight all that morning, but a small time while we were at breakfast. Neither I nor my son can think Quack that morning could have been from our house so far as the fort."

Adolph Philipse, Esq., Cuffee's master, speaker of the assembly and a vigorous seventy-six, testified on behalf of his slave, charged with burning the storehouse on New Street, "that the afternoon my nephew's storehouse was on fire, I had left Cuff at home at work, sewing a vane upon a board for my boat. After the fire was extinguished, I and Mr. Chambers were standing together in the garden near the storehouse, and somebody came up and told me that they had taken Cuff out of my house and were carrying him to jail, for it was he that had set the fire. I made answer, 'How can that be? I left him at home at work, making a vane for the boat.'"

Thus both slaves on trial had alibis, which their masters verified in court Friday, the twenty-ninth of May, not quite two weeks after Pursell's dinner just described. On that morning, in the assembly room at City Hall: the king against (Roosevelt's) Quack and (Philipse's) Cuffee, Negroes, both indicted for wickedly, voluntarily, feloniously, and maliciously conspiring with divers other Negroes to kill and murder the inhabitants of this city. Cuffee also indicted for setting on fire and burning a storehouse belonging to Frederick Philipse, Esq., against the king's peace. Quack also indicted for setting on fire, burning, and consuming the house of our sovereign lord the king, then standing at the fort in this city.

To the indictments each criminal has pleaded not guilty.

The attorney general opens the indictments and speaks to the court and jury:

"This is a cause of very great expectation, it being, as I conceive, a matter of the utmost importance that ever yet came to be tried in this province. Gentlemen, you will hear from the mouths of our witnesses that these two negroes with divers others frequently met at the house of one John Hughson, in this city. There they were harbored, and there was brooded a conspiracy to burn the king's house at the fort, as well as this whole town, then murder the inhabitants as they should come to extinguish the flames: crimes, gentlemen, so astonishingly cruel and detestable that none but a conclave of devils might be thought to execute them. Yet such monsters are these two criminals and the rest of their confederates.

"Gentlemen, the eyes of the inhabitants of this city and province are upon you, relying on and confiding in you that by the justice of your verdict in this cause this day, the peace and safety of province and city, at present very precarious until some examples are made, may for the future be secured to them. Gentlemen, it is in you that the people place their hopes and expectations that they may sit securely in their homes by day and rest quietly in their beds by night, no one daring hereafter to make them afraid.

"I shall now proceed to examine the witnesses for the king, to support the charge against each of these criminals."

Witnesses for the king called and sworn: Arthur Price, Jacobus Stoutenburgh, Isaac Gardner, Mary Burton, Abigail Earle, Daniel Gautier, Mr. Hilliard. Negro evidence: Sawney (Niblet's).

Arthur Price, the first witness called to give evidence, was the thief who had privately shared with Judge Horsmanden fruits of conversations he had had, through a hole between prison rooms, with the Newfoundland Beauty and Hughson's daughter Sarah. "Arthur having been found by experience to be adroit at pumping out the secrets of the conspirators, the under-sheriff had been ordered to put Cuffee (Mr. Philipse's negro) into the same cell with him, and to give them a tankard now and then in order to cheer up their spirits and make them more sociable. These directions were accordingly observed and produced the desired effects."

In court Price testifies for the king:

"I and Cuffee were confined in the same room together and talked over punch. Among other things he asked me what could be the reason that Peggy was called up so often? I answered him that I thought she was discovering the plot about the fire at the fort. Cuff replied that she could not do that unless she perjured herself, for he that had burned the fort did so after Peggy went to prison. His name, says Cuff, was Quack, that Hughson swore three times. I said I believed I knew that Quack, and that he lived with a butcher. Cuffee answered no, he lived with a house painter, whose name he understood to be Roosevelt, and was married to the wench who is cook to the governor at the fort."

COURT. Did defendant say how Quack set the fort on fire?

PRICE. I asked him how Quack did it, and he answered he could not tell, only that Quack was to do it and did do it. I asked him whether he did not think the firing would be found out? No, he replied, by God, he did not think it ever would. No more was he afraid that Caesar, who was to be hanged Monday, would discover the fires about the fort and town, for he was sure Caesar would let himself be burnt to ashes before he would discover it. Cuff would lay his life on that.

COURT. And did the defendant tell ye aught else?

PRICE. He told me he knew he was to suffer death, and wondered why they did not bring him to his trial, for he was sure he was to go the way the other went, meaning (as I understood him) Caesar, hanged.

COURT. What further said he? Tell the court all that the slave said.

PRICE. After his friend Quack was committed, please your honors, Cuffee never more mentioned anything concerning our former discourse, but read sometimes, and cried very much. . . .

Jacobus Stoutenburgh testifies for the king:

"I went to assist at the fire at Mr. Philipse's storehouse, and when it was extinguished was at the top of the roof. Somebody cried out there were negroes in the storehouse. A great many shingles being pulled off the roof, I could see down inside and espied out a negro in the storehouse next to that on fire. I began to let myself down through the laths in order to catch him, but was hindered by a nail catching hold of my breeches, or I believe I would have taken him. I saw him leap out the window at the end of the storehouse and make haste away, leaping over several garden fences and making his escape."

COURT. Pray tell the court what next you did.

STOUTENBURGH. I went back with the fire engines toward the City Hall, and the people were saying they had got the negro. There was a great crowd of people bringing him to jail, and when I saw him I knew him to be the same.

COURT. Is the negro that you saw present in this hall?

STOUTENBURGH. Yes, sir. Cuffee, the prisoner at the bar. . . .

Isaac Gardner testifies for the king:

"I saw Cuffee at the fire at the fort. There were rows of people in the garden, negars as well as white men, in order to hand water along to the fire. I observed that when the buckets came to Cuffee, instead of handing them along to the next man, he put them upon the ground and overset them, by which means the ground, which at first was dry and hard, became so wet that I was almost up to my ankles in mud. And Cuff would dance and whistle and shout when the flames blazed up. I said to him, 'You black dog, is this a time for you to dance and make game upon such a sad accident?' But he only laughed the harder and whispered to another negar who stood next him on the other side. Whereupon, seeing Colonel Moore, I said to him I wished he would speak to those negars, who only laughed and made game whenever I forbid them oversetting the water."

COURT. And did Colonel Moore do so?

GARDNER. Sir, he did. But after his back was turned, they went on again in the same manner, and so continued until they broke up from the fire. . . .

Mary Burton testifies for the king:

"Cuffee and Caesar used frequently to meet at my master Hughson's house. Quack I often saw at his door, though never within the house. I heard the negars talk of burning the fort, and indeed they used to say they would set fire to the whole town. They would do it in the night, and as the white people came to extinguish the flames, they would kill and destroy them every one. Cuffee was generally present and very active at those meetings, and said that the other negars durst not refuse to do what he commanded them. He was sure they had a number sufficient to stand by them. His master, he said, had too much money but would have less by-and-by. And he said, Damn his blood if he would tell of the plot even if he was burnt. Caesar swore that if ever I published their design to fire the town, he would burn me whenever he met me."

COURT. Did the prisoner Cuffee ever threaten you so?

BURTON. He and the rest of the negars all did. About three weeks after I came to Hughson's, which was about mid-autumn last, the negars were there talking of the plot, and some of them said perhaps I would tell. Cuffee said no, I would not. He said he intended to have me for a wife. And with that he run up to me, but I had a dishclout in my hand, which I dabbed in his face, and he ran away. . . .

Abigail Earle testifies for the king:

"Just before the going in of the afternoon church on the same Sunday that coals were found in Mr. Murray's haystack, I saw three negro men coming up the Broadway. I was then looking out my window up one pair of stairs in the house where Mr. Williams now lives. As they passed under the window I heard one of them say, '*Fire, fire, scorch, scorch,* A LITTLE, *damn it,* BY-AND-BY!' and then throw up his hands and laugh."

COURT. What did you thereafter?

EARLE. After the negroes were gone, I went into Mrs. George's house, which was the next door, and told her what I had heard. About an hour after, when church was out, I saw the same negroes coming down the Broadway. I shewed Mrs. George the negro that had spoke those words, and she said, "That is Mr. Roosevelt's Quack.". . .

Daniel Gautier testifies for the king:

"I was one of the first who went up to the fort upon the alarm of the fire. When I came up toward it, I observed that a great part of the outside of the roof was covered with smoke, but none for a considerable distance from the end next the chapel. I came upon the ramparts next the chapel and there asked how the fire had started. I was told it was occasioned by the plumber carrying his fire pot into the gutter to stop a leak."

COURT. Do you now hold that opinion?

GAUTIER. No sir, I do not. For seeing a ladder set up against the gutter, I went up and looked in at the dormant window at the end of the house toward the chapel.

COURT. And what saw you?

GAUTIER. The inside of the garret roof was in a blaze, but there was no fire within twenty foot of the end where I was.

COURT. What did you therefore conclude?

GAUTIER. I was of opinion that the fire could not have been occasioned by the plumber, who had been working twenty foot away, though upon my first view of the flames, I gave the house over for lost. . . .

Mr. Hilliard, plumber, testifies for the king:

"Indeed I carried my fire pot into the gutter, which I was mending between the house and the chapel of the fort, but I think the fire at the fort could not have been occasioned by my working there. I was very careful of the fire I carried up, and had a soldier to attend me. My fire pot was set on a board which was laid over the gutter from the chapel to the house, but was much lower than the dormant window."

COURT. Might not sparks of fire have flown out of the fire pot?

HILLIARD. I do not think so. It is an enclosed pot like a dark lanthorn, with an opening only before to put my soldering iron in. I was careful to put the back of it before the wind. . . .

Niblet's Sawney, Negro, testifies for the king. (This young slave, whom Schaw as messenger for the court had fetched from Albany, when first questioned some days earlier had denied he knew anything of the fires, or of any conspiracy concerning them. "The grand jury for a long time argued with the boy to persuade him to speak the truth. They told him if he would do so, the governor would pardon him, though he had been concerned in the fires. He answered that the time before—hinting at the conspiracy in 1712, thirty years ago—after the negroes told all they knew, then the white people hanged them. The grand jury assured him that it was false; for that the negroes which confessed the truth and made a discovery were certainly pardoned and shipped off—and upon this assurance he began to open.")

Sawney testifies against Quack and Cuffee.

"I heard them say they would set fire to Mr. Philipse's storehouse, and Cuffee said, Damn him, that hang him or burn him, he would set fire to the town and be rich like the *bacarara*, the white people. Both talked of killing the gentlemen and taking their wives to themselves. Then, in February late, Quack proposed to me to set the fort on fire."

COURT. When and where did defendant make that proposal?

SAWNEY. On a Sunday afternoon in late February or early March, on the street near Mrs. Ricket's. Quack asked me to set the fort on fire. I answered no, I would not run the risk of being hanged, but that he might go to hell and be damned. Then Quack said he would do it himself. The next day after the fire at the fort, I met Quack again, and he said to me, "The business is done." I asked him what business? He answered, "The fort is burnt. Don't you remember that I told you there would be great alterations in the fort?" . . .

Sawney's testimony concludes king's evidence. At the request of the prisoners, Adolph Philipse, Esq., and John Roosevelt are called as witnesses, testifying as noted in support of the prisoners' alibis. Cuffee and Quack themselves "being asked what they had to offer in their defense, they offered nothing but peremptory denials of what had been testified against them, and protestations of their innocency."

Mr. Smith proceeds to sum up.

"Gentlemen, it is hard to say whether the wickedness or the folly of the design of these wretches is the greater. That Hughson should become a king! Caesar, now in gibbets, a governor! That the white men should all be killed, and the women become a prey to the rapacious lust of these villains! That these slaves should thereby establish themselves in peace and freedom on the plundered wealth of their slaughtered masters! Had it not been in part executed before it was discovered, we should with difficulty have been persuaded to believe that such a wicked and foolish plot could be contrived by any creatures in human shape. Yet whence else could so many fires have been lighted up all around you in so short a time, with evident marks of willful design?

"Now, gentlemen, the prisoners at the bar stand charged with being principal parties in this tragical design, and the two of them prime incendiaries: Quack for burning his majesty's house in the fort, and Cuffee for burning Colonel Philipse's storehouse. And from the facts proved and circumstances attending them, there appears violent presumption of guilt, which the law esteems full proof.

"Gentlemen, the justice that was provoked by former fires, after innocent blood was spilt in your streets"—alluding to the conspiracy in 1712—"should have been a perpetual terror to the negroes that survived the vengeance of that day, as well as a warning to all that have come after them. But I fear we shall never be safe till that wicked race are under more restraint, or their number greatly reduced within this city. I make no doubt, gentlemen, but you will bring in a verdict accordingly, and do what in you lies to rid this country of some of the vilest creatures in it."

The jury are charged. A constable is sworn to attend them as usual. They withdraw, and soon returning, find the prisoners guilty of both indictments.

"Prisoners at the bar, what have you to offer in arrest of judgment, why you should not receive sentence of death?"

They offer nothing—those two bewildered, incoherent, terror-crazed blacks—but repetitions of protestations of their innocence. The court is unmoved. Judge Horsmanden proceeds to sentence:

"Criminals at the bar, Quack and Cuffee, ye cannot be so stupid as to imagine that when ye leave this world, ye shall become like the beasts that perish, that your spirits shall only vanish into the soft air and cease to be. No, your souls are immortal. They will live forever, either to be eternally happy or eternally miserable in the other world, where you are now going. There is a God above who has a clear view of all your actions, who sees into the most secret recesses of the heart and knoweth all your thoughts. Shall He not, do ye think, for all this bring you into judgment? Ye that were for destroying us without mercy, ye abject wretches, the outcasts of the nations of the earth, are treated here with tenderness and humanity, and (I wish I could not say) with too great indulgence also, for you have grown wanton with excess of liberty, and your idleness has proved your ruin. Now bewail your crying sins in this your extremity. Confess your whole guilt. Discover the whole scene of iniquity contrived in this monstrous confederacy—the chief authors and actors, and all and every the parties concerned aiding and assisting therein—as the only reasonable grounds ye can go upon to entertain any hopes of mercy at the hands of God.

"God may indeed then be merciful, but at the hands of men, here, ye must have justice. For the justice of human laws has at length overtaken ye, and we ought to be very thankful and esteem it a most merciful and wondrous act of Providence that your hidden works of darkness have been brought to light. Now the same mischief which you have contrived for others and have in part executed is at length fallen upon your own pates. Whereby the sentence which I am to pronounce will be justified against ye, as followeth:

"That you and each of you, Quack and Cuffee, on the morrow, the thirtieth of this instant between the hours of one and seven o'clock in the afternoon, shall be carried to the place of execution and there shall be chained to stakes and burnt to death.

"And may the Lord in His great goodness have mercy upon your poor, wretched souls."

* * *

They were to die, then, no later than the following day. The mild May evening that separated the trial of the two blacks from their scheduled execution found Francis Schaw "in a restless posture, turning to one thing and to another, wishing for company though when I had it wanting to be alone. I prayed to God that He would lead the current of my affections toward Himself." After dining in the late afternoon the schoolmaster had waited on his friend Corimer in King Street, "who invited me to breakfast with him tomorrow. I instructed my scholars under the steeple [*in a room at Trinity Church*], then returned to my lodging at eight o'clock, where the post being arrived, several were assembled in the parlor and discoursing noisily on the news. . . ."

Some of that news should have been cheering enough, to judge from the contents of the appropriate issue of *The New-York Weekly Journal*:

> Extract of a letter from a sailor on board his majesty's ship the *Lyon*, off Boca Chica fort, within the harbor, dated April 3, 1741. "* * * It is fine pastime to be among the Spaniards, fighting and cruising along in their harbors, for they are the cowardliest people that ever I saw. Our proceedings have hitherto been crowned with wonderful success, we being now in possession of Fort St. Philip, Fort Terra Bombo, Boca Chica, and Fort St. Joseph, and having obliged our enemies to sink and burn thirteen sail of men-of-war, a large merchant ship, a snow, and a sloop, with our bombs and ships now playing on the town and some fascine batteries they have raised to oppose us. Hope in a

few days to date a letter to you from *Cartagena,* where report of so much riches greatly animates the sailors and land forces to be within the walls of same. My service to * * *, and tell them we are very well and hope to see you all in a short time, as soon as we have given the Spaniards their belly full. . . ."

Yet for all that distant triumph, Schaw in his New York parlor continued "mighty uneasy." For one thing he had a toothache, a "hollow tooth accompanied with swelling," which was to do its part to keep him awake three hours after he had ascended the stairs to bed. In his room he tried reading Fiddes on morality, but his mind wandered and the candle burned down. A dog outside was barking insistently in the darkness. For a half hour and longer, Schaw lay listening to his landlady Mrs. Hogg— "could distinctly hear what she said"—at her prayers through the thin partition; she "groaned much in spirit." Finally he did fall asleep, but "my rest was broken all night, and once I woke from a confused dream about a horse dropping dead under me in the road. . . ."

His room facing east, at the back of the house, the morning sun roused him early. At eight the washerwoman came for his foul linen. He drank tea in the sitting room downstairs "a long time," then left his lodgings to keep his breakfast appointment. His toothache had eased, but he felt still "under a weight, though the sight of innocent birds in the branches and cows tethered in yards, who act according to the will of their Creator," tended to lighten the mental burden he carried.

Corimer at breakfast noted his friend's "increasing seriousness," remembering perhaps the vigorous, curious companion who had counted the steps in the Monument, enacted Aimwell with such spirit on the *Happy Return,* hallowed lustily to test the echo in the Middle Dutch church. "My friend C——— advised me to learn to think for myself—read Shaftesbury, Hobbes," Schaw recalled of that breakfast conversation years later. And he confessed of the occasion that "I was never more wretched, sad company in my life." He lingered, however, while Milne shaved his master, the servant chattering about local news: crowds forming along Wall Street, stakes sunk deep in place on the far side of the common, the brushwood gathered. As he was speaking shouts could be heard, even that early, from beyond the windows. Breakfast finished and shaving and powdering attended to, shortly after noon the two friends left Corimer's King Street home and made their way the little distance, no more than a couple of blocks, over to City Hall, before which a sizable part of the town was gathering to witness justice done.

* * *

"The spectators at this execution were very numerous," the record tells us, "and very impatient to have the piles of wood set fire to, their resentment being raised to the utmost pitch against the criminals, and no wonder." Many were waiting around the stakes in a field near the Collect south of Minthorn's farm, a short distance past the palisades out the Bowery Road. But many others were crowded together here on Wall and Broad streets and on the steps and very piazza of City Hall. Ladies were gazing with frank interest from upper windows of the nearby buildings, while atop the watch shed and the scaffold and into the branches of the limes and sycamores boys had clambered for the better view.

As one o'clock arrived and the prisoners were not promptly brought forth, the street mob began to yell for them—"Roast the negars! Baste and roast the negars!"—whistling and clapping and jeering their displeasure over the delay. A brief midday shower a few moments later set up an angry howl from some, but it seemed scarcely to dampen their impatient spirits; so that when, just before two, an oxcart was spotted rumbling from the Meal Market toward City Hall, a great cheer went up, and a way was elaborately opened to allow the cart to approach the entrance from which the blacks would emerge.

Corimer, with Schaw and various magistrates and officials in the council room, would move from time to time among those stored piles of city records to a front window, as shouts from below the balcony rose and subsided. Perhaps at first the Englishman had thought to glimpse Bonny Jack among the assembled citizenry, but only one Negro was to be seen abroad in the town that day: the lone carter stolid behind the dashboard of the oxcart that waited now by the steps, an armed constable at his side. As for the restless mob that Corimer looked down on, every face, like every visible face from the trees and at windows overlooking the street, was white.

At two-fifteen, to prolonged huzzahs, the prisoners Cuffee and Quack were brought forth. They were surrounded by a troop of twelve halberdiers and preceded by a drummer boy whose drum and scarlet coat were the first bright sights to emerge from the shadows of the arcade. Within the square that the advancing soldiers formed, the black prisoners as they descended the steps looked grotesquely awkward, their sweaty countenances—according to the record—"showing great terror," their shoulders hunched forward, their wrists manacled behind them, their legs in short chains that made their walk part hop, part waddle. Cuff, the larger of the two, a stout black over six feet tall, wore slops and the same tattered waistcoat he had worn in court, faded green with a red lining. His face was contorted, his bony cheeks tear-streaked, his eyes wide and glistening. Quack, barefoot, bare-legged, wore patched knee breeches and a chemise with one sleeve missing. Mouth hanging open, he moved forward reluctantly, in little jerks, cowering under the prods of the sheriff and three constables enclosed with him inside the square. The constables watched the crowd nervously, cudgels held ready; the soldiers, equally tense, gestured with their halberds as they stepped cautiously forward. Over the menaces of the multitude their captain, slight and anxious, was barking curt orders as best his tenor voice would let him, forcing those craning townsmen back from the cart so that the two prisoners could be brought alongside and lifted aboard.

Behind the dashboard the black carter never stirred, even

when Quack stumbled and the crowd hooted derisively—even then never took his eyes from the flies that vexed the rumps of the oxen. "Ha! Not so bold now, Quack!" the crowd was yelling; and "We'll warm you, never fear!" and "Some have too much, Cuff!" Volleys of dung were being thrown at the cart, and a tree branch hurled from overhead, and two or three cobblestones that fell short, and the discarded head of a chicken that struck a soldier's back. In the cart the two blacks were huddling between the constables, who frowned impatiently toward the blond captain, awaiting the order to start.

"By-and-by, Quack! Fire and scorch!"

"Idle bastards, there'll be work for you now!"

"You'll dance for us, lads!"

The justices, with members of the grand jury and the governor's council, had emerged in full solemnity at the head of the steps. Upon their appearance the young captain saluted, then at a nod from the first justice turned and shouted a command. The drummer beat advance. The driver whipped the oxen. The cart lurched forward.

"Give way! Make room ahead!"

At the movement most of the officials began to withdraw into the arcade, but a few, including the sheriff and the two court secretaries, descended the steps and fell in behind the cart. Up Wall Street it lumbered toward Broadway, turned north there, slowly, creakingly, with the taunting crowd growing larger at each successive intersection, citizens drawn by the noise and converging from King Street, from Queen Street, from Crown Street, from Maiden Lane, from John Street, from Fair Street, soldiers pressed now from each side, officials in the rear, blacks aboard shrunk small on the bench between their wary guards. North toward the common, out the Bowery Road that followed the present Park Row, through a gate in the decrepit palisades the cart advanced, coming finally to a halt within sight, in a field to the left, of the two stakes rising into the gray sky beyond the heads of another crowd, noisy and expectant.

Boys were straddling a fence at the edge of the field and

sitting high on the roof of a barn at a little distance. Beyond, trees covered hills to the west; to the north the freshwater Collect spread dull and flat under slate clouds. "The criminals," notes the record, "throughout the ride had looked as if they would gladly have discovered all they knew of this accursed scheme, could they have had any encouragement to hope for a reprieve." Now, confronting the stakes toward which they were being hauled—mob pressing and constables eager that the work be behind them—"as the case was, both prisoners were strongly inclined to make some confession"—Cuff's wet eyes fixed on the fagots, Quack's flashing over the faces of his captors both sides of him, as though in search of succor, while his lips moved frantically. By their shackled arms the Negroes were backed among the fagots and held tight against the roughhewn stakes. A smith fastened the bracketed chains first around Cuffee's waist and neck and chest, then around Quack's. Bound, the prisoners could see each other no longer, some five feet apart, one facing north up the island, the other south toward the town. Nor would their words have been audible to each other over the crowd's clamor. Quack had begun to moan, sounds in a strange tongue, softly as they secured him, then louder as the soldiers backed off and the mob roared its approval. While the bailiff stooped with more fagots to close the path to the stakes, some in the crowd started mimicking the high, inhuman sounds that were issuing from Quack's throat. Others threw their hands in circular motions over their heads and chanted the words that the black was alleged to have uttered in happier times: "Fire, fire! *scorch, scorch!* FIRE! FIRE! SCORCH! SCORCH!"

But in their desperation might not those two sufferers yet be made to unfold what they had so far kept secret? "Mr. Moore, the deputy secretary, now undertook singly to examine them both a last time at the stake, endeavoring to persuade them each to confess their guilt and all they knew of the hellish matter, but without effect; till at length the court messenger (Mr. Shaw) came up to him and said he would undertake Quack, whilst Mr. Moore examined Cuffee. But before they could proceed to the purpose, each was obliged to flatter his respective criminal that his fellow sufferer had begun. And the stratagem prevailed. . . ."

Thus the record, without ambiguity. The adulatory Edgar Desmond Griffith, weaving his colorful romance of Schaw's life that appeared in 1906, seizes upon the misspelling of the parenthetical name in that passage to deny that his hero, the future patriot, could ever have been party to so shabby a trick as here described. Yet though Griffith could not have seen it, I have the transcript of the document commissioning Francis Schaw as court messenger. And why might it not have been simple humanity to coax a confession from Quack and the other, a confession being all that might yet have saved those pathetic slaves, babbling, rattling their chains in terror? What sort of moralist, seeing the brushwood piled and the torch alight, would have clung to scruples and doomed them?

They did confess. The bailiff waited nearby, smoke rising from his torch. The crowd yelled curses and imprecations, and Quack confessed hurriedly and fully to all he was asked, first confirming to Mr. Schaw that Hughson indeed had been the contriver and promoter of the whole plot, which was to burn the houses of the town. Cuffee, for his part, admitted to Mr. Moore that Hughson had plotted to kill all the people. "What view caused the taverner to act thus?" Quack answered: To make himself rich. And yes, Mary Burton had spoke the truth and could name many more. How many, then, were involved in all? The crowd was screaming to know how many. Ask the negar how many in all? There was about fifty concerned, Quack supposed, but the record states that "this seems to have been a random guess under great confusion, for it is most probable he knew more." Who were they then? Make him name them! There was Albany, and Tickle, and Van Rant's Tom, and old Butchell ("It was not discovered who this negro was"), and Horsfield's Guy, and Worcester, and Codweise's Cambridge, and another short Negro who cooks for him. There were others, "but their names the prisoner could not recollect, the mob pressing and interrupting." Quack did fire the fort, though, by means of a lighted stick taken out of the servants' hall about eight o'clock at night on St. Patrick's Day. The governor had said that the slave was not to be let into the fort, even to see his wife, who cooked there. And some days earlier a sentry at his post had clubbed Quack over the head and thrown him into the street outside the fort. So on St. Patrick's Day, at night, he had entered the fort unseen, had stolen into the governor's house, had gone up the back stairs and through Barbara's room (his wife, the governor's cook), and put a firebrand near the gutter, betwixt the shingles and the roof of the house. And though it had not burned that night, he had returned next morning and blown on the brand and left it to catch the roof on fire. And yes, Cuffee did set fire to the storehouse, as sworn against him. When his master went to the coffeehouse, he had run out the other door and by the back way into the storehouse on New Street, bearing lighted charcoal in his pocket between two oyster shells. "Where did you set the fire?" Between ropes and boards in a corner, and left it and went home. To his interrogator, Quack at the same time was insisting that his wife at the fort was in no way concerned, "for I never would trust her with my schemes." And Denby, the governor's Negro boy: Denby knew nothing about Quack's intent to fire the fort. No, nor was Ellis's Jamaica concerned in the plot that he knew of, though frequently at Hughson's with his fiddle. Niblet's Sawney, however—so Cuff was confessing to Alderman Moore—he did set fire to Mr. Machado's house. . . .

The mob, meanwhile, jeered impatiently, the bailiff holding his torch high behind the tense soldiers, their captain scowling close beside the stakes. "After the confessions were minuted down (which were taken in the midst of great noise and confusion) Mr. Shaw desired the sheriff to delay the execution until the governor be acquainted therewith and his pleasure known touching the prisoners' reprieve." The three men were conferring in low voices. Sheriff Mills felt apprehensive, extremely so. "From the disposition observed in the spectators, he thought it much to be feared that there would be great difficulty, not to say danger in attempting to take the criminals from the stakes and back to jail." Yet reprieving them might be a means of producing great discoveries, so Mr. Moore argued, and he and Schaw accordingly demanded that they be allowed time to proceed separately through the unsuspecting crowds, in order to hurry across the field and down the Bowery Road for a judgment from His Excellency in town.

The streets of New York were all but empty that afternoon. Behind the two messengers ugly shouts grew fainter; the ruined fort lay ahead of them, as Alderman Moore stumped along with his limp and Schaw jogged in front. The latter was approaching Attorney Murray's great door that faced Broadway, had knocked, was gaining admittance to see the governor in the small parlor. "All was there represented to his honor": confessions extracted at the stake under promises of pardon, hopes for further discoveries. Behind a wide-eyed servant Mr. Moore entered breathless, in time to receive jointly His Excellency's "directions for a conditional and discretionary reprieve," with which assurance the two gentlemen took their hasty, grateful leave and passed again outside and up Broadway to make their way at all speed toward the field beyond the distant common.

"But," says the record, "before they could return from the governor to the place of execution, they were met by the sheriff upon the common, who declared his opinion that the carrying the negroes back to jail would be impracticable. If that was his excellency's order, it could not be attempted without a strong guard, which could not be got in time enough."

For somehow the mob had sensed what the two absent officials had been about. Loath to be cheated of a spectacle, it could be heard even then, in one outraged voice, chanting furiously: "Torch the negars! Torch the negars! Torch the negars!"

How had His Excellency meant his reprieve to be carried out? Had His Honor explained? Had he given instructions? Rain was threatening, and the citizens aroused. Did he not understand the situation? How is the sheriff to do his duty?

"Torch the negars! Torch the negars!"

Hobbling along the dirt road with the embattled Mills, Mr. Moore attempted to calm him. He must use his discretion, the alderman was saying. The governor himself had concluded as much: the sheriff must use his discretion.

Six words follow in the record: "For these reasons"—the need of a stronger guard, insufficient time to call additional troops together, the conditional nature of Governor Clarke's reprieve—"the execution proceeded."

Schaw did not witness it, however. Having failed to arrest it, he did not return to the site. Still short of breath, nauseous, his tooth throbbing, his heart beating fast, he sank to the ground where he had halted, by the roadside at the eastern edge of the common. From there a few moments later he heard beyond the palisades the chants of the mob "Torch the negars!" abruptly cease, and then a drum roll, interrupted by a wild cheer, followed by a sudden stillness. Flame must have been touching fagot. His loud heart beating, Schaw glanced upward toward a few first drops falling from the gray sky, up where geese were flying northward high overhead, squawking faintly over the green hills and the freshwater pond and the open field. Then a scream near at hand, and a second scream, and screams in rapid succession that Schaw and many another citizen would remember the rest of their lives: two human beings—Cuff, Quack— their chains slapping under those hideous cries, long, long, before a mob awed and grown silent, while two thick plumes of black smoke poured upward into the light rain, and on the wind soon the sharp stench of burnt flesh was wafted, long before the sounds at the stakes had at last diminished—finally had ended; and the cheers resumed.

* * *

Those confessions at the stake brought the town satisfaction. Specifically, "the testimony of Mary Burton and of Niblet's negro (upon the credit whereof the two criminals were convicted) had been by Cuff and Quack particularly and expressly confirmed in the midst of flames, which is the highest attestation." Moreover, the court could now issue a warrant for apprehend-

ing slaves on Long Island and elsewhere whom the prisoners
had impeached at the stake, so that Codweise's Cambridge and
Horsfield's Guy and Varian's Worcester and Kipps' Tickle-
pitcher, alias Will, found themselves among others committed
to jail on Sunday, the day immediately after the execution. Finally, both executed criminals had confirmed with almost their
last breaths that so far as they knew of the matter, John Hughson alone (not Romme or anyone else) had been the first contriver and promoter of the conspiracy.

Now that same Hughson wanted to speak with a justice.
About noon Monday, June 1, Sheriff Mills "informed the recorder at his home that Hughson in jail had been very urgent
that morning that somebody should go to the justices and acquaint them he was ready to open his heart to them. Thus,
pursuant to the white prisoner's desire, the recorder with the
court secretary did go up to the City Hall in the afternoon,
expecting he would make some material discovery."

The two officials followed the sheriff down the echoing stone
steps to the prisoners' rooms. The record discloses that precau-
tions had been taken earlier to keep criminals separate "as much
as the scanty space in the jail would admit of, new apartments
being fitted up for their reception." On the basis of this visit
Schaw subsequently described those same apartments as "surely
most dismal places. There were three of them, with partitions
and iron windows and within these strong iron bars. I did not
go in, nor did the justice, but stood in the court where were the
guards, one of a singularly blackguardly countenance. The sheriff had them bring Hughson forth from the chamber, he whom
I conceived to be possessed of a heart as diabolical as ever beat
in human breast."

The schoolmaster may have been remembering the pitiful
Quack's assertion at the stake that the blacks "would never have
thought of the plot if John had not put it into our heads."
Hughson could be heard now, "his chains rattling upon him,"
before he emerged from the dark cell into the torchlit forecourt
between two guards stooping under the lintel. His beard was

tangled and filthy. There was a sly look about him, his lank form bowing slightly as he kneaded a gray knit cap he had pulled from his head.

"What does the prisoner want with the judges?"

"Please your honor, is there a Bible? I desire to be sworn."

Judge Horsmanden cast an irritated glance in the sheriff's direction. "No oath will be administered to the prisoner. If the prisoner has anything to say he has free liberty to speak."

"Ay, but saving your grace, I want much to be sworn. I pray you—."

The judge "thereupon reproached the prisoner with his wicked life and practices, for debauching and corrupting of negroes, and for shewing his children so wicked an example, training them up in the highway to hell. He further admonished him to lay open the whole scene of the dark tragedy that had been brooding at his house and discover the several parties he knew to have been engaged in it, in doing which he would make some atonement for his past villainies—or the recorder expressed himself in words to that purpose."

Throughout the admonishment, forcefully delivered, the prisoner was twisting his cap and attending, torchlight flickering over his haggard face. But when the judge had ended, "Hughson put a soft smiling air of innocence upon his countenance, again desiring that he might be sworn. The request was again refused him. He then declared that he knew nothing at all of any conspiracy, and called God to witness his protestations, that he was as innocent with respect to the charge as the child unborn—as were his wife, his daughter, and Peggy, for aught he knew."

"The fellow wastes our time. Remand him to jail."

Chains rattled as guards turned the prisoner roughly about, dragging him toward the barred door that the sheriff was unlocking. From the rank darkness came scarcely determinable sounds of life astir: a stumble, a deep sigh perhaps, or snoring. Horsmanden moved impatiently before Schaw toward the archway and the stairs, a moment later had ascended them and reentered the fresher world above—afternoon of a bright June day.

Annoyed, he was in no mood now to renew an earlier conversation with the secretary concerning Governor Clarke's promised reprieve of those blacks at the stake. He was wondering, rather, what Hughson may have intended by requesting that fruitless interview. Yet in the end the judge was able to settle on no better explanation than those that the record itself guessed at later: "The man may have been struck with compunction, or he may have flattered himself with making a merit of his discovery and thereby recommending himself to mercy to save his life. Or he may have imagined that if he could be sworn and then protest his innocence most solemnly with the sanction of an oath, he would give such strong impressions as to prepare the way for his escape." Whatever his purpose, "several there were with him, when he had first expressed a desire of addressing the judges, who concluded from Hughson's behavior that he was at that instant really in earnest to speak home truths. However, if such was the case, before two or three hours had passed and the recorder arrived at the City Hall, the taverner's wife or others must have got the better of the wretch, prevailing upon him to change his mind and desist from his former resolution."

* * *

Supreme court. Thursday, June 4, 1741.

The king against John Hughson, Sarah his wife, Sarah their daughter, and Margaret Sorubiero alias Kerry. To the indictments entered against them, defendants all plead not guilty.

This being the day appointed for their trials, whereof they have had due notice, the court proceeds thereupon as followeth:

CLERK IN COURT. Cryer, make proclamation!

CRYER. O yes! Our sovereign lord the king doth strictly charge all manner of persons to keep silence upon pain of imprisonment. If any can inform the king's justices for this province of any treason, murder, felony, or other misdemeanor done by the prisoners at the bar, let them come forth, and they shall be heard; for the prisoners stand upon their deliverance.

CLERK. Cryer, make proclamation!

CRYER. O yes! You good men that are impaneled to inquire

between our sovereign lord the king and the prisoners at the bar, answer to your names. Charles Arding. Frederick Becker. Robert Benson. Samuel Burdet...

CLERK. Prisoners at the bar, hold up your hands. These good men that are now called and here appear are those which are to pass between you and our sovereign lord the king upon your lives or deaths. If you or any of you challenge any of them, you must speak as they come to the book to be sworn.

Prisoners, upon explanations from the court, agree that John Hughson will challenge. Sixteen jurors he challenges peremptorily, among them "a young gentleman, merchant of the town, which puts Peggy out of humor, who intimates that he has challenged one of the best of them all: an exchange between the prisoners occasioning some mirth to those within the hearing of it."

Jurors are sworn: ... John Lasher. Henry Lawrence. Edward Man. Francis Roswell. John Troup. Peter Vergereau. Peter Wendover.

CLERK. Cryer, make proclamation!

CRYER. O yes! Keep silence upon pain of imprisonment.

CLERK. You, gentlemen of the jury that are sworn, look upon the prisoners and hearken to their charge.

Plot to set on fire and lay in ashes the king's house and his whole town ... kill and destroy the inhabitants as they should come to secure their effects and extinguish the flames ... took its first rise at Hughson's house in this city ... the three last named criminals, as well as Hughson himself, present at divers meetings of great numbers of negroes, joining with Hughson in inciting the negroes to commit felonies ... swore the negroes ... received from them money to buy arms and ammunition to kill and destroy their neighbors ...

Prisoners rise.

THE ATTORNEY GENERAL. Gentlemen, this is that Hughson! Behold the author and abettor of all the late conflagrations, terrors, and devastation that have befallen your city. This is the man! whose name will no doubt be held in everlasting remembrance, to his eternal reproach, and stand recorded to latest posterity. Were he not sunk below the dignity of human nature, were he not abandoned to all sense of shame and remorse, were he not void of all feeling for the dreadful calamities he has brought on this city and his fellow creatures, he would from a consciousness of his monstrous guilt be so confounded as not to be able, without the greatest confusion of face, to look up or stand before this court and audience. Yet stands he boldly there before you, he with his wretched confederates, so that now you may behold at this bar the ringleader and some of his principal contrivers of those destructive fires which elsewhere at other times your eyes have woefully gazed upon. Gentlemen, we shall call and examine witnesses who will prove the crimes charged upon each of these four criminals. When we have done, I doubt not but that you will find them all and every one of them guilty.

As counsels for the king, with Mr. Attorney General: Joseph Murray, James Alexander, William Smith, John Chambers, esquires.

First witness for the king: Mr. George Joseph Moore, clerk in court. Alderman Moore proves the arraignment and conviction of the two negroes Quack and Cuffee. Proves their confessions at the stake, "that Hughson was the first contriver and promoter of the plot to burn the houses and kill the people . . ."

COURT [*to the prisoners*]. Have you any questions to ask this witness?

The prisoners have none.

Second witness for the king: Joseph North, constable. Proves there was a cabal of negroes at Hughson's last Whitsuntide was twelve months. Ten, twelve, fourteen of them. Eating, drinking, meat on the table, knives, forks. Negroes calling for what they wanted. At his appearance they made off as fast as they could. North laid his cane about them, soon cleared the room of them. . . .

COURT [*to the prisoners*]. Have you any questions to ask this witness?

Prisoners have nothing to ask.

Third witness for the king: Peter Lynch, guard. Proves that Cuffee, led into prison with Quack immediately after their conviction, as he passed Hughson said, "We may thank you for this, for this is what you have brought us to."....

COURT [*to the prisoners*]. If you have any questions to ask this witness, now is your time to propose them.

Prisoners have no questions.

Fourth witness for the king. Francis Sylvester. Says that when Hughson lived next door to him upon the dock, kept a very disorderly house. A very disorderly house: sold liquor and entertained negroes. Sylvester often saw many there at a time. Once in particular. A great many of them in a room dancing to a fiddle, Hughson's wife and daughter along with them. Sylvester reproached Hughson more than once with keeping such a disorderly house, an offense to his neighbors....

COURT [*to the prisoners*]. Any questions of this witness?

The prisoners have no questions.

Mary Burton called and sworn.

"While Mary Burton is delivering her evidence, Hughson and his wife in the dock begin bemoaning themselves, embracing and kissing their daughter Sarah, intimating what care they have taken in catechizing her and the rest of the children and teaching them to read the Bible and breeding them up in the fear of the Lord. And in order (as may be supposed) to move compassion in the jury, Hughson's wife has brought thither a sucking child at her breast, which is ordered to be taken away."

Twenty or thirty at a time in the kitchen, eating and drinking [*says Mary Burton*], but most of a Sunday. Negars used to bring provisions, particularly Carpenter's negar, whose mistress is a butcher. My master swore the negars into the plot, and themselves, and Peggy. He carried the negars into a private room, and one of the daughters followed with a Bible, and when they come down again—

"Ah ha!" screams forth Hughson's wife, interrupting, "now, trollop, you are found out in a great lie, for we never had a Bible in the world!"

Order. Prisoners will keep silent.

The audience, considering Hughson's protestations "but a little before" concerning his teaching his children to read scripture, are much diverted by this.

Order in the court. Witness will proceed.

When they come down to the rest of the negars, my master says they are all sworn, though I did not see them sworn. I did see Vaarck's Caesar pay my master twelve pounds in silver Spanish pieces of eight to buy guns, swords, and pistols. And thereupon my master went up into the country and returned with seven or eight guns and swords, which he hid in the house. And I've seen a bag of shot there, and a barrel of gunpowder. They often tempted me to swear, and offered me silks and gold rings to prevail with me, but I would not. Caesar offered me as much speckled linen before Peggy as would make me an apron, that Sunday morning after he had robbed it of Mr. Hogg. But I said I would not have it, and threw it down upon the floor, and told them I did not want it. Want it I did, but I would not have it in that manner. I told them I believed they did not come honestly by it.

COURT. Does witness have further testimony concerning the plot?

BURTON. Only that the day the fort was fired, I went to Mrs. Masters and said to her, "Now you see this is the beginning of it, Mrs. Masters. You did not seem to take much notice of what I said to you earlier." Lud I was that frightened and much perplexed, and told her it were a thousand pities the plot should not be discovered. "But," says I to her, "if I was to speak what I know of it, I know they would not believe me." And yet when I looked upon the houses that afternoon, I thought what a pity it was that they must all come down. . . .

COURT. Do the prisoners have questions of this witness?

The prisoners ask Mary no material questions, "such only as seem to imply their guilt. But some of them during her testimony have thrown up their hands, and cast up their eyes as if astonished, and have said she is a very wicked creature, and protested all she said was false."

COURT [*to the prisoners*]. Have you witnesses to call?

PRISONERS. Yes, sir. We desire that Eleanor Ryan, Mr. Blanck, and Peter Kirby be called.

Ryan sworn. I and my husband lodged two months at Mr. Hughson's house last winter. Saw no negroes there but Philipse's Cuff and the negro that was hung in gibbets, three or four times is all. Never saw any entertainments there for negroes, though I lay sick in bed in the kitchen day and night almost all the time.

Blanck sworn. I saw Hughson give a dram to a negro, but I thought him a civil man, and still do.

Kirby sworn. I know nothing of the character of Mr Hughson's house, but I never saw no harm of him.

COURT [*to the prisoners*]. Have you any more witnesses?

PRISONERS. Yes sir. We desire that Gerardus Comfort and Adam King may be called.

Comfort sworn. I saw nothing amiss of him, though my business being a cooper, I'm often abroad, and went very seldom to Hughson's house.

COURT. Mr. Comfort, you are a next-door neighbor to Hughson. You live opposite to him. Surely you must have seen negroes go in and out. Pray what have you observed of the house since Hughson came to live there?

COMFORT. I have seen nothing amiss. I have seen no harm there.

COURT. You may step down. Call the next witness.

King sworn. Says that of late he took Hughson's house to be disorderly. Saw whole companies of negroes playing at dice and papa there. Wincoop's negro once carried a silver spoon there that was hammered down. Saw no harm of Hughson himself, however.

ATTORNEY GENERAL [*dryly to the defendant*]. Have you any more such witnesses as this?

HUGHSON. We have no more witnesses, sir.

COURT. Then now is the time for you the prisoners severally to offer what you can in your defense, that counsel for the king may sum up the evidence.

"Prisoners speak in their justification in turns"—the illiterate taverner, his wife, the prostitute, the child in her midteens—"protesting their innocence and declaring that all the witnesses have said against them is false. They call upon God to witness their asseverations."

But according to counsel for the king in summing up, it was through God—"by the blessing of heaven"—and through the uncommon diligence of the magistrates that such a detestable piece of villainy had been uncovered in the first place. That any human creature, he wondered, could be so lost as to have conceived of such a plot! "More wonderful is it, then, that so great a number should unite and conspire in a scheme so hellish. Yet that the cruel design was set on foot has been occularly demonstrated for us in the late fires enkindled in divers parts of this city. Witnesses declare the principal contriver of those mischiefs to be John Hughson, that wicked man whose crimes have made him blacker than a negro, the scandal of his complexion and the disgrace of human nature. Yet, gentlemen, in matters that affect life, you ought to have the most convincing evidence: the trial of the fact is your province. To condemn the innocent or acquit the guilty is equally criminal. If you can, therefore, after what you have heard, think the prisoners innocent, you ought to acquit them. But if you find them guilty, you cannot acquit them without the greatest injustice and cruelty to your country and yourselves."

The jury withdraws. "In a short time," to use the language of the record, they return from their deliberations, "having found Hughson, his wife, and Kerry guilty of all three indictments charged against them, and Sarah Hughson, the daughter, guilty of the second and third."

* * *

At the start of the following week, Monday, June 8, the prisoners received sentence. "You, and each of you, at the place of execution on Friday the twelfth day of June instant between the hours of nine and one, are to be hanged by the neck until you are severally dead, the body of John Hughson to be afterward hung in chains." The record observes that the four white people merited a more severe death, "their crimes being much worse than those of the negroes. However, we must not act contrary to law."

On the morning after their sentencing, the condemned in jail were visited by Rebecca Hogg, storekeeper, whose goods worth £4 and upward had been stolen one fateful winter night: an event that had inaugurated all these present calamities. She brought along melons and various pickled foods. A kindly soul, Mrs. Hogg may have felt uneasy at the dimensions of civic misery occasioned by her personal losses last February. Or she may have been merely curious. In late April and early May she had visited the cellar under City Hall in order to talk with the slave Caesar, "several times, as well before his trial as after his conviction." Those visits had yielded information not disclosed elsewhere. The slave convicted of stealing her coins and linen had for whatever reason confessed to Mrs. Hogg what he had refused to confess in court—a version of events the truth of which she may have doubted but, as was proper, she had passed on to the authorities. They let it enter the record without comment.

Caesar had told his visitor (this much she had known already) that the sailor Wilson discovered where was good booty to be had. Wilson had described the house and shop to Caesar and informed him of what money lay in the Hoggs's bureau drawer. "The slave," as Mrs. Hogg deposed to the justices, "did not know my husband and me, but told Wilson he knew the house if it was where the widow Scott lived formerly. No more did Hughson know of us. Notwithstanding, he and Caesar contrived together how to commit the robbery.

"On the Saturday evening following"—February 28—"the negro, who had had much to drink that day, dropped asleep on a table at Hughson's, having gone there to see Peggy Kerry.

About 10 o'clock John came to him in the kitchen and waked him and reminded him of what he had promised, to go to the house in Broad Street and get that booty. Thereupon Caesar went out, but not (so he says) to our house. He went rather to the house of Cuffee's master, in John Street.

"Finding nobody at Mr. Philipse's, Caesar sets himself down in the cellar kitchen by the fire. By-and-by, he hears his confederates outside. At the sound he feigns himself asleep. Soon Cuffee and Quack come in bearing a large bundle, and—as Caesar discovers by their talk, they thinking him asleep—they hide it in a bran box in the stable in the yard. Making no attempt to wake him, they go out again in search of further prey.

"When they leave, says Caesar, he takes the bundle they've hid and carries it to the shoemaker Romme's at the New Battery, who opens the door himself and lets him in. Caesar throws the bundle, which is tied up in a large tablecloth, in a chair. Romme takes out some pieces of linen and a pair of silver knee-buckles belonging to Mr. Hogg. Caesar then carries the remainder of the bundle to Hughson's, climbing upon the shed and getting into the house (the family all abed) and going to bed to Peggy.

"In the morning when he awakes, he gives snuffboxes, a pair of earrings, and a locket with four diamonds to Peggy, and bids her give an apron to the servant girl. Caesar then goes jauntily downstairs and distributes money to Hughson, his wife and their children, and likewise to that same servant girl, Mary Burton. . . ."

Thus went the slave's version, self-serving, of course, though he had been too sure of his doom or too proud to bother the court with it. Mrs. Hogg had heard the account after the trial, from the slave during her visits in the rooms under City Hall, rooms she was approaching again on this bright June morning following other trials, this time in company with her lodger Mr. Schaw.

Sheriff Mills searched the Samaritan's basket briefly, then got keys from his quarters off the arcade and led the two visitors down. A guard preceded them with a torch and victual bowls

Despite a small, barred window open near the ceiling, the cell was dark and stifling. The guard's torch burned low, though enough to reveal lurid shimmerings against the walls and in puddles on the floor. At one end of the room the Newfoundland Beauty was sprawled in shadows, mumbling drunkenly. She had got rum from somewhere, perhaps by obliging her keepers; the smell of it combined with excrement and vomit and staleness to sting Schaw's nostrils and make his eyes water. He breathed into his palm. Plump Mrs. Hogg for her part seemed oblivious of unpleasantness, familiarly offering the other three prisoners the contents of her basket. Hughson's wife held off, sullen against the damp stones at her back, but the girl Sarah took a melon and soon had broken it open across a stool and fallen to devouring the meat—welcome supplement to the usual black bread and meal mush. Hughson himself, Schaw noted, was required to stand still near the cell door, "a smith taking measure of him at the time for his irons, he alone having been ordered to be hanged in chains." But upon recognizing Schaw in the murkiness—court secretary who had recently accompanied the justice with the carbuncle nose down here—the taverner began fervently proclaiming his innocence, "imploring God to witness that he knew of no plot against the town or any townsmen." Mrs. Hogg was emptying contents of the pickle crocks into wooden bowls that the guard provided her, while the child Sarah went on slobbering over her melon and Peggy crooned stupidly in the corner and voices howled in the rooms adjoining. Tears streaming down his face and into his knotted beard, Hughson cried out his innocence again and again as the stolid smith measured neck and chest and arms. "Why has God done this to me? I, who am innocent of plots as is the babe unborn!"

Schaw approached the wretch and bade him be calm. Briefly they spoke together, during which time Hughson, earnest in his knit cap, "admitted freely that he deserved death for receiving stolen goods. He did not doubt, however, but some remarkable sign would happen to show his innocence of any conspiracy. . . ."

Alongside, blacks were shouting in the neighboring room beyond the partition. One voice rose roundly above the others, cursing the taverner in bastard English. Hughson ignored the voice, as well as sounds of scuffling and of something thrown against the timbered wall that made it rattle. "I am innocent," he was exclaiming amid tears, while the smith worked indifferently about him and the guards were moving to still the rowdy blacks. "As God is my witness, I swear I am innocent!"

That visit to prison clouded Schaw's mood through the rest of a long summer day and beyond. Not that he doubted the taverner's guilt, to which many had already testified and many others would soon: "The judges every day were gaining new knowledge concerning it." Yet the sight of such misery was humbling. "How wonderful are the ways of Providence, and by what severe discipline are we taught the value of life's common blessings." An innkeeper who would be rich, who would be king! And would crown his wife and daughter! Reverence and humility: not my will, oh Lord, but Thine be done.

"I went from there up to my friend P—— and discovered at home his sister, who gave me dried figs. I sat with her alone half an hour. We found it difficult to discourse for so long a time, and seemed both uneasy. She told me some old stories." This from a portion of Schaw's *Reminiscences* where he reproduces verbatim one week of a journal no longer extant, representative of the clouded state of his mind and the aimlessness of his days as a young man not yet reborn. Though undated, and included earlier in the work among concerns of the preceding fall, internal evidence dictates its proper placement here in his life, near the middle of June 1741.

"Miss E—— entered, has a great deal of sweetness and civility that is taking. The son, an only one, grows into a young man of good temper and tolerable conversation, but little as I have been able to discover extraordinary in him. Soon after P———with my friend C—— arrived from bowling on the green. A turtle was barbecued for us on the lawn by the river."

Corimer, who had recently arranged his passage home to

England, was as sanguine that afternoon after his bowls as
Schaw was downcast after his prison visit. The *Charming
Nancy,* Captain Carr, was to sail for Plymouth on the fifteenth,
less than a week away. Meanwhile, "C——— was out to please
the women in conversation, at no loss to entertain Miss E——
and her mother and aunt with discourse and laughter and light
raillery. He tells a story well and with a great deal of wit. I was
but very dull company in turn."

Yet Corimer's own, carefree mood was to receive a shock
before that same day ended. "In the evening to Downing's."
And Elizabeth's sixth letter to Sophia Milner, the last of those
that I own, begins with melancholy news that the English aristocrat had abruptly learned that day from the papers at the
tavern. In the issue of the *Weekly Journal* dated Monday, June 8,
1741, we may still read the item that Corimer would have encountered Tuesday, after he had left Pursell's and was lounging
in Pearl Street before the assembly of the Hungarian Club:

> Thursday last arrived here Capt. *Hill,* from *Jamaica,* by
> whom we have the agreeable confirmation of the taking of
> six castles in the harbor, &c., of *Cartagena,* among which is
> the castle of *Boca Chica,* which was taken by the land forces
> under the command of General Wentworth. The loss sus-
> tained by the English forces were two Cols. *Douglas* and
> *Santford,* the brave Captain *Provoost* of this city (who had
> gained great reputation among the officers on the expedi-
> tion), one lieutenant aboard his majesty's ship *Boyne,* and
> one ensign Aubrey, *Lord Byles* and his lieutenant and about
> 200 men. . . .

Aubrey, Lord Byles. Heir to the earldom of Cavendham.
"Mr. C, now Lord Corimer, is greatly distressed with the news
of his brother's death on his majesty's service, learned in so
unexpected a manner, from the papers here. His lot has been
very hard indeed. He has received no notice otherwise." But the
news that Elizabeth was soon relaying to her friend Sophia

proved true enough. Admiral Vernon's fleet on March 4 had stood down to leeward and come to anchor in Plaza Grande, the roadstead off Cartagena along the South American coast. Troops had been landed ashore. Nineteen days later five ships of Vernon's fleet, including the *Boyne,* had been moved in to attack the fascine battery and the formidable St. Louis Castle. The depth of water in the harbor had not permitted the ships to get closer in than seven hundred yards, at which range they had found themselves at a grave disadvantage. Nevertheless, for two days the English had kept up a gallant, futile attempt to batter the castle. Then, their ammunition expended, they were ordered to withdraw. Ensign Lord Byles—blown to bits the morning of the second day when a rocket exploded on the port side of the *Boyne's* gun deck—was one of the large number of men killed in the engagement, which had disabled all five vessels without producing any effect of consequence on the castle. Indeed, the entire campaign was disastrous. What Spanish guns could not do, rains, yellow fever, and the appalling incompetence of General Wentworth ashore did to the English for them. By May 6 Vernon had been forced to abandon the campaign. His fleet put out to sea that day, bound for the sanctuary of Port Royal. By then the unsuspecting Charles Corimer—last of a noble line— had already for six weeks been heir to Cavendham.

* * *

The taverner Hughson, his wife, and the whore Peggy were hanged at New York Friday, June 12, in the morning, as ordered. But on the next-to-last day of their lives the court had been moved to show clemency of a sort to Hughson's daughter: "As to this miserable creature under sentence of death, to be executed with her father and mother and Margaret Kerry tomorrow, the judges wish that she would furnish them with some pretense for recommending her as an object of mercy. But they wait for it in vain. She is a wretch stupefied and hardened in wickedness, and seems void of all sense of a future state. However, it is thought proper to respite Sarah's execution one week, to Friday, 19th June, in hopes that after her father and mother have suffered, the girl may be mollified to a confession of her own guilt and raise some merit by making a further discovery—or at least, by confirming what has hitherto been unfolded concerning this accursed scheme."

So ordered, the court adjourning soon after. The same evening, the evening before she would hang, Peggy Kerry "sent a message to Mr. Justice Horsmanden signifying her desire to speak with him." That patient man "accordingly went to her and saw her at the sheriff's quarters. There Peggy declared before him that she had earlier perjured herself in her voluntary confession, for all that she had said then about the shoemaker Romme was false. It was all false, excepting as to his receiving stolen goods of the negroes."

Then if not at the shoemaker's, would the whore confirm that the plot had been hatched at the innkeeper's where she lodged? "The woman was interrogated very strictly to that purpose, the judge admonishing her in the most solemn manner to declare the whole truth if she intended to do herself any service or induce him to recommend her as deserving of the pardon which had earlier been prepared. Yet," the record reveals, "she absolutely denied to the last that she had ever heard at Hughson's any such discourse as of firing the town."

To the last she denied it: that night at the sheriff's before the justice, next morning when they came for her and the others to take them to the field beyond the palisades, in the field itself as she stood in terror by the tree, halter around her neck and the howling mob before her.

Schaw was among the official party attending the execution. He would have arrived at the City Hall about nine in the morning, though his *Reminiscences* deal with that public event only in general terms. By contrast, an encounter at City Hall, before the prisoners had been summoned to their doom, he does describe fully and vividly; it is as though the effect of so unexpected an encounter marked his consciousness grievously enough to efface much of what followed. He had arrived about nine, and was surprised when the guard of the "blackguardly countenance" whom he had noted on an earlier visit approached him with a request that the court secretary descend to the subcellar dungeon, below the jail rooms where Hughson and his confederates were incarcerated. No doubt Sheriff Mills had learned in conversation of Schaw's apprenticeship to a surgeon at sea in the West Indies and had passed that information along. The town's only doctor having found reasons why he couldn't attend at the subcellar, would the secretary take a moment? It wasn't jail fever exactly; the guard knew jail fever when he saw it. But if the gentleman would come with him for a moment.

They clattered in torchlight down the stone steps. Iron gates creaked. Into the dank corridor, cells emitted their stenches; a door wicket framed briefly the bonneted face of Sarah Hughson, child reprieved for a time to ponder her parents' hanging. At the end of the corridor another gate was unlocked and opened, and Schaw, with a guard ahead of and one behind him, descended to the suffocating quarters that had enclosed the slave Caesar, gibbeted now and rotting in chains at the edge of town.

It was a single room ten feet square, stone walls, earth floor, no windows, only one faint, flickering light at the far corner. The torch that the guards had brought with them glowed dully over as many as a dozen figures in the tumbling shadows, Spanish Negroes and six or eight others, "in a wretched condition, in rags, dirt and vermin abounding. All the horror I ever had an idea of," writes Schaw, "falls short of what I saw these poor creatures in, chained to iron bolts in the walls, collars and horse locks about their necks. Their distress appeared so great as to have benumbed them, in that seat of woe just this side of hell. At the sight of so many objects of pity I was sensibly touched with a fellow feeling of their miseries."

Two or three whose chains permitted had gathered around something lumpy in the corner. It was a human being. A feeble flame from oil in a calabash lit the body, supine, that trembled uncontrollably on the damp earth. One black had dropped into the flame powder or dirt that made it smoke; another with some tattered feathers waved the smoke toward a crude idol at the feet of the body, then prostrated himself, mumbling.

Schaw approached, and the nearer blacks gave way. The man they had huddled over "lay in a blanket thin and meager, and little else but skin and bones in chains. His skin was sooty, all glistening with sweat that ran down his face and neck and chest. His breast heaved against the iron; his heart panted. The whole man was in a bitter agony, looking up at me through ghastly eyes."

Not until some time afterward did Schaw come to realize who lay suffering there before him. Now, according to the *Reminiscences* (p. 37), all the schoolmaster could consider was that this was a soul for whom Christ had died. "For our conduct toward him we must answer." After a moment, however, he did manage a word with the guard: "The man must be got from the others. Find a space apart, in the almshouse, wherever—but quickly. The magistrates shall be apprised of this."

With a haste that made him ashamed, he turned to leave that pestilential hole, perhaps reminding himself gratefully that his presence at the forthcoming execution of the Hughsons and Peggy was expected.

As it happened, not until he had reached the street again, under the summer skies in the crowds swarming jubilantly toward the gallows, did Schaw suddenly see past the transformations that illness had imposed on that suffering face behind him in the subcellar. Something about the contortions of pain—no malingering this time—abruptly recalled shipboard writhings of a black apparently seasick unto death on the voyage from England last summer. And the scarified cheek, sunken now, and the brand on the glistening forehead, and even the rags of a checked shirt. The slave in his death agonies was Corimer's Bonny Jack.

That realization may account for the court secretary's reticence as an old man about the Hughsons' execution: scarcely more than a mention of the effect that attendance at so mournful an occasion had on him. "There was a most prodigious crowd of spectators. I got upon a scaffold near the fatal tree. My mind," he wrote, "was opened then to meditate on hearts loaded with grief; I was much affected and brought into a feeling of the state of sufferers"—presumably blacks in the bowels of City Hall as well as the three white people who had been carted through sunlight toward their deaths along the streets above.

The record provides some of what Schaw, for whatever reasons, omits from his *Reminiscences*. "The magistrates [*it tells us*] observed John Hughson, when he was brought out of jail to be carried to execution, to have a red spot on each cheek about the bigness of a shilling, which they thought remarkable, for he was always pale of visage. Those spots continued all along to the gallows. Hughson stood up in the cart all the way, looking round about him as if expecting to be rescued, as was by many conjectured from the air he appeared in. One hand was lifted as high as his pinion would admit of, with a finger pointing, as if intending to beckon. At the gallows his wife stood like a lifeless trunk, the rope about her neck tied up to the tree. She said not a word, and had scarce any visible motion. Peggy seemed much less resigned than the other two—or rather, unwilling to encounter death. She was going to say something, but Hughson's wife, who hung next to her, gave her a shove with her hand, so Peggy was silent.

"They all died having protested their innocence to the last, touching the conspiracy."

One additional point the record mentions, foreshadowing matters to come: "The wife was bred a papist, as it has been generally reported, and Peggy was much suspected of the same persuasion; though perhaps it may seem to be of little significance what religion such vile wretches professed"—dangling there, necks awry, eyes bulging in death over the stained field near the bright water's edge.

IV

From *The New-York Weekly Journal,* Monday, June 15, 1741:

In a former paper we gave an account that two negroes were burnt here, who at the stake confessed they were guilty of the crimes for which they suffered. With their last extremity upon them, they discovered a most horrible plot formed in this city and in part carried into execution. Since then we have learned that the conspiracy has been a long time in agitation and almost general among the negroes. John Hughson (executed last Friday with his wife and Margaret Kerry) was a grand promoter of the detestable scene of villainy, which was calculated to ruin and destroy not only the city but the whole province.

It appears that to effect Hughson's design, the conspirators would first burn the fort, and if opportunity favored, seize and carry away the arms in store there. Afterward they would set fire to the town, murdering all the male inhabitants (the females they intended to reserve for their own use). This was to be effected by seizing their masters' arms for a general rising. It appears also, as we are informed, that these designs were not carried on in this city only, but had spread into the surrounding country.

The Spanish negroes (of which there are many in this place) were deeply concerned and active in the business. It seems they persuaded the others that an attempt on the province would be made by the Spaniards and French, for whom all agreed to wait some time. If it happened that our enemies should invade us, they were to rise and join with them, Hughson having bought and procured arms, ammunition, and powder for that purpose. If such an invasion should not occur, they were to carry their diabolical scheme into execution themselves. Indeed, so far had they gone that their captains and other officers were appointed, the particular buildings to be first burnt were laid out, and the places of general rendezvous were fixed.

The number of negroes concerned is almost incredible, and their barbarous designs still more so, especially when it is considered that white people were privy to and fomenters of so unparalleled a villainy. Moreover, by keeping their intention private, and the concerned so artfully bound by the most horrid and execrable oaths, in all probability the plot would have remained a secret till they had done much more mischief, but by the mercy of God and through the indefatigable pains and vigilance of the magistracy and the present worthy grand jury, their deeds of darkness are now we hope almost (if not quite) brought to a full light.

Since our last, fifteen negroes have been capitally convicted, whereof seven have been burnt, one reprieved, and two have been pardoned on their confessions. Five are to receive sentence this day. Hughson, his wife, and Margaret Kerry have been hanged, and Sarah, the daughter of Hughson, reprieved until Friday next. Five Spanish negroes have also been arraigned, who are this day to be tried, and many more are now in jail.

As soon as we can obtain a full account of the plot, and leave from the magistrates, we shall publish the same.

* * *

Corimer had not been present at the execution of the Hughsons and Newfoundland Peggy. Instead, he had spent much of that Friday getting ready for his impending departure from New York. "June 12. This day I again awoke in low spirits, being called by Milne according to my directions a little after six. Some time was employed in the morning sorting papers and reading family letters, till about noon, when I put them into the new trunk, under wearing cloths, and prepared in other ways for the removal to England. At three through empty streets to dine on board the C Nancy. Capt. Carr a most civil host; shewed me his daughter's performances in writing, ciphering, etc. I took my leave about 6 o'clock and was rowed ashore. . . ."

But after all, the low-spirited heir to Cavendham would not be back on board the *Charming Nancy* as she weighed anchor in the East River early Monday and dropped with the tide toward the open sea. For Francis Schaw had come to his friend, that evening of the Hughsons' execution, with news of Bonny Jack: ". . . Found S awaiting me when I reached home." Together the two Englishmen had proceeded to City Hall. Sheriff Mills was away, but the high constable had admitted them, accompanied by guards, to those fetid regions that Corimer's journal describes no less vividly than does Schaw's *Reminiscences:* "Held to my nose a handkerchief soaked in rose water . . . floor resembled a slaughter house, mucus and blood in pools. Slaves along walls like resurrections from the grave. One was eating earth." Jack lay where Schaw had seen him that morning; and after Corimer had approached and was standing in bewilderment and anger over the shrunken form—the chained body "as dry as a chip"—his runaway slave, now found, opened his eyes, the eyeballs dull yellow by torchlight, and smiled faintly. "Master," Jack whispered, "don't you know me?"

Ill as he looked, the black did seem to Schaw to be in a

condition less desperate than earlier that day, when his sweat-glazed chest had been heaving in "bitter agony." Now the sweat had dried on the shriveled flesh: the fever was down. He could speak, he knew his surroundings. At Corimer's insistence, the turnkey fetched a litter, and while Schaw held the torch, the fragile Negro was placed on the litter and carried out of the dungeon and up the stairs. At the ground-floor arcade High Constable Schultz himself authorized the removal, deferring to the wishes of an earl's son, presuming the slave's death to be imminent in any case, and willing enough to have the plague-ridden body taken from the premises.

Yet Bonny Jack did not die; perhaps the ministrations of those fellow blacks over their calabash lamp had worked a miracle. In the loft of Corimer's stable he lay on straw through succeeding days of mid-June, and before long was taking porridge that Milne brought him, soon—though chained and guarded still—was squatting under the sloping roof and gazing, through an opening formed by adjacent knotholes, down to the back garden and the rear of the brick houses facing Crown Street opposite.

Angry at first, the slave's owner soon felt his anger give way to relief at having recovered lost property of considerable value. In days ahead he listened with gratification to Milne's reports of the steady improvement in Jack's health. The magistrates had concurred in High Constable Schultz's decision to let the nobleman care for his slave during convalescence, provided the prisoner was available to the court on demand. Now a couple of times a day Corimer came out of his house and crossed the yard to where a neighbor boy, hired to keep guard, would rise from his stool and unbolt the stable door and precede him inside. The first time Corimer's hand had been on the new sword at his waist, but the precaution seemed unnecessary. Jack, still weak, would usually be near the knotholes, chained, mindless of wasps that came and went, and nothing about his appearance or posture gave any sign of threat. His elbows and kneecaps protruded knobbily; his legs were like stalks too brittle to support him upright. Having learned some English during the months of his absence, he would respond to Corimer's greeting with deferential sounds, grinning his skull-like grin. Once or twice he felt encouraged to talk when his master lingered. Much of it was hardly intelligible—some about his life since the September morning of his flight from the landing wharf. He had found his way eventually to "a farm in the country," where his feet had been frozen in the first great snow. A slave at the farm had dressed his feet. The mistress, an old lady, had come to regard him as "a fellow that did not want sense," and her husband had talked of making him a cooper; then he would give Jack to his son, who had been bred a merchant and lived in a city at a great distance. The farm itself lay beyond a river, a day off walking at night in the direction away from where the sun crosses the sky.

The twentieth of June, a week and more after Corimer's recovery of Bonny Jack, was the second anniversary of the death of Susannah Pursell; so that her sister Elizabeth's English friend on King Street left home to attend readings and remembrances that Saturday morning with the Pursell family, who thereafter, according to an odd entry in his journal, "dined in the graveyard." Was it a summer picnic, brought from the Broadway mansion by Venture and other servants to the grass at the site of Susannah's grave? Two days later, the twenty-second, was Elizabeth's birthday, her seventeenth, though the occasion was destined henceforth (as she wrote her friend in London) "ever to be solemnly observed," being the anniversary of her sister's funeral as well. In the early afternoon Schaw and Corimer called at the Pursells' with their condolences and felicitations, and the three young people sat together in the grape arbor by the river and "drank lavishly of weak punch, which was requisite," the weather having turned disagreeably hot. "The chief talk now in town is about the negroes' conspiracy," so Elizabeth was writing under this date to Sophia Milner. No doubt conversation in the arbor had included that direful subject. "A negro of our neighbor's cut his throat last night; I suppose he knew himself guilty and did it to prevent a harder death. Hughson, the manager and ringleader, was hanged with his wife ten days ago, having been proved to be a most vile wicked wretch. . . ."

We feel, in fact—reading such sentiments fashioned in Elizabeth's beautiful hand—something of the intensity of fear and repugnance felt at the time among those respectable citizens: "They talk that the Spaniards are concerned. Two of the conspirators who were burned last month confessed their setting the fort on fire and other places, and that their intent was to burn the city and murder the whites. I think," this gentle girl, just seventeen, adds grimly, "no death can be too bad for such. . . ."

After dining that afternoon at the Pursells', Corimer returned home ("Mr. C, now Lord Corimer, is greatly distressed with the news of his brother's death on his majesty's service"), but Schaw remained, accompanying Elizabeth and her brother on a promenade along Broadway, when the sun was low in the sky and after the heat of the day had eased. It may have been this very walk that provoked the schoolmaster's undated, appealing confession of awkwardness in his later *Reminiscences* (p. 33): "Walking with Miss P———— a little perplexed how to behave with respect to the giving her the right or left hand when we turned back. At first changed sides with her to keep her on my right hand, but at last observing that ceremony not much regarded by others, I kept my own side in going backward or forward." The triviality merited inclusion in an old man's recollections as one specimen of what had come to seem foolish, youthful preoccupations before the experiencing of his spiritual rebirth. That the moment is applicable to the present afternoon is supported by reference in the same sharply focused passage to the heat and noisomeness of a city in summer: "disagreeable stench off the kennels"—those gutters down the center of the cobbled streets—"full of oyster shells, feathers, eggshells, all kinds of excrementitious and offensive matter. Flies and musketoes were troublesome. We ended at the Queen's Head at Whitehall, where we eat raspberries above stairs and heard a tolerable concerto of music performed in the garden below. Insects clamorous in the trees. Toward evening new hay piled in rucks on the islands cast a sweet and agreeable smell with the onshore breeze. On the balcony E——— spoke of David's psalms and Mr. Addison's genius. I found I was using 'I profess' at almost every sentence when conversing. Am resolved to avoid the frequent use of any word, which tires like a peculiar suit of clothes worn a long time. I talked pretty well, however, without that bashfulness that sometimes takes off from the gracefulness of speaking. Vessels were sailing apparently round the house, within fifty yards of us, out of the harbor and turning through sunset up Hudson's River. At dusk the garden was illuminated, very pretty with musical entertainment. . . ."

On the tip of the island, one day's ending. Exactly three evenings into the future, Schaw's aristocratic friend was passing a later warm twilight less agreeably, alone at the front window of his home nearby, shelves behind him emptied of books packed days ago for his now delayed departure. The night would be too hot for reading anyway, by a light that would have attracted insects. Accordingly Corimer stood in that later dusk before an open window of the drawing room, awaiting a breeze while listening to the neighbor's cattle bellowing over the smell of skunk from some nearby cellar. Beyond the window, Milne was throwing buckets of water on the front pavement, though on this particular evening the ritual offered "no sensible cool." For a moment the Englishman musing within the darkening house had tried to recall winter's feel—icicles glistening from the eaves, chill winds, deep snow, boys on barrel staves sledding noisily down Flatten Barrack Hill. But the present muggy stillness rendered such recollections incredible. Soon he abandoned the effort, returning to more immediate concerns. This same day Jack had been moved down from the loft—made insufferable by the heat—and sat secured now in an empty stall of the stable. But the slave's communicativeness had increased with his appetite and strength, so that during this very afternoon he had been talking animatedly with Corimer about the occasion of his only two visits to York from the farm beyond Harlem. Those had been in the fall before the snows, once when his new master had wanted to hear a man speak to crowds at a stone church and had brought three of his slaves along, two to watch after the third; the other time had occurred when there were fires at the street corners and the first snow fell. Two weeks had passed after that second visit, and Jack's feet had been frozen badly as he was working in the woods at the farm, so that from then on he had been bedridden until spring. One mild evening some days after his feet had healed, he had stolen away and, traveling at night, had returned to York, to the company of blacks met on those previous visits. One had led him at that earlier time to a tavern for a dram, and at the tavern there had been warmth and food and drink—and talk after the cloth was taken away of all the drink he could want. He had found his way back there this spring, but the whites had come for him and put him in the dungeon and had left him to sicken and die in the darkness.

What Corimer could understand of his slave's story was troubling. Growing stronger each day, Jack would, of course, run off again soon. Yet the Englishman, repossessed of lost goods, was now determined to return to England before that could happen, return promptly and with all that he had brought to America nine months earlier intact. Or with what could be gathered together, at any rate: Milne had left a gate ajar on a recent evening, permitting the escape of Vixen, one of the grey-hounds, not seen or heard from since. But nothing more should get away. The heir to Cavendham meant to set off for London, after already too long a delay, accompanied by his remaining possessions—bed, pot, books, clothes, flute, monkey, and Bonny Jack worth £40. All the more eager was he to be gone, inasmuch as a letter from his father, bereft so recently of two sons, had arrived during the week just past to add its gloomy voice to the surviving son's several other importunate motives for leaving.

The heir must take passage by early July, and intent on doing so he called on his neighbor, Judge Horsmanden, the following morning, presuming that an official intercession might facilitate the removal of Jack. The judge, however, was at court, exceedingly busy in these times of public crisis, so that it was not until the twenty-eighth, Sunday before church, that the magistrate found an hour to return Corimer's call.

The morning of the visit offered rare sunlight after a succession of humid, overcast days. Indeed, Horsmanden, at the window seat in Corimer's bare parlor, began by commenting to his host on the unseasonably wet weather, which brought with it rising civic fears of epidemic, five cases of distemper within the city limits having already been noted this month. Cellars were flooded all over town, and slips and wet ground needed draining if the suffering province were to avoid an additional grief. These were difficult times forsooth. Behind the frowning magistrate, the boy on watch could be seen seated on the water trough at the end of the garden, smoking his pipe near the stable door. Horsmanden, attired in Sabbath splendor, taking a cup of chocolate from the servant Milne, thought to offer his host sympathy on the death of Lord Byles, that news having come late to the justice because of the press of official duties. He spoke feelingly of those duties, enlarged by the great numbers of Negroes who, in his words, had "begun to squeak" in the aftermath of the governor's recent renewal of pardon for prisoners now in jail willing to confess their crimes before the end of the month: "Be assured, my lord, that a great many negroes have begun to squeak." Even so, the jail remains packed with prisoners—upwards of seventy or eighty of them, every day more—and steaming down there. Vermin. Always and increasingly the threat of plague. When shall we see an end to our ordeals?

Corimer spoke of his plans to return home.

Of course. Quite understandable under the present lamentable circumstances. And once back in London, my lord will be so kind as to assure our fellow countrymen that no one in His Majesty's plantations entertains a thought of allegiance other than to the crown of England. If on occasion his provincial assembly may seem unresponsive to the wishes of the royal governor, no part of our local contention should be interpreted as casting doubt on the loyalty to their sovereign of his dutiful subjects in America. My lord will be pleased to assure our friends in London of those heartfelt sentiments, universally held?

But one other matter the judge's host would speak of. The slave out there, in the stable. Soon he would be strong enough to be up and about. Corimer had no wish to delay longer on the slave's account in any case, having postponed his departure already, and so would thank his friend for some official word authorizing Jack's removal from the province.

The justice's expression had grown cloudy. "My lord, forgive me." He set down his cup, speaking with gentle reproach. "Throughout these recent trying weeks, our most difficult task in prosecuting has been not the slaves, but rather—excuse me— their masters. All are of course loath to lose the value of their property. The court is alive to their hardship, yet my lord will understand that we must not officially admit such concerns. Our task is with justice. In the present case"—and he dabbed at his lips with a kerchief—"the county might indeed be persuaded to prize the negroman somewhat higher than customary. The fee has been £25, my lord, though the county might allow, say, £35 in the present instance, with the charges of prosecuting and, if need be, executing also paid by the county—"

Executing? But I have spoken at length with Jack. Throughout most of these months of turmoil he has not been in York at all. Since soon after taking flight upon landing he has been at a farm to the north of the city at some remove—he describes it very particularly—and was much of that time disabled with his feet frozen, so could have formed no part of any conspiracy here . . .

The justice smiled as one who had heard such tales often in recent weeks. He had risen from his seat. Services would begin soon; steeple bells were pealing their summonses beyond the sunny window.

"This Jack," Horsmanden interrupted when he could, "has imposed upon your lordship. Nay, 'tis true; you are deceived, I promise you. The servant girl under oath has positively identified that same runaway slave as one of the deepest-dyed of all the confederates who have been scheming these many months against our peace and safety."

* * *

She had done just that, and some time ago. The servant girl Mary Burton had identified Jack as a conspirator as long ago as late May, when he had been brought before the court with a number of other blacks implicated by the slave Sawney, who himself had earlier been fetched from Albany and was now testifying fluently enough to earn a pardon. Of those whom Sawney named as present during his own rare visits to Hughson's, one was a Negro "in a checked shirt, with a scar." Accordingly, Jack, come upon soon with another slave at the Center Market, was brought in. Confronting the latest lot of prisoners a day or two afterward, Mary Burton, the court's principal witness, said yes, she had seen Capt. Marshall's Ben, and Mr. Shurmer's London, and Mr. Van Borsom's Scipio, and Mr. Furman's Harry often around the table at Hughson's. And yes, that one too, whose name she knew not, but he had been present many times, he in the checked shirt, and she had heard him say that "soon they would all be free, and free from trouble," and had seen him whetting a knife on a brown stone that lay in the yard by her master's door.

Taken as a whole, the girl's testimony had grown more ample and precise as the court continued meeting into the summer. She would sit on the bench holding her rag baby and answer the gentlemen's questions with growing assurance, so that even the second justice, Horsmanden himself, though much obliged to her for her civic zeal, was led to conclude, in the formal record of the proceedings that he later prepared and had published: "She was of a warm hasty spirit, had a remarkable glibness of tongue, and uttered more words than people of her supposed education usually do." Yet the glib tongue had managed, through May and early June, to give so persuasive an account that no contradictions or discrepancies, no protestations of innocence by the accused or alibis by their friends or owners had been able to gainsay her version of the truth. Thus, on the very day that the Hughsons and Newfoundland Peggy were hanged, three more blacks were chained and burnt at the stake in a nearby field—three of a growing number who had been and would be burned or hanged or transported from the colony, sometimes on the girl's word alone, as summer days passed on.

Her version of events continued to acquire elaborations, but by mid-June its pattern was clear. That included accounts of two large meetings at her master's tavern, one around Christmastime, another in late February, three weeks before the fort was fired. It revealed "black stuff" that the Spanish negroes had contributed to the enterprise, "to set houses on fire." It disclosed oaths that Hughson had administered to his recruits, "on the book, of damnation to eternity to them who failed or discovered." Blacks were sworn by thunder and lightning, of fearful efficacy to the heathen mind, whereas any white man who betrayed the plot was to be hanged by his confederates "at low-water mark, his privy parts were to be cut out and thrown in his face, his belly ripped open, and his body eaten by the birds of the air." The court heard her enrapt. Mary told her listeners, during numerous sessions and with mounting volubility, that she had overheard the Spanish Negroes plotting at Hughson's to burn the house of Captain Lush, who in the role of privateer had earlier taken the *Soledad* as prize—burn the captain's house and "tie Lush to a beam—damn that son of a bitch—and roast him like a piece of beef." The slave Manuel, who claimed to speak no English, she had seen at Hughson's about new-year, or so she thought, "but am sure I saw him there often in March, and he often spoke to me in English, and I heard him say that while the York negars were killing one, the Spaniards could kill twenty." York and Spanish Negroes together, under Hughson, had hatched their plans in her master's long parlor, where the taverner, his wife, and their daughter "sat down to eat with the negars after frolics to a fiddle, though they sat on one side of the table, and the negars on the other.

The cloth was laid on several tables put together, and some boards laid upon tubs." Punch was made from a flask of rum, and some drank dry drams, and all the negars agreed to what was proposed. In a little while war would be proclaimed against the French, and then the French and Spaniards would come here. Meanwhile the plotters were to stay till they came, about a month and a half; and if they did not come in that time, they were to begin themselves by first setting fire to the fort. From there they would fire both rows of houses on Stone Street, the Fly, and so on up the town, and the negar in the checked shirt would be an officer, a captain, a commander of a hundred at least, and all were to turn on their masters as the fires blazed, and kill them and send them to their long homes, then come abroad, out in the streets, to fight. Hughson said that after the negars had killed the white men, they were to marry the gentle-women. And the slave London told her, Mary Burton, that his master would trust him anywhere in the house, so he could get into any room and murder him. And once, when they had done eating over the table where the girl was serving, Hughson brought forth more drink and said the country was no good, too many gentlemen here who made negars work hard; they must set fire to their masters' houses, and get guns, swords, and knives when they came out. And after the business was done, the taverner would put the blacks in a ship and carry them into their own country. And Vaarck's Caesar had said that it was a hard case upon the poor negars, that they could not so much as take a walk after church-out but the constables took them up. Therefore, in order to be free, they must set the houses on fire and kill the white people, but for that they would wait until the wind blew hard. Which is what they did. In mid-March, on the night of St. Patrick's Day with the white men carousing, Quack did put a lighted brand against the roof at the fort. The roof had not taken fire, though, until he went back to the fort the following morning and blew on the brand where it lay hidden under the rafters. Thus by nightfall the governor's house was burned to the ground, and the slave Patrick said he wished the governor himself had perished in the flames, and Manuel said that by-and-by this would be put in the news that the fort was destroyed, and then the Spaniards would come and assault a city made weak by the fort in ruins. And with many of the best men of the city away in the Caribbean, the Spaniards would come and take us all.

Those were the principal features of the servant girl's account, confirmed in the main by the desperate confessions of Quack and Cuff at the stake, and by the abundant testimony of the slave Sawney upstairs in City Hall. True, some of the blacks that Sawney named as present at the taverner's Mary said nothing of, and some that Mary had implicated Sawney did not mention. Times that they assigned to the tavern meetings differed, and Sawney had the Hughsons sitting among the blacks instead of on the opposite side of the table. Moreover, he added details omitted from her accounts, that Vrelandt's Starling, for example, "brought out about eleven penknives, which were rusty, but had said his own knife was so sharp that if it came across a white man's head it would cut if off" (to which the righteous Sawney had answered, according to his testimony, "If you want to fight, go to the Spaniards, and don't fight with your masters"). But in essentials Mary's version and his were in agreement, an agreement less remarkable, perhaps, considering the leading questions that the court was accustomed to pose to witnesses ("all the gentlemen taking testimony being well acquainted with the account of the plot"). Moreover, what Cuffee and Quack had confessed in May had soon become common knowledge among the prisoners, as was the importance, in turn, of those surviving blacks' providing the justices with certain answers when they were questioned—that is, answering "so as to be believed." Again, crowded conditions in jail had allowed many besides the white thief Arthur Price to converse with others confined there; talk was circulating regularly through the dungeons that spring and summer—as, for example, when Mr. Moore's Cato was able to advise Braveboy, newly incarcerated, "to bring in many negroes"—give the authorities names of many negroes to round up and imprison. "He [*Braveboy*] would certainly be burnt or hanged if he did not confess, but if he brought in a good many negroes it would save his life, for Cato had found it so himself. Braveboy must say he was to set his master's house on fire, which would make the judges believe him. . . ."

Those blacks devising means of salvation were only two among a multitude implicated by the testimony of Sawney, of Mary Burton, and of others whom Sawney and Mary had cited. Such testimony had led to the incarceration of Brazier's Tony and Lowe's Sam and Van Horne's Bridgewater and the widow Fortune's Robin and Hunt's Warwick and Burke's Sarah ("one of the oddest animals," the record tells us, "amongst the black confederates, a creature of outrageous spirit who foamed at the mouth when interrogated, and absolutely denied she knew anything of the matter")—all those and fifty or so additional slaves besides.

Indeed, so crowded had the prison become that by mid-June drastic steps were required to be taken. "We were apprehensive that the criminals would be daily multiplying on our hands, with fears of infection and harm to the poor debtors, for it seemed very probable that most of the negroes in town were corrupted." Accordingly, to relieve the congestion, the governor, "with the advice of his majesty's council," had renewed his proclamation June 19 "promising his majesty's most gracious pardon to any and every person or persons, whether white people, free negroes, slaves, or others, who have been or are concerned in the conspiracy, who shall on or before the first day of July next voluntarily, freely, and fully discover and confession make of his, her, or their confederates, accomplices, or others concerned in the said conspiracy. . . ."

The response to that offer could hardly have been more gratifying. In the two weeks thereafter, before the month ended, seventy additional Negroes were arrested on the word of those in jail, as slaves already imprisoned sought to save their lives by naming conspiratorial blacks still at large. Fifteen prisoners, for instance, confessed in a single day, June 27, each one specifying two or three additional blacks for the constables to gather in. Such cooperativeness kept the gentlemen of the law busy, during sweltering June mornings and afternoons, filling in their several columns with maximum efficiency, "viz., one for the name of each negro; another for his respective owner; another for the matter or substance of the confession; another for the negroes he accused. These gentlemen," the record asserts, "(considering the great number to be examined) for the sake of dispatch only minuted down what came from the examinant which they judged to be most significant, which is the reason that the examinations and confessions taken at this time are so concise."

Even so, they are full enough to establish the repetitiveness with which Mary's and Sawney's testimony was confirmed.

No. 1. Dublin (Breasted's) said that Vaarck's Caesar (hanged) carried him to Hughson's; that Hughson told him he must join in a plot they were making and swore him to set his master's house on fire and cut his mistress's throat. Saw Gomez's Cajoe, Bound's Jasper, and Pemberton's Quamino there.

No. 2. Provost's Ebony said that the taverner gave him the book to swear to stand by them to overcome the city. Saw Philipse's Frank and Bayard's Phaeton at Hughson's.

No. 3. Horsfield's Guy said that Quack and Albany swore him at Hughson's, where he also saw Van Horne's Kid and Tiebout's Wan, Indian.

No. 4. Cruger's Deptford said that DeLancey's Cataline and Pintard's Jupiter first engaged him to be concerned in the conspiracy, and Ward's Will afterward.

No. 5. Ten Eyck's York said that Cuff carried him to Hughson's; that Cuff there talked of the number of Cuba men gone off to fight in the West Indies, and said he believed an hundred and fifty men might take this city. Wendover's Manuel was there, and Murray's Adam, who brought turnips. . . .

Generally such cooperativeness with the magistrates produced the results that the prisoners had hoped for. For instance, on Saturday, July 4, a list of Negroes was "recommended by the

judges to his honor the governor for transportation," a list that
included Breasted's Dublin, Provost's Ebony, Horsfield's Guy,
Cruger's Deptford, Ten Eyck's York, and thirty-seven other
names of blacks who had confessed their own culpability while
implicating others. Those forty and more were to be resettled in
Hispaniola, Surinam, Cape François, or some equally remote
dominion. "Dublin (Breasted's) being set to the bar and asked
what he had to say why execution of his former sentence should
not be awarded, he produced his majesty's most gracious free
pardon, and prayed that the same might be read and allowed of,
which being read, was allowed by the court accordingly. The
said Dublin then proceeded to give evidence against the prisoners . . ." As did those others in court, before their pardons,
too, were finally granted

To be sure, some Negroes were not so lucky. Mr. Murray's
Adam, for example, "was very willing to lay hold of the benefit
of the proclamation, but would entitle himself to it by saying as
little as possible to enlarge the discovery of the confederates in
this dark scheme." In other words, he would not implicate fellow blacks. Adam "was under examination several hours, several
days running. But the information that he gave came from him
slowly and by piece meals, which was tiresome, and gave so
much trouble that he was several times remanded to jail and
told what he said would do him little service. But as the constable was taking him away, he would beg to stay, and say he
would tell of all he could recollect. Yet he mentioned very few
but what we were apprised of before, and who had been either
executed or apprehended already." For his pains Adam died in
the fields after all, "behaving at the gallows like a mountebank's
fool, jumping off the cart several times with the halter about his
neck, as if sporting with death. Some conjectured he was intoxi-
cated with rum."

Othello, too, was ill-fated. Imprisoned, that Negro of Mr.
DeLancey's "began with exclamations and protestations of his
innocence, declaring it was nothing but damned lies that
brought him there, and that he knew who was the author of

them, and would be avenged even if he died for it. His examiner reasoned with him, telling him if he was innocent to insist upon it and not be afraid, for he might be assured of having justice done. Othello considered those words awhile, then desired to know his accuser. They told him they believed it was Goelet's Neptune, which as soon as he heard, he said, 'Then I am a dead man,' striking his head against one of the beams of the jail, and said further that he had been afraid the dog would serve him so. Then he gave the examiner his shoe and knee buckles, being silver, and desired they might be delivered to his brother Pero (another negro of Mr. DeLancey's)." Thereafter Othello provided testimony that confirmed the existence of the conspiracy, but falteringly, with reluctance. From what he said and how he said it, the judges were led to conclude that his confession "did not come within the intent, nor did it entitle the slave to the benefit of his honor's proclamation lately published, offering mercy." Accordingly Othello, like Adam before him, was carted to his execution. "The pile being kindled, this wretch set his back to the stake, and raising up one of his legs, laid it upon the fire, and lifting up his hands and eyes, cried aloud, and several times repeated the name Neptune Goelet, Neptune Goelet. . . ."

Many others were put to death during those summer days. Burke's Sarah, who had earlier foamed at the mouth insisting on her innocence, now "pleaded guilty, but the court passed sentence upon her to be hanged; for this reason, that she had prevaricated grossly. Indeed, we could give no credit to her evidence, so that she deservedly drew the rope about her neck." And after she had "hung the common time, and they went to cut her down," to the astonishment of the crowd the body still showed symptoms of life in it, so that a soldier was ordered to mount the gibbet hurriedly and hang her up again.

As for the five Spanish Negroes—Mesnard's Antonio, Becker's Pablo, Sarly's Juan, McMullen's Augustine, Wendover's Manuel—during their trial counsel for the king felt constrained in summing up to remind the jury that the servant girl had been the only one who had testified against them: "to prove the charge in this indictment, there was the testimony of Mary Burton. I must observe to you that her testimony is single; there is no other witness. Nevertheless, gentlemen, one witness is sufficient, and if you give credit to her testimony you will no doubt discharge a good conscience and find them guilty." Find them guilty even though the Negroes themselves had from the beginning protested that they were all free subjects of the king of Spain, unjustly sold into bondage when their ship was taken as a prize of war. Find them guilty though Captain Jacob Sarly had testified that "when the fire was at Mr. Thomas', Juan [*his Spanish Negro*] first discovered it to my wife; I never had a more faithful servant." Find them guilty though Mrs. Mesnard told the court that "Antonio was not down stairs from November till the 17th of March; I believe it was not possible for him to be abroad at that time." Find them guilty though Frederick Becker testified that "Pablo was brought into this country by Captain Boyd in January last, and was sick in my house till some time in March." Find them guilty though Augustine's master McMullen told the court that his Spanish slave "was sick all the winter with an ague, as the doctor said, and kept to his bed most of the time, but always behaved very well." Others who had known the Spaniards—families of their masters, neighbors, lodgers in their masters' homes—testified to the same purpose, about the illness of each of those unseasoned blacks spending the first winter of their previously sunwarmed lives in so brutal a climate. Like Corimer's Jack, Wendover's Manuel had frozen his feet: "Dr. Depuy, junior, said that the latter end of November and December last, this negro was ill, and he saw his toes in December, and they were bad, so that he could not walk. Mrs. Wendover, his mistress, said he came downstairs about the latter end of February, when his feet grew bad again, for they had been better before." Those and other witnesses had spoken for the accused; only Mary Burton spoke against them. Counsel instructed the jury: "The prisoners seem all to be equally involved by her testimony, and therefore you will either acquit them all or find them all guilty.' The jury withdrew, and "in about half an hour returned, having found them all guilty."

All were accordingly sentenced to be hanged, though in the event, for reasons the record leaves unclear, four were ultimately pardoned and transported, and only one, Wendover's outspoken Manuel, was executed, "on Friday the third instant. And ordered, that the body of Manuel shall be afterward hung in chains on the same gibbet with John Hughson."

On that third day of July, Manuel went to his death with the dignity of a Spaniard. The "well favored Moor," whom Corimer had seen the preceding autumn being cudgeled on the waterfront by his irate master, now passed along Broadway in the oxcart, "neatly dressed in a white shirt, jacket, drawers, and stockings. He behaved decently, prayed in Spanish, and kissed a crucifix, insisting on his innocence to the last." And after life had left it, the corpse of the Spaniard was carried across the field to the gibbet where Hughson the taverner and the slave Caesar still hung in chains, corrupting the midsummer air on the edge of town.

The black man had hung there, not far from the water's edge, for seven weeks, the white man for three. "Some few days following this," the record tells us, pursuing what occurred after Manuel's execution, "the town was amused with a rumor that Hughson was turned negro and Vaarck's Caesar a white. For when they came to put up the Spaniard in chains by those other two, as much of Hughson as was visible—viz., face, hands, neck, and feet—were of a deep shining black, rather blacker than the negro placed by him, who was one of the darkest hue of his kind. The hair of Hughson's beard and neck (his head could not be seen, for he had a cap on) was curling like the wool of a negro, and the features of his face were of the symmetry of a negro beauty: the nose broad and flat, the nostrils open and extended, swelled to a gigantic size. As to Caesar (who had been hung up in chains a month before Hughson, and was also of the darkest complexion), his face was at the same time somewhat bleached or turned whitish. Beholders were amazed at these appearances. The report of them engaged the attention of many, and drew numbers of all ranks who had curiosity to the gibbets for several days running, in order to be convinced by their own eyes of the reality of things so confidently reported, and many of the spectators were ready to resolve these wondrous phenomenons into miracles."

For New Yorkers, a unique summer outing: along the Bowery Road to see the conspirators who had exchanged colors. The record proceeds, relentlessly: "The sun at this time had great power, and the season was hot, so that Hughson's body dripped and distilled very much, as it needs must, from the fermentation and abundance of matter within the extraordinary bulk of his body, though considering the force of the sun and the natural meagerness of his corpse, one would have imagined that long ere this it would have been disencumbered of all its juices. At length, about ten days or a fortnight after the taverner's black mate Manuel was hung by him, Hughson's corpse, unable to contain its load, burst and discharged pailfuls of blood and corruption. This was testified to by those who were near, fishing upon the beach when the irruption happened, to whom the stench of it was very offensive."

A Monday or Tuesday of mid-July 1741. "Earlier Hughson had declared in life that he did not doubt but some remarkable sign would happen to shew his innocence. And if his corpse become monstrous in size (nay his arms, legs, and thighs were swelled to amazing bulk in proportion to the body; this is submitted to the consideration of the curious and connoisseur in physic), and if his complexion (for once to use a vulgar similitude) becoming as black as the d——l can be remarkable signs or tokens of innocence! then some may imagine it has happened according to the taverner's expectation."

An outcome fraught with such meaning excited much comment at the time, so that one more arrest that same week went all but unnoticed in the general amazement. The girl Burton had borne witness before the court that Benjamin

Pursell's Venture had been often at Hughson's among the conspirators: "said he would set the houses a fire, and he was to have a pistol." Accordingly, constables came in the middle of the morning Wednesday, July 15, and fetched the merchant Pursell's trusted servant from the yellow brick mansion on Broadway.

* * *

The conclusion of Elizabeth Pursell's sixth letter to Sophia Milner, last of the letters in my possession, this portion dated Monday, July 20, 1741:

> My friend will grieve over a most melancholy event that has happened here to throw our family into deep distress. On Wednesday last, our Venture—kindliest and good-naturedest soul that ever I knew—was come for by two constables, one a giant of a man in stature, who bearing warrants led him away, over the expostulations of my mother (Papa being abroad in the town at the time), whilst my brother and I could but watch helpless at the door, our hearts up at our mouths. We were to learn later that the poor old man was dragged into court, where he has been examined and pronounced *guilty*! of plotting with others to fire his master's house and *kill us all as we slept within it*! And now for sure, says Papa, Venture will be hanged, except he confess to what could never have been or ever could be.
>
> The charge against him is false, a vile and execrable lie. O Sophy, when will this state of barbarousness end! I have been alarmed to see my dear mother and aunt made dispirited by so sore a misfortune (for my aunt has ever been beholden to the good old man), and indeed, myself have been but in a most miserable humor. Add to our distress that the weather continues wretchedly hot and troublesome, as it has been for days past, and the heat makes us unfit for anything. I have now an ill cold upon me, and the distemper is in the town and everywhere increasing. But

most distressful is the terrible apprehensions of all our
family concerning our loyal friend, which is all our care and
cuts us to the heart, grieving as we do for one who has
served us faithfully all my life and longer.

We are persuaded the evidence against him is mistaken,
and I fear maliciously so, for it comes from the creature of
whom I wrote to you earlier, whose indentures were purchased then sold by Papa under trying circumstances some
time past. The city is now possessed of them, so that doubtless the girl will have her freedom and a reward of money
besides. Yet she is a wicked, envious child, as Father has
represented to the court (though all to no purpose), who I
doubt not has been embroidering on a tale before her bet-
ters these many weeks that may have begun as artless truth
but now is lies fantastical. Three whites and no more was
all she named when first she spoke of these things before
the magistrates in the spring, and only a dozen or twenty
blacks stirring discontent among themselves in some idle
house. But lo the tale has swollen to prodigious size, to
include whites in ever increasing numbers—soldiers and
dancing masters and Romish priests and even some that she
swears (but will not name) who "wear ruffles" as she says—
all those and half the negroes in town by now. Sure one, at
least, that she charges is guilty of nothing but too kindly a
nature and too trusting a heart. Yet I doubt not that the
trull will continue instructing our magistracy with her
fancies until such seeming innocence and simplicity hath
corrupted the entire province!

And was it this same creature who was wont to slouch
through our halls and chambers, to come whining late
through that very door, she who is now of such consequence that all the town listens, ay and trembles, too, when
she speaks? And now do I recollect Venture's bluntness
with her idle ways, that she would answer pertly to, so that
my brother once heard the baggage exclaiming by the
kitchen stairs that "no negar was to scold her, no, but only

her mistress that was ill could do that." It is too much! from her whose spite extended even to that dear soul, even as the poor innocent lay feverish and untended— The tavern wench, too, she that was hanged last month protesting her innocence to the last, as indeed did the wretch Hughson and many another who has perished besides. How the wench's very name (called by her sable admirers the Beauty) must have waked spite in so hard-favored and ill-natured a child as was this muddy-faced, toothless— (I do verily despise her, and God forgive me), slopping pigs in the tavern yard whilst the other lounges by the fireside within, sporting her rings and stolen favors. Lord C has theorized on this, that causes me to see things plainer than before. As doubtless the taverner Hughson found leisure in jail or on the way to the gallows to regret whatever scoldings he had uttered as provoked by the insolent bearing of that beggarly serving maid.

She is a deep one, depend upon it, and has paid them back forsooth. Mr. Schaw, who stopped with us this morning, brings accounts of doings in court that amaze us. The thing is quite out of hand. True is it (and no one misdoubts it) that Hughson received from his circle of black thieves goods, nor is it to be wondered at that some in their carousings have spoke ill of their masters while belaboring the times around his tavern table. The various fires have been too real, and frightful spectacles indeed. But now we hear from some that *scarce ten grown negroes in all the province* but are implicated in this swelling conspiracy! Meanwhile, Mr. S brings news of one slave who yesterday admitted to having threatened to call in every black man in York rather than surrender up his life, and in that seems to have spoke as have others, with the voice of desperation, regardless of truth. Another having confessed to the most enormous crimes recanted of them afterward, saying he never so much as saw the tapster in all his days, nor knew so much as where his house was, but only talked thus after some in jail had instructed him what to say an he would have his life spared.

Such circumstances as these at present summon forth the trial of our faith. I am much mistaken if frightened, pitiful wretches such as that latter slave will not hang or burn, say whatsoever they will. As indeed will our friend, so Papa fears, except he confess to what he has been charged withal. I cannot think on it. To fire this house! He who has comforted me a thousand thousand times! When my red squirrel Amos died, and I was near dying myself for weeping, Venture helped me to bury the dear creature near the river's edge, at evening with water reflecting on the trunks of the willows. Lindsay would go with him partridge shooting, and Venture it was taught him to mount the pony, and to shoe and curry her. And he clipped the wings of my brother's pet crow, and made it a hardwood perch, and made a wicker cage for my canary that later flew away. Now this same black man—our kind friend—sits broken-spirited and miserable in the dark cell, where Mr. S saw him yesterday, scarce able to speak for despair.

We know not whether to go or stay, or what we do. Mother longs to remove to Flatbush, away from the heat and turmoil, yet dares not leave us, who cannot go whilst Venture languishes. Last evening being even more hot than usual, and the night bringing no relief, my aunt and I drove in the fields by moonlight, then supped at our return by the same light, without candles. She remains indifferent well, her spirits made listless with the troubles of these days. As for me, I write none but my friend Sophy, scarce willing to write of what can bring no pleasure, scarce knowing indeed how the days pass. Last fortnight I received dear Mrs. W's kind favor and was truly concerned for her affliction, though I doubt she bore it with her usual resignation. Have not found means to respond, thus will thank you to express to her our hope that domestic happiness has succeeded by now to the afflictive scenes in her family.

This scribble, how unwelcome soever its news, would ere this have been dispatched but that I remembered me of your removing from London through the heat of July and have accordingly held it against your return, which I suppose to be in August late. The brig *Narrow Seas* is cleared for Greenwich tomorrow, whose captain will take letters. Lord C, as now is, longs to return to his father, made disconsolate by his own recent misfortunes (such sadness on all sides!), and had hoped to be among you ere you receive this. He is determined to leave here within the month, though without his slave Jack as now appears, remanded to jail again to Lord C's great annoyance. He will have much to tell you that will doubtless seem scarce to be credited. Yet could dear Sophia and I be together for the refreshment of converse, she must hear perforce what his lordship relates of matters in York confirmed on all counts, with grief and regret, by her distressed though ever most affectionate friend,

E.P.

* * *

From the *Reminiscences* of Francis Schaw (pp. 34–7):

I had all along been deeply affected with the oppression of the negroes. When apprenticed a young man to a ship's surgeon I had beheld at Antigua a parcel of slaves, newly landed from Guinea, marched in file to drum and bagpipe through the streets of St. John's like so many shuffling skeletons, their nakedness rubbed with lime and gunpowder so as to shine, pates of the older ones shaved lest some gray show. The ragged parade ended at the town square, where they were drawn into a ring and bade to jump and stretch forth their arms, and were most strictly examined by various planters and their ladies without the least distinction or modesty, as though they were cattle or horses and not our fellow creatures unwillingly in bondage.

A practice so inconsistent with the very idea of liberty and justice as is slavery seems of all others matter for temporal concern. Notwithstanding I was on that wretched isle but briefly, I witnessed there unspeakable cruelties for the most trivial of offenses (floggings, maimings, burnings, stakes driven through limbs into the ground), the least of which troubled me greatly. I am aware that it is a tender point to speak to, but apprehend I am not clear in the sight of heaven without I speak to it. On the ship that brought me to America after my return to England was a young black man, slave to my friend C———, who in the course of the voyage desired me to teach him to read, that he might read the Bible. The slave came to my cabin when not in the throes of seasickness, which to say truth was seldom (or so it seemed), yet in such times was I moved to feel the common humanity we shared as equally subjects of redeeming grace, his voice speaking the strange, new sounds I uttered, his somber head bent over the page as we sat on the ground on a mattress in the close cabin, afloat together on a wide and empty sea. He shewed himself an apt pupil, and my heart reached out to him in kindness, even unto the morning of his flight (on limbs too sturdy to have been after all much discommoded by sickness) from the quay and into the labyrinth of lanes and alleyways as soon as ever we landed at York. Seeing him disappear I was provoked at the man's deceit and as it then seemed ingratitude, which only later appeared to me in a different light. For I was led finally to wonder what might I have done in the black man's stead, ashore in a strange land where I had not sought to come? And might not my white man's resolution have appeared mere obstinacy, my resignation under adversity like the black man's indolence or stupor, what wisdom I had naught but craft and cunning?

In York in that first year after my arrival, I beheld so many vices and corruptions spreading that were in a measure occasioned by this trade in human souls and way of life of which I write, that it came to appear to me as a dark gloominess hanging over the land. Surely, surely bondage is inconsistent with the plainest precepts of the gospel, the dictates of reason, and every common sentiment of humanity. Those were fearful months in truth, the town gripped by terrors of the Negro Plot so called, of which I have writ and mean to write elsewhere in these pages. Among the conspirators named in time was this same escaped slave, taken up at one of the markets some months after. Being persuaded of his innocence (the slave having been in the country and abed with frostbite through much of his absence), his master, my friend C———, determined to save him if he could, and thus seek to affect certain persons in high station with the desire to put an end to a phrenzy that was every day more firmly and grievously established. Being a gentleman of influence, as belonging to a family of great consequence in England, C——— seemed likely to press his point to some purpose, the more so as the net of conspiracy was spread ever wider during those days to include some, white and black, who appeared maliciously accused, and in no way capable of the villainies charged against them.

One such was an old black man in the family of her who later became my wife and helpmeet.* So evident was it, to all that considered the matter dispassionately, that the slave was unjustly accused, that my friend C——— (among others) found himself henceforth grown outspoken and in ever warmer disputes with some about the town, going so far finally as to utter doubts of the very hatching of a conspiracy, even though some to whom he put forth that opinion were heard to mutter that he was "like to get his guts squeezed out" and such like talk, did he not study to hold his tongue. For the fever of fear that had seized the town raged on, notwithstanding the growing number that

---

*One of three references to Elizabeth Pursell in all the *Reminiscences,* and resembling the other two in its brevity.

were coming to question the worth of confessions extorted, and the justice of punishing crimes of such hazy substance.

It will be observed that two black men had earlier confessed at the stake to the firing of the fort, &c., but had not those same two wretches been importuned with promises of a pardon for doing so, who perished nonetheless to gratify a raving multitude? From the confessions of others the town had learned of plots to burn the houses at night (as was confirmed by many), and yet each of the several fires had occurred in the light of day. The town, it was said, was to be burned upon signal, yet the fires had happened singly. Indeed, thirty or forty blacks, as we were first to believe, would do battle with all the whites of York, no fewer than two thousand or more adult males, armed and ever on their guard for such a rising. To that add that there was much disagreement among the prisoners as to when the plot had been first hatched, some saying later, some earlier, some as far in the past as Whitsuntide was twelvemonth, some even so distant in time as two years or more. We were to believe that recruits were got drunk and then sworn at the tapster's, but would such a terrific conspiracy be manned in so easy a style, and so early, too, before being put into effect, to include most of the blacks in town, nay throughout the whole province (as was finally affirmed), and not a word leak out to a single slave's master before the first fire was set?

Having considered these things, I felt difficulties in increasing numbers arising in my mind, though being young and new to the land it was not pleasant to find myself under a necessity to question the judgment of elders, and such more especially as had a good character (counselors, justices, aldermen, and the like). Nevertheless, I did in midsummer, not trusting myself to speak (as diffident of speech then, and scarce able to frame words when discomfited), write and dispatch the following to the recorder, who was sitting as one of the justices in the trials of the negroes:

Your honor will apprehend the design of what follows is to endeavor the putting an end to the bloody tragedy that is acting amongst us in regard to poor negroes and whites too. As is known, five negroes were recently executed in one day at the gallows, a favor of sorts, for one next day was burnt at the stake, where he impeached several others, and amongst them some whites. What grounds the court proceeds upon I must acknowledge myself informed of in part only, but these five who were but a short time ago put to death denied any guilt, as have many others so dealt with.

Having refrained of late from attending at court, I know little of its present proceedings. But I am humbly of opinion that even had all who have been hanged or burnt first confessed, what they said (unless certain overt acts appear to confirm the same) would have been scarce worth the effort to set their words down. Many times such confessions are obtained by questionable means, by force or torment, by surprise, by flattery, by distraction, by prisoners' discontent with their circumstance, or through envy that they may bring others into the same condemnation, or in hopes of a longer time to live, or to die an easier death, &c. For anybody would choose rather to be hanged than to be burnt, tho' one would say much to avoid either the one death or the other.

It is true the fort was fired, but that might have been by accident, as first supposed, or as the single act of some malicious person or persons of whatever color. (As to a brand lying under the rafters all night without burning until breathed upon the morning after, sure that marvel seems scarce to be credited.) Concerning the other fires about town, some such are not to be wondered at after the long winter through which we have passed, with chimneys of houses put to much hard use. Feats may indeed have been performed against us, but perhaps none so grave or so numerous as to petrify our hearts against all the poor blacks of the city, and some of our neighbor whites as well. One thing for a certainty seems impossible *in rerum natura:* that the blacks (among whom are rational persons) should attempt the destruction of a city when it is impossible they should escape the just and direful vengeance of the countries round about, which would immediately and unavoidably pour in upon them and destroy them all.

Doubtless there have been some murmuring amongst the negroes, and a mad fellow or two has threatened and designed revenge for the cruelty and inhumanity they have met with, which is too rife in the English plantations. But if that be all, it is a great pity there have been such severe animadversions. And if nothing will put an end hereto till by God's will some of higher degree and better circumstances be accused, may that come soon, lest all the poor people perish in the merciless flames of an imaginary plot.

In the meantime excuse me and don't be offended, if out of friendship to my neighbors and compassion to the negroes (who are flesh and blood as well as we, and ought to be treated with humanity) I entreat the court not to go on to massacre and destroy your own estates by making bonfires of the negroes, thereby loading yourselves with guilt far greater than any of theirs. For we have too much reason to fear that the Divine Vengeance does and will pursue us for our ill treatment to the bodies and souls of the poor slaves.

All which is humbly submitted by a well wisher to all humane beings and one that ever desires to be of the merciful side. . . .

* * *

Three entries from Corimer's journal:

Sunday, July 19. Met with the second justice in the churchyard and walked toward home with him in company with

213

several others. Turning on King Street, "there be amongst us," says H to a gentleman at his side, "some wanton, wrong-headed persons who take the liberty to arraign the justice of our proceedings." I felt myself grow warm, but with an effort remained in countenance. My slave Jack, as your honor well knows, is back in custody, and yet is innocent. "That remains to be determined," says H with a smile. "But I am surprised, my lord, that you make such a difficulty about his obstinate silence"—that the man will confess to no wrongdoing. He will (said I) confess to nothing he did not do, and indeed, so I reminded the justice, many of those punished early had protested their innocence before God. Such protestations troubled me then. They trouble me now, since the governor's recent proclamation, when it has become the very fashion amongst blacks to name new conspirators. To accuse whites too, though until a fortnight past but two or three whites were named and not another besides. *Facile est inventis addere.* Nay, sir (I pressed on), too many questions remain unanswered for me to be easy. As, why did not the blacks arise at the first firing of the fort, in the manner they are said to have plotted to do? "Why, sir, because Major Van Horne drummed forth his militia and paraded them through the streets. For that fortunate reason only." But can it be credited that an ignorant taverner meant in truth to erect a kingdom, with himself as king and his pitiful daughter as princess and the black man Caesar as governor? "Nay, sir, I do not believe so. That was but to impress fools and negroes." Yet surely a train of policy has been set in motion here that, if report is to be trusted, goes far beyond what could be expected from such an one, and him with a wife and house full of children, and scarce any visible business or means of subsistence. How, pray, was Hughson able to support such extraordinary generosity to the blacks of the town, as feasting large numbers of them and giving them drink? "From the profits of their thievery," says Horsmanden in reply, "and from the Spaniard." The Spaniard? "Ay," and he pulls forth from his waistcoat, with a sort of flourish that was very vexing (the others relishing the moment), a paper on which proved to be written the text of a letter from my father's old friend, General Oglethorpe, to the governor of New York. "Your lordship will please to read this," cries H, "and favor us with an opinion of its contents."

It was writ from Georgia in mid-May last, and told of a party of Indians that had brought a Spanish prisoner to Gen. Oglethorpe after an engagement near Augustine. The prisoner gave an account of a certain villainous design, viz., that the Spaniards were employing emissaries to burn all the magazines and considerable towns in English North America, to prevent the subsisting of the expedition to the West Indies, employing for the purpose many priests posing as physicians, dancing masters, and such like. "Well, my lord?" says H, all but prancing with impatience. Yet I scarce knew what to answer, this rumor of mischief seeming so flimsy a reed to build upon. Suppose for a moment (said I, changing the subject) that some one of us, ruttish and in his cups, had toyed in a dark lane with that beauty that was hanged some weeks back. Nay, for a moment only, suppose it so. If she in the last court session had pointed the accusing finger our way, would not any one of us here have denied it, even to save such a trifle as our repute amongst the gentlemen at the club? What, roger a nigger's whore? And yet how much more cause do those in prison have to abuse the truth. "It pleases your lordship to be whimsical," says H. Nay, sir—but they only smiled and sauntered on. . . .

Tuesday, July 21. This morning Milne and I took to the Boston road and found ourselves at mid-day in the village of Harlem. Stopped at the sign of the Dove, situated prettily at the foot of a hill, cattle grazing on the plain in one direction, a little river passing through a meadow before it. Commodious kitchen within. Dined upon what I never had eat before in my life, a dish of fried clams, of which shell fish there is abundance on the island. Landlady spoke only Dutch, but her husband some English. He knew whom I inquired for by my description, and set us on our way well-fed and content. In the afternoon passed a prodigy: a fat sheep riding in a chaise, a negro upon the box. Milne asks, Is that your master? No, says the black solemnly; was a weather belonging to Mr. Lovel, which had strayed and would not come home without being carried. Road stony and uneven. Rested a portion of the afternoon in shade, then well before sundown came upon the farm as Jack had described it. Three trees and a pond in the front; across the road trees hung with gray moss; roof of the corncrib caved in. Inquired of the mistress of the house where was the master. In York, at one Comfort's, a cooper, but the man's father was there, venerable, with long gray hair, seated in the sun in the vegetable garden, who recollects Jack perfectly well and confirms all that the runaway has said. Mistress brings tea, chimes in with further corroboration and some queries: will he be coming back then? Are we to have him back? Stayed the night. Milne's room in the rear, though cramped, appears more airy and pleasant than my own.

Wednesday, July 22. Concerning the slaves, Judge H earlier brooded much, as he told me, whose mind is now fixed and settled. More than once in times past have we spoke of it. Against the cry of a gentleman of his acquaintance that wished all blacks back where they came from, to leave us in peace amongst ourselves: "We must ransom them from their national tyrants," said H, "however disagreeable the task, and transplant them under the benign influences of the law and gospel." It is an onerous duty of ours, says he, to wean them from idolatry and afterward keep them Christians; the negroes among us meanwhile have been advanced to much greater degrees of felicity than those left behind, though not (to be sure) to absolute liberty. With more of the like. To seal the point he is pleased to quote scripture—*Both thy bondmen and thy bondmaids, which thou shalt have, shall be of the heathen that are round about you. . . .*

Late this afternoon return with Milne to town. Pursell's new greenhouse with more than half the lights in place. S with his tooth out retires to P's for solace that E's attentions provide, tending him with porridge, etc., and making the ordeal near easeful. The family generally despondent, however, and concerned for their servant Venture, so that I did not stay to trouble them long. Hughson's draggletailed daughter has this day confirmed the negro's guilt in court. . . .

* * *

The confirmation had occurred in the course of testimony by Sarah, fifteen-year-old offspring of the doomed taverner, during her second examination before the magistrates

As far back as June 11 that same child had heard her death date postponed for the first time, on the evening before her father, her mother, and the Newfoundland Beauty had been taken to the fields and hanged: "it is thought proper to respite Sarah's execution one week, to Friday, 19th June, in hopes that after her father and mother have suffered, the girl may be mollified to a confession of her own guilt and raise some merit by making a further discovery . . ."

Thereafter she had been subjected to an ordeal in prison that might have unhinged the most settled stoic. When the initial week had passed, the date of her execution had been "further respited until next Friday sevennight, though this is a mere act of mercy, for she remains inflexible." Having once more approached to within a day of her end, the child learned Thursday, June 25, that her trip to the gallows had again been deferred, "until tomorrow sevennight." But as the new date came round, she did reluctantly make a first confession, one that was immediately retracted upon her returning to jail, so that the exasperated judges "thought themselves under a necessity of ordering her execution once for all, as the last experiment to bring her to unfold her infernal secret."

Accordingly, the girl, who was just fifteen, had been assured Friday, July 10, that she would be executed on the morrow, "between the hours of nine and one." Yet during the course of the following morning, and despite "the continued untoward behavior of this wretch," her execution was postponed another week. That most recently designated date arrived, but again Sarah was granted a reprieve to live beyond it, so that at the beginning of the following week, Monday, July 20, part of the court's business was taken up ordering her execution "Wednesday sevennight next."

At that, Sarah Hughson's "stubborn deportment," her "untractable temper" gave way. Within two days she was responding amply to a second examination, finally telling the magistrates what they wanted to hear. The slave Venture had indeed been often at her father's. Ury the priest was many times there as well, as charged by both Mary Burton and one William Kane. Other interesting testimony was on her tongue, so that it came about, after having lived six full weeks almost daily at the point of death, and having had her sentence deferred six separate times, Sarah Hughson was thought fit at last to be recommended to the governor for a pardon as an object of mercy, "having discovered some truths not before brought to light, and having given very material evidence against John Ury, now in custody and soon to be tried, with her assurance that she will keep to her history concerning him. . . ."

The priest Ury will be dealt with in a moment. William Kane, whose testimony against him the girl's had confirmed, was a soldier stationed at the fort, "aged about forty, born in Athlone in Ireland, who had been in this country four and thirty years." In a recent appearance at court Mary Burton had accused Kane of being often at Hughson's, "amongst Hughson, his wife, &c., and the negroes, when they were talking of the conspiracy, and that he was one of the confederates." Interrogated separately, Kane had denied it: "never was at Hughson's house, nor did he know where it was." So flat a contradiction had impressed the chief justice, who thereafter "thought proper to admonish Mary Burton in an awful and solemn manner concerning the nature of an oath and the consequences of taking a false one, more especially as it affected a man's life." But the servant girl had answered back smartly enough "that she was acquainted with the nature of an oath very well, and that she would not take a false one upon any account. She repeated the charge against Kane over and over, and persisted in it, that what she said was truth. All which Kane, when informed of it, as positively denied."

The two had been brought into the same room to confront each other: a teenage serving maid, the gruff, forty-year-old soldier. "As Kane entered, Mary shook her head at the sight of the man, and being asked upon the oath she had taken whether she had seen him before, and what she knew of him? she declared to his face to the effect aforesaid. But the soldier stoutly denied all she charged, and declared he had never seen her, at which the girl laughed."

By now a laugh from that source could kill. "Mary was then ordered to withdraw, and Kane was apprised of the danger he was in, and told he must not flatter himself with the least hopes of mercy but by making a candid confession of all that he knew of the matter. For a while he continued to deny what Mary had alleged against him, till upon most solemn admonition he began to be affected. His countenance changed, and being near fainting he desired to have a glass of water, which was brought him. After some pause, he said he would tell the truth, though at the same time he seemed loath to do it. Nevertheless, the man began slowly to open, and several hours were spent in taking down heads of his confession, which were afterward drawn out at large and distinctly read over to him. Being duly sworn, he made oath that the same was true, and (not knowing how to write) put his mark to it."

Kane had confessed to some novel enormities. After being relieved at nine one night near Christmas last, he had been approached, so he said, in the guardroom at the fort and taken to the Fighting Cocks on New Street in order to witness a christening by a Romish priest. "They had a child there and christened it, and the priest handed the book about." The acquaintance who had taken him to the ritual was one Corker, who three or four days later had remarked, "By God, I have a mind to burn the fort." And some time after the fire at Fort George, that same Corker had gone to work in the country, out about the White-plains, so Kane believed. There was a little man had lodged at Corker's who was a priest, and many Negroes had been christened by the same when visiting at Hughson's, where he often was, and where he had endeavored to seduce Kane himself to the Romish religion, telling him what a fine thing it was to be a Roman, for they could forgive sins and would not go to hell. At Hughson's, "there was a ring made on the floor," according to Kane, "about two feet and a half diameter, and Hughson bid everyone pull off the left shoes and put toes within the ring, and Mrs. Hughson held a bowl of punch over their heads as the negroes stood round the circle, and Hughson pronounced the oath, swearing by thunder and lightning that God's curse and hellfire fall on them that first discovered the plot to so much as a cat or a dog." That same Hughson had designed to burn the English church last Christmas Day, but Ury the priest had said they had better let it alone until good weather, when the roof might be dry and a larger congregation gathered within. Roosevelt's Quack often said that after he had destroyed his master he would ride in a coach. And Holt the dancing master, who had since thought proper (like the shoemaker Romme whom Peggy accused) to ship himself off to Jamaica, once whipped his Negro Joe very severely; Joe meeting the soldier Kane on the street next day had said, "That cursed dog my master is the greatest rogue in the world. He would burn all the town to get money. If you knew what was between him and Hughson it would make you stare."

This and more from Kane were in the possession of the examiners when the first of Sarah Hughson's two confessions was given before them in July. To be sure, that first provided the gentlemen little or no satisfaction, because (as the record states) it was so scanty, because it came from her "after much difficulty, with great reluctance," and because immediately afterward she had retracted the little said, denying any knowledge of a conspiracy after all. The examination had occurred July 3, "upwards of three weeks since the execution of her father and mother," on one of the several days she had been scheduled to hang. That morning the girl was brought up to Mr. Pemberton, who came to pray by her. "After all his admonitions she still denied her guilt, but being carried back to her dungeon, at last owned to another prisoner that she had been sworn into the plot. The prisoner, a negro wench, (thinking as may be supposed to make a merit of it) soon after told what had passed to the under-sheriff, who acquainted the judges, and they sent again for Sarah." She now admitted that she had seen the soldier William Kane sworn into the conspiracy one Sunday evening sometime before Christmas, she could not tell exactly when. He had threatened to kill her if she discovered, and the Negroes threatened the same. When an east wind was blowing, the confederates had meant to begin burning the town at the upper end. Ury she knew. The first time she had seen the priest was with the Campbells, on May Day, when they came to take possession of her father's house and take her room from her. Sarah had heard Peggy the Beauty say that Roosevelt's Quack was her sweetheart, and she thought him the handsomest among the Negroes. A middle-sized white man had been at Hughson's, with black hair always cut, of a sharp chin, and also a fresh-colored, long-haired man, both often among the Negroes, drinking with them.

That was the gist of the girl's brief first confession, promptly disavowed and in any case hardly comparable in fullness to the second, three weeks later. "The reader will be apt to conclude that there could be little or no dependence on Sarah's veracity, or that her evidence at best would deserve but slender credit; and indeed the case would have been so if her testimony had stood single." But Kane was testifying as well, and so was Mary Burton, who by this time had learned on the stand to fit herself all too comfortably into the role of witness.

"Mary, tell the story in your own method, but speak slow, not so hastily as you usually do, that the court and jury may the better understand you."

Why, I have seen Ury very often at Hughson's about Christmas and new-year, and then he stayed away a fortnight or three weeks, and returned about the time that Hogg's goods came in our house. And next day the constables came and searched and stepped over the stolen goods several times, and one even poked a stick into the broken stairs where they were, so that I could scarce forbear laughing to see how dumb they were, yet dared not tell them. And I have seen Ury with a book in his hand and heard him read from it, though I did not understand the language. And once I opened a door upstairs and heard him saying to some negars that they need not fear, for he could forgive them their sins as well as God Almighty. But when he saw me at the door, he bid me go away, and asked me what business I had there. He was angry and shut the door to, but I looked under it after, and there was a black ring upon the floor, and things in it that seemed to look like rats, I don't know what they were. [*Here the record—ignoring or unaware of the impossibility of discerning through the crack beneath a door a circle drawn on a floor within—obliges us in a footnote by identifying what Mary saw as the black toes of the Negroes, "as might be supposed."*] Another time I heard Ury talking with the negars, Cuff and others, about the plot, and he turned the negars out of the room and asked me to swear, and Hughson and his wife fetched silks and gold rings and offered them to me in case I would swear. But I would not, and they said I was a fool. And one night I was listening at the door of the room upon the stairs, some time about new-year, and I looked through the door and saw upon the table a black thing like a child, and Ury put salt on it and was reading from a book in a strange language, and having a spoon in my hand I happened to let it drop upon the floor, and Ury came out of the room running after me downstairs, and he fell into a tub of water which stood at the foot of the stairs, and I ran away. When they were doing anything extraordinary at nights, they would send me to bed. But I verily believe they meant to murder me, or send me away in a boat, and would have, but that Goody Kannady relieved me from the hands of my enemies by taking me from Hughson's, and she has been better than ever my mother was to me, she and Mrs. Masters have.

Thus the rambling testimony of the king's principal witness, confirmed at certain points by the soldier Kane and by Hughson's daughter Sarah, the latter testifying finally to the examiners' satisfaction July 22. Points of similarity in the statements of the two girls might have seemed all the more remarkable considering what the record notes as Sarah's "inveterate spleen" toward Mary, "who was the cause of the conspirators' detection." The version of events that Sarah provided did differ in some respects from those of Kane and of Burton, each of which had presented its own discrepancies. For example, Sarah placed Ury, not Hughson, in the chalk ring drawn on the floor of the tavern room: "he stood in the middle with a cross in his hand, and there swore all the negroes to be concerned in the plot." Moreover, she claimed to have heard Vaarck's Caesar, Philipse's Cuffee, and other Negroes say that they used to go to Ury's lodging, where they prayed in private after the popish fashion, and that the priest forgave them whatever sins they would commit in burning the town and cutting of the people's throats. Ury christened many Negroes, according to Sarah, "crossed them on the face, had water and other things." He had once told her, Sarah, that she, too, must confess what sins she had been guilty of to him, and he would then forgive her them. "I answered him that I had been guilty of no other sins but cursing and swearing in a passion, and that I did not believe anybody could forgive my sins but God." But Ury had insisted that yes, he and all priests could, if the people did but do what priests bade them and followed all their directions. To Ury, Peggy the Beauty used to confess in private the sum total of the wickedness she had done in the world. And the soldier Kane used often to come there to Hughson's with the Negroes. But the slave in the checked shirt, he that went by the name of Jack, Sarah had seen only once at her father's, and did not believe he was in the conspiracy. Pursell's Venture was, however, and Kortrecht's Frans and Van Rantz's Diego, and some others as not yet named.

For such candor, and her pledge to the court to stand by the vivid testimony concerning Ury that she had provided, Sarah did gain her pardon, which was applied for to the governor July 27.

That was three days after another group of Negroes, among the last so dealt with, had been taken to the fields as conspirators and put to death. About noon Friday, July 24, "Van Rantz's Diego, Ryker's Frank, Pursell's Venture, Walton's Fortune, and Rutgers's Galloway were executed according to sentence. In the afternoon Harry, the negro doctor, was executed; in the way from the jail to the stake there were several endeavored to persuade him to make a confession, but Harry's heart was hardened, and he would discover nothing."

Nor would Venture, about whom the record says only that he "had more sense than the common rank of his tribe." Not sense enough, to be sure, to save his life with a lie. Of what the Pursells were feeling on that midsummer Friday, no trace survives from their own hand. Indeed, Venture's would have been simply one more name among those inarticulate, scarcely distinguishable slaves, his plight and the effect of his fate left mute like the others, had it not been for Elizabeth's agonized letter to her English friend that by chance has come into the possession of her descendants—that and a brief entry in Corimer's journal. Whether the English aristocrat attended the execution is unclear. Did he see Venture go to his doom, or was Corimer only recording what he had heard of the manner in which the black met "the terrors of death and the lighted pile"? However the facts were acquired, his lordship's journal for the twenty-fourth contains a single terse, affecting notation: "This date Venture with four others are murdered before the rabble by judicial order. In his behavior the man shewed a brave and undaunted mind, nothing like fear appearing in him. He died without acknowledging any guilt."

* * *

Sarah Hughson's pardon was applied for three days later, shortly before the trial of John Ury as Romish priest and conspirator, at which trial her testimony, with Burton's and Kane's, provided the principal evidence.

The twenty-ninth day of July, in the fifteenth year of the reign of our sovereign lord George II, by the grace of God King of Great Britain, &c.

At the city of New York, the king against Sarah Hughson, daughter.

This criminal convict being set to the bar, the court demanded of her why execution of her former sentence should not be awarded against her? She thereupon produced and pleaded His Majesty's most gracious pardon, and the same was read and allowed of.

The king against John Ury.

Prisoner brought to the bar. Court proceeds upon his trial.

Gentlemen of the jury, look upon the prisoner and hearken to his charge:

Said John Ury, private schoolmaster . . . of his malice aforethought did feloniously counsel, abet, and encourage the negroman slave called Quack to enter into a certain dwelling house of our lord the king, then standing within the fort of New York, and there wickedly and wilfully to set on fire and destroy the said dwelling . . .

The attorney general opens the indictment.

"Gentlemen, the prisoner will be shown to have been at Hughson's house, counseling and encouraging the divers negroes there, baptizing, swearing them into a plot to kill and destroy. This that I allege, as well as his counseling of the slave Quack to burn the fort and much more besides, you will hear fully proved by the witnesses for the king.

"But before entering upon their examination, give me leave,

gentlemen, to say a few words concerning the popish religion in general, a murderous religion for which the prisoner will be shown to have manifested much zeal. For murderous it is. They who profess it hold the killing and destroying of all that differ in opinion from them to be not only lawful but meritorious, if so doing may any way serve the interest of their crafty and deceiving church, the whole scheme of which seems to be a restless endeavor to extirpate all other religions whatsoever, more especially the Protestant religion, which they maliciously call the Northern heresy. And to attain their wicked ends, they scruple not to use subtle arguments to persuade the laity out of its senses, devising to get an absolute dominion over the conscience that they may the more easily pick the pockets of credulous people. Witness their pretended pardons and indulgences. Witness their masses to pray souls out of purgatory, which they quote (or rather wrest) scripture for, when no such thing is to be found there—mere inventions and cheats to gull the simpleminded. Witness their doctrine of transubstantiation, so big with absurdities that it is shocking to the reason of mankind, for were that doctrine true, their priests by a few words out of their mouths could make a God as often as they please—and eat Him too. And this they have the impudence to call honoring and adoring Him. Blasphemous wretches! for hereby they endeavor to be exalted above God himself, inasmuch as the creator must necessarily be greater than his creature. These and many other such juggling tricks have they in their hocus pocus bloody religion, which has been stripped of all its wretched disguise and fully exposed by many eminent divines, more particularly by the great Dr. Tillotson, whose extraordinary endowments of mind and exemplary piety have gained him such universal esteem as no doubt will endure as long as the Protestant religion lasts, which I hope will be to the end of time.

"Now, gentlemen, hear the witnesses prove what I have alleged against this popish prisoner. After, I make no doubt but you will, for your oath's sake and for your country's peace and future safety, find him guilty."

Call Mary Burton.

Mary Burton sworn. She gives her testimony, following which the prisoner is allowed to put questions to her.

PRISONER. You say you have seen me several times at Hughson's. What clothes did I usually wear?

MARY BURTON. I cannot tell what clothes you wore particularly.

PRISONER. That is strange, and know me so well.

BURTON. I have seen you in several clothes, but you chiefly wore a riding coat, and often a brown coat trimmed with black.

PRISONER. I never wore any such coat. What time of day did I used to come to Hughson's?

BURTON. You used chiefly to come in the night time. When I have been going to bed I have seen you undressing in Peggy's room, as if you were to lie there; but I cannot say that you did, for you was always gone before I was up in the morning.

PRISONER. What room was I in when I closed the door in anger upon you, as you said?

BURTON. In the great room upstairs.

PRISONER. And what answer did the negroes make when I offered to forgive them their sins?

BURTON. I don't remember. . . .

Call William Kane.

William Kane, soldier, sworn. Testifies. Prisoner puts questions to him.

PRISONER. You say you have seen me very often, and several times at Hughson's. Pray what clothes did you see me in?

KANE. I have seen you in black. I have seen you in a yellowish great coat, and sometimes in a straight-bodied coat of much the same color.

PRISONER. You say you saw me christen a child in New Street. How was the child dressed, and what ceremony did I use?

KANE. The child was not naked; it was dressed as usual. You put it on your left arm and sprinkled it with water three times and put salt in its mouth and crossed it.

PRISONER. Who was present at the christening?

KANE. Eight or nine persons, I think: you, the mother of the child, myself, Jerry Corker, three or four more. . . .

Call Sarah Hughson.

PRISONER. I except against her being sworn, for she has been convicted and received sentence of death for being concerned in this conspiracy, and therefore cannot be a witness.

ATTORNEY GENERAL. But, Mr. Ury, she has received his majesty's most gracious pardon, which she pleaded in court this morning before you was brought up, and it has been allowed of. Therefore, the law says she is good evidence. H. Hawk. title pardon. Chap. 37. §48.

COURT. By law she may be admitted.

Sarah Hughson sworn. Testifies. Prisoner puts his questions to her.

PRISONER. How did I swear you into the plot at Hughson's?

HUGHSON. On a book. I believe it was an English book.

PRISONER. Who was present when I swore you?

HUGHSON. My parents, Peggy, Kane, and others.

PRISONER. You say I baptized several people. Pray what ceremony did I use at baptizing?

HUGHSON. You made a cross upon the negroes' faces, and sprinkled water. You used something else, but I cannot tell what. And you talked in a language that I did not understand.

PRISONER. Whom did I baptize?

HUGHSON. Caesar, Prince, Bastian, Quack, Cuffee, and several other negroes. . . .

COURT [to king's counsel]. Have you any more witnesses?

COUNSEL. Sir, we shall rest here at present.

COURT. Mr. Ury, have you any witnesses? For now is your time to produce them.

Prisoner calls his witnesses.

A Mr. Webb testifies that he became acquainted with the prisoner November last, learned he was a schoolmaster lately come from Philadelphia, and asked him would he teach a child of the witness. "I sent my child to him, and he taught him Latin, and after this I recommended him to Colonel Beekman, to teach his daughter to write and cipher. Ury and I growing more intimate, I observed a poor appearance in his habit, which I thought his pocket might be answerable for. Accordingly I gave him an invitation to my house, telling him he should be welcome at my table noon and night, and he frequently came during the winter and would stay late discoursing, after which I have often accompanied him home to his lodgings. He told me he was a nonjuring minister, ordained by the senior nonjuror in England. I asked him what was the signification of nonjuror. He answered that the difference between nonjurors and others was in this: in the prayers for the king and royal family we mention no names, as others do. I asked him if then he prayed for the Pretender? He said he prayed for the king, let him be who he will, he mentioned no names. . . ."

Mr. Campbell is called and testifies. Witness says that Ury to his knowledge never was at Hughson's "till I went in his company to take possession of the house at May Day last. As we were going there together, Mr. Ury said he did not know the way thither, and he took Gerardus Comfort's house for Hughson's. I regard Mr. Ury as a grave, sober, honest man. . . ."

Mrs. Campbell is called. Accused addresses her thus: "Will you please to give an account to the court of what you know of me, and of what passed between Sarah Hughson and me when you and your husband and I went to take possession of your house?"

A. CAMPBELL. I went with my husband and Mr. Ury on May Day last to take possession of the house that had been Hughson's. When we came there, Sarah Hughson the daughter was in possession, and we told her she must go out of the house, for my husband had taken it. Whereupon the girl swore and cursed at me. Mr. Ury said to her, "How dare you talk so saucily to an old woman! Come out of the house, or I will turn you out." But the girl bolted the door and was got out only by the timely arrival of constables that had come to fetch her to jail. And as they were removing her, she swore miserably and shouted at us, "You have a house now, but shall not have one long." As for Mr. Ury, I will say that I have often heard him pray and sing psalms, and he prayed by a sick woman. I never saw any harm in him at all, a good sober sort of man. My husband and he were to keep school together. . . .

COURT [*to prisoner*]. Will you ask your witnesses any more questions?

PRISONER. No, sir. I have nothing more.

King's counsel addresses the court.

"Before the prisoner enters upon his defense, we conceive it will be proper to read to him some passages out of sundry books that declare the customs and usages of the church of Rome. Unless he can make it appear that his own practices as a cleric are warranted by the usage of any other church, the passages will likely convince everybody that he is a priest of the Roman church and no other. First, as to the use of salt. Peter de Moulin, in a book entitled *Anatomie de la Messe,* part 2, p. 94, gives us the form of the priests' exorcising salt in order to prepare it for their superstitious uses. Because the prisoner professes himself a scholar, I shall first read in the original, then render it into English. '*Exorciso te, creatura salis, per Deum vivum, per Deum verum, per Deum sanctum . . .*' In English thus— Creature of salt, I exorcise thee by the living God, the true God, the holy God, &c. . . . As to the popish use of salt in baptism, we have testimony in their catechism, 66th question: 'Why is salt put to the mouth of the person that is baptized?' As to the point of absolution, we have the Jesuits' doctrine in *Les Provinciales, ou Lettres écrites par Louis Montalte,* Tom. 2, lettre 10: "*On peut absoudre . . .*' In English thus—A man may be absolved who confesses that the hope of absolution encouraged him to commit sin with the greater ease. This is the doctrine of the church of Rome, contrary to that of St. Paul, who says, *Shall we continue in sin that grace may abound? God forbid.* May it please your honors, this is all we shall mention at present, that the prisoner in his defense may take notice if he choose. But that the prisoner is a Romish emissary, sent according to the intimation in General Oglethorpe's letter of May last, I think must be concluded from what has been given in evidence against him."

COURT. Mr. Ury, now is it time for you to make your defense.

PRISONER. May it please the king's judges and the gentlemen of the jury. How could I have had a hand in this plot that I am charged with and yet have acted such a lunatic part as to continue in the city, even publicly advertising myself for teaching of grammar? Why would I have behaved thus? Nay, a week and a few days before I was taken into custody, Mr. Webb had given me caution that the eyes of the city were fixed upon me as a stranger to the place and a suspected Roman. But I valued not what the world said, answering him that my innocency would protect me. Were my actions then or thereafter those of a plotter and a guilty man?

"Again, the negro who confessed that he set fire to the fort: why did he not mention me in all his confession? And why did not Hughson once name me in all the time before he was finally put to death? And his wife, and the creature that was hanged with them, and each of those that have been put to death since: why did not one of them mention a single word of me? No, what is of note is that Hughson himself was sworn to be the whole projector of the plot. . . .

"Now certainly, gentlemen, priests are crafty and cunning. If I am a priest, as you take me to be, could I have been so foolish as to bind myself with a cord for negroes or profligate whites to make an halter for me by their babbling? Had I done so, would not such a plotter, and he a priest, have been the next person after the discovery of the conspiracy to have been brought on the carpet?

"Gentlemen, as there is a great unknown and tremendous being whom we call God, I never, excepting in his last moments, did see the negro that is said to have fired the fort. And as there is a God, I never to my knowledge knew or saw Hughson, his wife, or the creature that was hanged with them, living, dying, or dead.

"As to my professing to be an ecclesiastic of the church of Rome, how can I prove myself not to be what I never was? Yet is it probable, given the penalties, that I would be so childish as to admit as much to any person out of communion? And how came those three illiterates who have spoke against me to know so much of arcane matters? To wit, if their evidences saw me celebrating of masses, they must have seen more, for there can be no masses without two and sometimes four at the altar. Yet such persons know nothing of what mass is but by conjecture, no more than they know a vesper from a compline.

"Gentlemen, I am no popish priest, but a nonjuring minister of the English church, a true Protestant and far from having regard for any popish prince. Much this afternoon has been offered here to show my innocency of the charge against me. Now I must ask that you gentlemen consider all that has been said with minds unprejudiced, being as you are lovers of truth, with a tender regard to life.

"Your honor, I have no more to say."

The court then calls counsel to sum up the evidence for the king, which is done in a flood of imagery. Works of darkness have manifested themselves among us in many blazing effects, yet the secret springs of the mischief have lain long concealed. At length we may conclude that they have taken their rise from a foreign influence. The monstrous wickedness of the plot might impeach its credit among strangers, but when considered as the inhuman dictates of the public enemy and a bloody religion, the wonder ceases. Cruel and unnatural have been the attempts of popery: the valleys of Piedmont, the ashes of the Waldenses and Albigenses, the massacre at Paris, the horrible slaughter by the Duke of Alba—all sacrifices to the Roman idol, to the scarlet whore perpetually drunk on an ocean of foreign blood. And nearer home, the execrable design of the gunpowder treason, to blow into bits king, lords, and commons, the intestine fire in the late unnatural civil war, the bloody massacre of thousands of Protestants by the Irish papists, who like their cohorts never boggle at the vilest means, sanctifying their villainies and canonizing their monsters of iniquity.

"The mischiefs we have suffered or been threatened with are now seen to be but a sprout from those evil roots of Spain and Rome, a small stream from those overflowing fountains of destruction. Nor need we wonder to see a popish priest at this bar as prime incendiary. When a man has imbibed such principles, he can easily divest himself of everything that is human but his shape. And that the prisoner has imbibed them, and has abetted the slave Quack to burn his majesty's house in the fort, has been fully proved by the testimony of three witnesses. Two, indeed, have been concerned in the plot, but we have shown them under present circumstances to be legal witnesses.

"As for the prisoner's own defense, he tells you that he must have been a lunatic to have stayed in town after notice if he had been guilty. But, gentlemen, all wickedness is in some sort madness. He lays stress on his rough language to Sarah Hughson at Campbell's, but this may be accounted for as proceeding from causes other than his innocence. Perhaps he resented a supposed injury to himself, who wanted the room she took up in that house. Or perhaps he designed to make a show that he never had been acquainted with her—for priests, as he tells us himself, are artful and cunning. As to what he alleges concerning the conspirators who died not having accused him, we think little can be inferred thence in his favor. Quack accused in general terms many more than he particularly named, and indeed the confession that the negro made was in the hurries of death, after he had been fastened to the stake. Hughson, his wife, and the creature that died with them confessed nothing at all; therefore, nothing can be inferred from their not accusing the prisoner. It does seem strange, by the way, that Mr. Ury could not give us the name of that creature with the Hughsons, seeing as Mary Burton says he was so well acquainted with her as to have had the liberty of undressing himself in her bedroom.

"As to the prisoner's appeal to God for his innocence, this we conceive manifests nothing in his favor, but rather against him; for we often find that the wickedest of men will attempt to cloak their villainies thus, whereas good men are ever sparing in their appeals to heaven. . . ."

Much more followed in the same vein of eloquence before counsel ended at last, leaving members of the jury to the direction of their consciences. But the outcome of this contest between the king and one of his humbler subjects was, of course, inevitable. Two weeks before the trial, at his arraignment July 15, John Ury had "prayed a copy of the indictment" against him, a request that the court had refused. The prisoner had thus entered on his defense scarcely knowing what he was charged with, unaware of which witnesses he would confront or what they would testify, unprepared for rebuttal, without counsel, a stranger and suspect, alone in an atmosphere of hatred and terror. His trial had been fair by the lights of the time, but the glare of those lights showed a man foredoomed. "After staying out about a quarter of an hour"—one-quarter of an hour; fifteen minutes!—"the jury returned, having found the prisoner John Ury guilty of the indictment."

* * *

"The old proverb has herein been verified, that there is scarce a plot but a priest is at the bottom of it." So Recorder Horsmanden, in a letter to an absent friend, summarized the conclusion to be drawn from proceedings that had led to Ury's conviction. Now the recorder's fellow townsmen could begin to hope that he and their other magistrates had indeed plumbed the very depths of the conspiracy. Most of those townsmen were eager to rid themselves promptly of the foiled emissary of the antiChrist, the papist schemer against the peace, though at the prisoner's own request this latest execution was deferred a month, until August 29, "for the settling of his private affairs."

In the interval the officers of the city were not idle. Numerous additional blacks were gathered into the jail for trial during those late summer days, as were a number of white people—Andrew Ryan, Edward Kelly, David Johnson, and others—all implicated by Mary Burton. Yet at the same time was arising from certain quarters "a clamor against the girl. So many negroes being daily taken into custody, some people began to be afraid of losing their slaves; for as matters were then likely to turn out, there was no guessing where or when there would be an end of impeachments."

The grand jury was meanwhile drawing near its discharge. As the conclusion of its term approached, members grew importunate with Burton once for all "to discover every person, black or white, she knew to be engaged in this villainous design; for about this time she had suggested to some that there were white people of more than ordinary rank above the vulgar that were concerned, whom if she named they would not believe her. This having been intimated to the grand jury, they were very pressing with her to discover all she knew, whoever they were. But the girl stood mute. She complained that she had been ill-used, that her life had been threatened by conspirators of both complexions, and she frequently insulted by people of the town for bringing their negroes in question. People did not believe what she said, so what signified speaking? Notwithstanding, she intimated withal that there were some *in ruffles* (a phrase as was understood to mean persons of better fashion than ordinary) that were concerned."

The grand jury turned the girl over to the judges, who now demanded that she hold nothing back. "At last, having been threatened with imprisonment in the dungeon, Mary did name a person which she said she had seen at Hughson's amongst the conspirators around the table, a person of known credit, fortune, and reputation, at the naming of whom the judges were very much astonished."

As well they might have been. The citizen the youthful informant now impeached was Benjamin Pursell, merchant and member himself of the grand jury. The identification was made before the first and second justices Thursday, August 13.

That same day the brig *Roscoe* arrived in the East River from Margate, bringing consequential news concerning another matter to an English friend of Pursell's in the town. As soon as the *Roscoe*'s captain came ashore he sought out the young lord from Hinstead, to whom was conveyed the news that the gentleman's noble father was dead, had taken his own life two months before. In the aftermath, Charles Alexander Corimer had become what he may never have expected to be: the fifth Earl of Cavendham.

V

John Corimer, fourth Earl of Cavendham, K.B., was born April 16, 1687. He succeeded to the title on the death of his grandfather in 1710. His lordship married, first, Charlotte McAleer, daughter of the Earl of Chantry, who died childless in 1713. He next married, in 1714, Anne, Lady Aberway, the mother of his three sons. She dying in 1739, his lordship the following year married Martha, Dowager Lady Galt (later Boswell's confidante), then twenty-two years old; the earl was fifty-three. But within twelve months of the wedding, good fortune forsook his lordship. Two of his sons were dead, one in Rome, the other off the coast of Cartagena; moreover, his third wife had withdrawn her affections to bestow them scandalously on a certain notorious nobleman and gallant at court, pursuing a course of behavior that was reckless enough to provoke universal comment.

Saturday, June 27, 1741, the earl, accompanied by only one servant, set out from his London home and late that same afternoon arrived at Hinstead. It was noted that he seemed "under some discomfort of mind." The next day, according to a contemporary account, "he dined quietly at an early hour. Complaining of indisposition, he declined to take the air but retired early to his chamber, ordering broth to be prepared. The servant that brought the broth found his master at the fireplace burning private papers. It was the last time he was seen alive. Early the next morning, Sunday, June 28, about seven of the clock, he was discovered in the lower part of the garden, next the labyrinth, suspended from a fence and strangled in his handkerchief."

When word of the earl's death reached New York seven weeks later, the authorities there, despite their many preoccupations, were prompt in responding appropriately. Monday, August 17: "On being informed that Alexander, Lord Corimer, has been newly elevated to the earldom of Cavendham, the common council resolves to wait on his lordship and present him with the freedom of the city." Three days later members of the council and principal officers of the city regiment were formally introduced to His Lordship at His Majesty's garrison, in the parade ground of the burned-out fort. In the name of the corporation, Recorder Horsmanden delivered "a very elegant speech" on the occasion, and the mayor presented His Lordship with the copy of his freedom, enclosed in a gold box that was engraved with the arms of the city: "Charles Alexander Corimer, Earl of Cavendham, is hereby admitted, received, and allowed a freeman and citizen of the said city of New York, to have, hold, enjoy, and partake of all and singular the advantages, benefits, liberties, privileges, franchises, freedoms, and immunities whatsoever granted or belonging to the same city, to him and his heirs forever." Next day Bonny Jack was delivered into His Lordship's keeping: "Earl Cavendham's Jack having been indicted for the conspiracy, his master agrees to enter into recognizance to transport him forthwith." And before the following week was out, on the evening of August 28, Corimer set sail with Jack aboard the *George William,* Captain Beck, bound for England.

The long-delayed departure occurred on the eve of the schoolmaster Ury's execution. *The New-York Weekly Journal* for August 31, 1741, takes note of that conclusive event, which Corimer did not stay to see: "On Saturday last was hanged John Ury, known by the name of the popish priest in all the public papers. He persisted in asserting his innocence as to any plot, as well his ignorance of persons concerned therein, although this was proved against him. He died intrepid and without showing the least concern at death." On the scaffold Sheriff Mills had asked the condemned man, before removing his wig that the rope might be noosed about his neck, whether he had any words to deliver. This, in part, was what Ury is recorded as having said:

Fellow Christians—I am now going to suffer a death attended with ignominy and pain. But it is the cross of my dear Redeemer, and I bear it with alacrity; it is the cup that my heavenly Father has put into my hand, and I drink it with pleasure. Now am I to appear before that same awful and tremendous God, a being of infinite purity and unerring justice, a God who will by no means clear the guilty, that cannot be reconciled either to sin or sinners. This is the being at whose bar I am to stand. And in the presence of such a being, the possessor of heaven and earth, I lift up my hands and solemnly protest that I am innocent of what is laid to my charge. I appeal to that great God, that never in my life have I so much as seen Hughson, his wife, or the creature hanged with them, nor never had I knowledge or confederacy with white or black as to any plot. Upon the memorials of the body and blood of my dearest Lord I protest that the witnesses against me are perjured. I never knew the perjured witnesses but at my trial.

Having said thus much, I have no more to say by way of clearing my innocence, knowing that to an unprejudiced mind I must appear guiltless. However, I am not very solicitous about it. I rejoice, and it is now my comfort, that my conscience speaks peace to me, and I depart this waste, this howling wilderness, with a mind serene, free from all malice, with a forgiving spirit, hoping and praying that Jesus, who alone is the giver of repentance, may convince, conquer, and enlighten my murderers' souls. . . .

One of those murderers, as denominated by Ury moments before his death, was Mary Burton, whose burgeoning testimony during these late weeks had been raising doubts among growing numbers of people. "At length there was reason"—so the record concedes—"to conclude that the girl had been tampered withal. Might it not have been suggested to her that she was already sure of the reward offered for discovery of the cause of the fires, and might she not have been tempted to make her own advantage of the affair? Upon this supposition, the surviving conspirators could not have devised a more effectual means to put a stop to further inquiry than by prevailing upon her to call persons into question whose fortunes and characters set them above suspicion"—persons such as the estimable Pursell, merchant and jury member. "Her advisors would thereby not only halt additional discovery, but likewise would have occasion to clamor loudly that there was no plot at all! It was a mere dream! notwithstanding the ruins of his majesty's house in the fort that remain before our eyes as daily evidence of it."

At the end, then, even the record grants that Mary "had told some things incredible at the winding up of this affair." Nevertheless, "but for her, next under the interposition of Divine Providence, this town would in all probability have been laid waste in ashes, and many families massacred." A grateful City Corporation accordingly granted the teenager her freedom from indentures, and almost exactly one year later, Thursday, September 2, 1742, it "ordered at a common council that the mayor should issue his warrant to the treasurer to pay Mr. Moore, for Mary Burton's use and benefit, eighty-one pounds, which with the nineteen pounds before paid by the corporation for the freedom and other necessaries to and for the use of the said Mary, made in the whole one hundred pounds in full of the reward offered. The mayor accordingly issued his warrant, and the money was paid to Mary Burton."

A very substantial sum, far more than an orphan bondwoman might ever have hoped to see in all her life. With it, Mary thereafter was to disappear among the ranks of those many others on this island who have lived out their days unremarkably and left no trace. What finally became of her? After that last mention in the autumn of 1742, no written word survives to give a clue.

Of Pursell, it is clear that his eminent standing in the community protected him from any injury that might have come from Mary's preposterous accusation. Although the serving girl and those who had joined her in testifying had ultimately brought twelve blacks to the stake, eighteen to the gallows, with seventy-one transported from British North America, and although her testimony and that of others who generally corroborated her had led to the arrest of twenty whites and the execution of four of them, she could convince not a single citizen that what she had charged against Benjamin Pursell had any foundation in fact. Indeed, in the aftermath of the charge, when other whites whom she had accused—Andrew Ryan, Edward Kelly, Peter Conolly, David Johnson, John Coffin, Edward Murphy— were placed at the bar Monday, August 31, and proclamations made, no one appeared to prosecute, so that they were promptly discharged. The conspiracy had run its course at last.

But if the reputation of the merchant Pursell survived unscathed through events of that woeful year, his life would soon be troubled from another quarter, by the marriage of his beloved daughter Elizabeth to the itinerant Francis Schaw. Among the endless array of prices, ships' names, ports, and cloth patterns that bestrew the arid prose of his published correspondence, Pursell does make one reference, in a letter of early January 1743, to "the late ills that have agitated me, as my sister's death (tho' to say truth hers was an easy end, the oil of the lamp as 'twere but used up), and more particularly the recent loss of my only daughter in a match beneath her station, from which those who have her interest at heart can hope to take little comfort, and any who know her may expect but little happiness to ensue. . . ."

Schaw's letter on the public hysteria of midsummer, 1741, questioning the justice of trials and punishment then being imposed on so many blacks in town, had been widely circulated, generally to its author's discredit, so that the newcomer from England had found it preferable to remove that fall to Philadelphia, a hundred miles off, either because of hostility expressed toward him by various New Yorkers, or because of his own distaste for remaining in a community manifesting such evidence of civic mania. Again, the record is sparse. "I saw clearly the hour was come for leaving this place"—but his motives for doing so must be conjectured: perhaps some summons from the neighboring city, unrelated to events at York? Likewise the basis for his marriage the following summer (June 1742) to Elizabeth Pursell can only be guessed at, no further letters of hers having survived. As for his own *Reminiscences,* they contain but three uninformative references to his "dearly beloved wife" and family. Henceforth over great portions the pages of those reminiscences are filled instead with a joyous account of his spiritual rebirth, which granted him answers to questions of such moment then: Is atonement necessary in the nature of divine decrees? Does man await God's pleasure, or can he prepare himself as a fit vessel of divine grace? Is God's great design to save souls merely, or to redeem the society of mankind?

There are, to be sure, passages in the writing from this period of Schaw's life that suggest grounds for sharp differences between him and a New York merchant. "So great is the hurry of this world to do business quick and to gain wealth that the spirit at the day doth loudly groan." "In the love of money the eye is not single to God, and the understanding is closed up against the counsel of truth. Some with large possessions go on arraying themselves in purple and fine linen, faring sumptuously every day, yet the channel for business that their urgency opens serves only to please a mind that wanders, with people laboring as in the fire and wearying themselves for very vanity." Those sentiments, which some in our own more secular age may subscribe to, would not have been hospitably received, perhaps, in the yellow brick mansion on Broadway. Nevertheless, Schaw had found himself back there in the late spring of

1742, and by midsummer he and the merchant's daughter were married. "About noon July 2 we set out from New York on our return, and arrived Philadelphia July 4." And thirty-four years later to the day, in that same city, the rugged old minister that Schaw had become would learn with rapture of the declaration of independence from their mother country of Pennsylvania, New York, and the various other colonies, united now as sovereign states.

By then he had lived more than a quarter of a century as a widower. Elizabeth Pursell Schaw died in Philadelphia giving birth to her third child, in 1749. She was twenty-four years old.

The surviving record of her husband's life from that early severance onward is for the most part an account of travels among towns and villages in America to preach the gospel of the new birth at clapboard churches as far south as Georgia, in brick meetinghouses as far north as Boston. In his sermons he became an increasingly outspoken opponent of slavery, and increasingly a defender of the rights of colonists against an unresponsive Parliament on the other side of the ocean. In 1769 occurs one rare glimpse of the minister, then in his mid-fifties, before the congregation of a Tidewater church, "a lean, freckled, elderly man," so the eyewitness records, "his hair smoothly combed, wondrous clean, a very actor in his delivery." The inarticulateness of younger days was behind him by then; other contemporaries would refer to his pulpit eloquence. And after the Revolution had finally commenced, and General Washington was wintering his army near Philadelphia, Schaw was with that ragged band subsisting on firecake and water on the snowswept hillside, ministering to the spiritual needs of those desperate few on whom so much depended. Two included among their number were the old man's sons.

Schaw died the year after Yorktown, on the eve of triumph for the American cause, in 1782. The final thought in his *Reminiscences* is expressed in these inspiriting words: "Our Provider keeps His best wine till the last. And though He may cause us to drink of the cup of affliction in the way to heaven, He sweetens it with a sense of His goodness, and makes it pleasant drink, such as my soul doth love."

The minister's life had ended before his father-in-law's, doughty old Tory who, almost ninety by then, was helped on a November morning one year later aboard a ship of Sir Guy Carleton's fleet in the East River, at the tip of Manhattan, to join his grieving son and those last few other Englishmen forced in the end to abandon all that they had held precious—all except loyalty to their king—as they set out on the long voyage eastward to a bleak future in the land of their ancestors, driven by rebels from homes in the New World they would never see again.

That sad fleet with its burden of exiles would follow roughly the route that Corimer had taken on his return to London forty-one years before. Near the outset of the earlier voyage the young earl had lingered on Burling Slip with his friend Schaw, Elizabeth Pursell, and Elizabeth's maidservant Annie, all melancholy enough at the moment of parting. The Pursells had "loaded me with things convenient for my journey. E wished me a good passage and a speedy return." And with Schaw the earl was exchanging sleeve buttons as remembrances, while sailors lifted his various possessions onto the skiff. Then all was suddenly bustle and noise, and Corimer, holding his white monkey, was calling to his friends from the boat in the river, then was ascending the side of the brig, and the anchor was weighed, and the ship was moving slowly seaward with the tide. A last wave of the hand across the widening distance, later a last gaze above the Narrows at the little town receding— spires, belfries, steeples, charred ruins of the fort, cupola of the City Hall, brick walls, windows and weathercocks agleam in the late sunlight—before wooded islands intervened, green land gliding along the horizon to hide the town from view.

Much of what remains to tell is familiar enough that it may be dealt with briefly. Becalmed beyond the Narrows, the *George William* lay for an hour within sight of—and stench and sounds of moaning from—a cursed object that graved itself on Corimer's imagination for the rest of his life: Dutch slaver awaiting the turn of the tide to enter port. In time a breeze did spring up, and the departing vessel commenced what would prove to be a remarkably speedy voyage home, day after glorious day of sailing over sparkling seas, canvas bellying, booms creaking, shrouds briskly snapping. Each day on deck near the hen coops an English earl and an African slave would form an unlikely tableau, teacher and pupil: "Set to work almost immediately after hoisting sail, and within a fortnight had taught Jack the alphabet and how to spell almost any single syllable when distinctly pronounced to him." The ship reached Greenwich in mid-October, her hardened sailors by then so impressed with Jack's "good nature and affability that, sailing up the channel, some pointed out to him the headlands and other interesting places. . . ."

Having reached home, Cavendham was not long in taking his seat in the Lords, in time to participate in the tumultuous days of Walpole's downfall, joining heated debates over the conduct of the war and the Prince of Wales's allowance. He voted against the government, in early February 1742, on the decisive question of the Chippenham election petition. But along with the Duke of Montague, the Earl of Pembroke, and two or three other influential humanitarians of the age, His Lordship was to take as his special cause the horrors of the slave trade, which he made it his business to become informed of during succeeding years, having as guests in St. James's Square ships' captains, factors, Quakers, anyone who might add to his understanding of the issues. "We ought," Cavendham would write, "to deal the death blow to that most infernal of all commerce, the traffic of our fellow creatures. There is no reason that is not sordid for our violating the native liberties of man even in a savage state." And again: "To fancy that superior power or superior knowledge gives one race of people a title to use another with haughtiness and contempt is to abuse power and science, and in spite of both to shew ourselves worse men than those who have neither."

In regard to Jack, Cavendham had acted on his convictions soon after returning to London. We read of the former slave, now dressed in "a silk damask gown, a black velvet cap, and voluminous breeches," having "the honor to be sent for by many of the gentry, who were mightily pleased with his company and concerned for his misfortunes." We learn of Jack's admirable quickness of mind: a plow and a grist mill having been taken to pieces before him, he was able to reassemble both without further directions. We are told that "his time is much occupied by one or another, and he has many gifts, among others a watch with which he is very much pleased. He collects all his things together and packs them up, that he may be in readiness."

For the black, now a free man, would be returning to Africa. Of all those millions who had been and were to be brutally forced to travel westward from their African homeland, he is one of only two slaves on record destined to make the journey back. "Know all men by these presents that I Corimer Earl of Cavendham have acquitted and do by these presents acquit and forever discharge Jack, otherwise called Bumdou Tuaco, a black lately brought over from the province of New York, of and from all manner of claims and demands of me against him on any account whatsoever. And I do further hereby for me and my successors declare that from and after this day the said Jack, otherwise called Bumdou Tuaco, is a free man at liberty to take his passage to Africa in any ship which he shall chuse, in order to return to his native country. In witness whereof I have caused my seal to be hereunto affixed this seventeenth day of October in the year of our Lord one thousand seven hundred and forty-one."

The certificate of manumission, sighed "Cavendham," handsomely engrossed and authenticated, is stored in Box 1407-D3 at the British Museum. The same box contains other documents of interest, including a receipt for the 12s.6d. that the earl paid for "a suit of bedding" for Jack's use aboard the *Dolphin,* snow of eighty-six tons, which the free black boarded Saturday morning,

October 31, with assorted tools and goods that included gifts from well-wishers. Late the same afternoon the ship slipped her moorings at Gravesend and proceeded toward the Downs, and on the second of November began sailing along the coast to the Solent, starting point for voyages to West Africa. To the Solent, then southward the *Dolphin* sailed, close to the wind through the Atlantic, clawing back against the northerlies that blow round Cape Bojador. From there she shaped a course down the Atlantic coast of Africa, and in late December put in at the Gambia. Having left the fort near the mouth of that river she passed alongside Guinea—white surf, golden beaches, green jungle beyond—and proceeded on to the marshy delta of the Bonny, though the last word from Jack, taken down by a scribe who translated it into English, was dictated at James Fort, to be delivered to Cavendham as addressee: "I am very well, and have been used with civility all the way. I give you my service greatly. You have done great favor and are my best friend. I wish from my heart that all that you have may prosper, and that you have long life and happiness in this world and the world to come. . . ."

Jack's wish would not be granted. Although Cavendham became a hero to later abolitionists, he was to enjoy a life too short to make much immediate difference among his countrymen. He died at London in the same year as Elizabeth Pursell on the other side of the ocean. "One night," writes the earl's betrothed decades after the event, "in the beginning of November, 1749, as his lordship was returning to St. James's Square by moonlight, and about ten at night, he was attacked by two highwaymen in Hyde Park, and the pistol of one of them going off accidentally (as attested to by the footman), the ball passed through his lordship's head and lodged in the top of the chariot."

Corimer had been killed instantly. His assailants fled and were never found.

To the young third wife of the earl's late father a son had been born seven years earlier, some eleven months after the fourth earl's demise. With a few objects that had come into his mother's possession that son set sail for America in 1762. He cleared a farm in the wilderness northwest of Marietta, and there he begat a family, native Ohioans who remained in the vicinity until the line died out in the early twentieth century. In 1918 the last descendant, Clara Walker, succumbed to influenza in her late fifties. Miss Walker's best friend lived the length of her own long life in the house next door, in what was by then a village; and upstairs in a cedar chest of the Finney farmhouse, in that village of Vinton, my uncle was subsequently able to locate Corimer's journal, the small volume that I hold open now, musing over the shorthand of a late, faded entry at the bottom of a water-stained page:

Thursday, September 24. Spanking breeze at an early hour in the morning, though it soon died. This day we get our new awning up to keep us from the sun. Picked over my sound apples from the rotten. Two sails are seen to leeward about midday. Read to Jack in the afternoon. Ate some hashed fowl and hogs' haslet for dinner. Milne I doubt not to have been at the brandy, though he denies it. About 9 retire but couldn't sleep because of noise aboard.

That same day, September 24, 1741, in the town at the edge of America that Corimer had left behind him, no servile labor was being performed, for this was a day of thanksgiving observance. "Whereas it hath pleased Almighty GOD of His infinite goodness and mercy to save the people of the province from the late horrid and dangerous conspirators bent on the destruction of this city, when for our manifold iniquities He might have given us over to their cruel and bloody hands and have suffered us to perish by their barbarous machinations, which only Providence hath prevented; therefore, it is our duty to return humble and hearty praises and thanksgivings to Almighty GOD for His late mercies vouchsafed to us."

Thus, divine services were being held that Thursday morning in all the churches, chapels, and other places of worship throughout New York: in the English church on Broadway, in the old Dutch church on Garden Street, in the Middle Dutch church on Crown Street, in le Temple du Saint Esprit on King Street, in the Lutheran church on Rector Street, in the Presbyterian meetinghouse on Wall Street, in the Quaker meetinghouse on Little Green Street, in the Jewish synagogue on Mill Street. And at the parade ground a chaplain, kettle drum for his lectern, was praying with the regiment, praying fervently beside the ensign's standard and the charred timbers of the governor's house, praying even as the indifferent trees, there and all over the island, were being stirred anew—oak and hickory and maple and fragrant locust—by the first faint changes that would turn them again to crimson, to gold, there at the end of another season.

Note

Readers will have recognized entries in Corimer's journal as echoing and sometimes reproducing those found in the journals of James Birket, Dr. Alexander Hamilton, Warren Johnson, William Byrd, Peter Kalm, Robert Hunter Morris, Dudley Ryder, the young James Boswell, and others of Corimer's approximate contemporaries. Similarly, Elizabeth Pursell's letters will have been seen to be based in the main on those found in such sources as the letters of Lady Mary Wortley Montagu, *Dear Miss Heber, Letters of a Loyalist Lady* [Anne Hulton], and *The Book of Abigail and John* [Adams]. Corimer and the Pursell family are of course fictional, as is Francis Schaw, whose *Reminiscences* are derived from the writings of George Whitefield, John Woolman, the Wesleys, Anthony Benezet, and other likeminded contemporaries. The fictions have been composed thus in order to avoid intruding twentieth-century attitudes on eighteenth-century people. In the midst of a factual world those few authentic fictions may have helped bring closer a distant year in the past of an American city.

To focus events of that year, I have on occasion tampered with the historical record. For instance, Judge Horsmanden as recorder would have been appointed to the Common Council, not elected like other members, despite a suggestion to the contrary early in these pages. Two blacks, not one, were hanged for the theft at Hogg's. After he absconded, John Romme was captured in New Jersey and returned to New York, though ultimately he escaped execution, perhaps through the intervention of influential relatives. Roosevelt's Quack has been merged here with Walter's Quaco, and some others of the historic slaves have been brought together as single characters. Names have occasionally been changed to avoid confusion: Downing's for Todd's (cf. Hogg's), those of various Caesars in order to distinguish them from a principal in the action.

For readers interested in examining the historical record intact—or as much of it as can accurately be pieced together—the best modern account is unfortunately the least accessible: Walter F. Prince's "The Great Slave Conspiracy Delusion," published in spring and summer issues of the New Haven *Saturday Chronicle* for 1902. Among other treatments are T. Wood Clarke's "The Negro Plot of 1741," in *New York History* XXV (1944), pp 167–81; Annette K. Dorf's "The Slave Conspiracy of 1741," an unpublished master's essay (1958) at the Butler Library, Columbia University; and Ferenc M. Szasz's "The New York Slave Revolt of 1741: A Re-Examination," in *New York History* XLVIII (1967), pp 215–30. The contemporary source (here referred to as "the record"), written by "The Recorder," Daniel Horsmanden, in order to prove the existence of a conspiracy, was first published in 1744, three years after the events it recounts, as *A Journal of the Proceeding in the Detection of the Conspiracy Formed by Some White People in Conjunction with Negro and Other Slaves for Burning the City of New York in America and Murdering the Inhabitants*. As *The New-York Conspiracy, or a History of the Negro Plot . . .* , it was reissued in 1810 and again, with an introduction by Thomas J. Davis, in 1971.

P.M.